D0485024

25 YEARS
BUILT to LAST

A TOUCHSTONE BOOK

PUBLISHED BY SIMON & SCHUSTER

New York   London   Toronto   Sydney   Tokyo   Singapore

AT THE BAR

The Passions and Peccadilloes of American Lawyers

DAVID MARGOLICK

Illustrations by Elliott Banfield

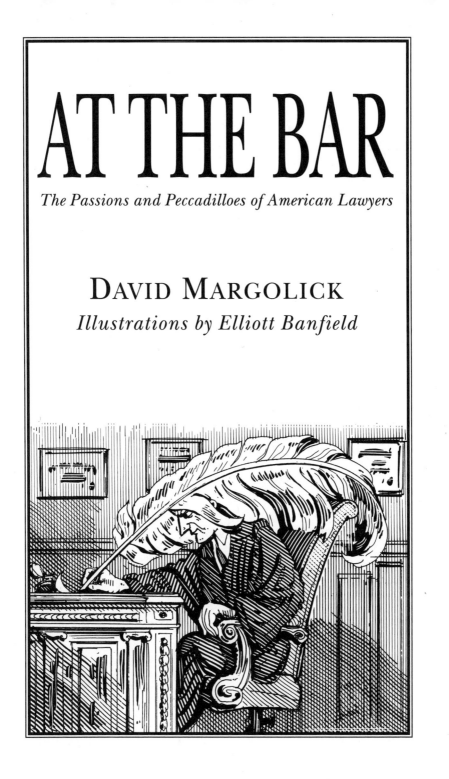

⊼⊼

TOUCHSTONE
Rockefeller Center
1230 Avenue of the Americas
New York, New York 10020

Designed by Hyun Joo Kim

Manufactured in the United States of America

10   9   8   7   6   5   4   3   2

Library of Congress Cataloging-in-Publication Data

Margolick, David.
  At the bar : the passions and peccadilloes of American lawyers/
David Margolick.
    p.   cm.
  "A Touchstone book."
  1. Law—United States—Anecdotes. 2. Law—United States—Humor.
  3. Lawyers—United States—Humor. 4. Lawyers—United States—
    Anecdotes.   I. Title
  K184.M367   1995
    349.73—dc20   94–45229
    [347.3]   CIP

ISBN: 0-671-88787-4

To

Lucjan Dobroszycki,

Elizabeth Cohen,

and

Douglas Lavine,

with

love and thanks.

ACKNOWLEDGMENTS

I'D LIKE TO THANK THOSE EDITORS AT THE NEW YORK TIMES WHO CREATED "At the Bar" and asked me to write it, particularly Max Frankel, Arthur Gelb, John Lee, and Soma Golden. My thanks go also to the many conscientious and good-natured law editors with whom I've worked over the past seven years, who were forced to put up with late copy, squabbles over pet phrases good and bad, and other assorted nit-picks: Martin Arnold, Andy Malcolm, Daryl Alexander, Jonathan Landman, Peter Kaufman, David Corcoran, Norma Sosa, Dave Stout, George Kaplan, Lad Paul, and Margot Slade. Then there are the wonderful copy editors of The Times's National Desk, especially those unlucky enough to show up early on Thursdays—notably Irv Lipner, Jim Barden, and Bob Thibault. Thanks, too, to Linda Mathews, who was happy to let me write the column as long as I wished, but who also encouraged me to seek new journalistic challenges.

In the ephemeral world of daily newspapers, every writer dreams his work will have a second life. I am grateful to all those who helped make this possible for me. They include Dennis Stern of The Times, who cut through the red tape concerning permissions; my agent, Esther Newberg, and Alice Mayhew of Simon & Schuster, who nailed down the deal; my editor, Becky Cabaza, who helped put this collection together with taste, skill, good humor, and patience; and various others—D. S. Aronson, Fred Chase, Tony Davis, Ani Go, and Hyun Joo Kim—who turned it all into a book.

Finally, I want to thank Elliott Banfield, my illustrator and friend. From the first week of our collaboration, his sophisticated and elegant drawings have been the indispensable signature of the "At the Bar" column, and I'm grateful that they are now gracing this book as well.

—*David Margolick*
Los Angeles, January 1995

CONTENTS

INTRODUCTION

A RESEARCHER IN ATLANTA ASKS LAWYERS TO SPIT INTO TINY LABORATORY vials to test whether litigators really do have more testosterone. Bar-bashing has become big business: A cottage industry of "Let's Kill All the Lawyers" items—coffee mugs, pillows, T-shirts, etc.—has sprouted up; one lawyer sends a "Let's Kill" plate to his old buddy, Justice David Souter of the United States Supreme Court. Meantime, publishers peddle whole libraries of lawyer jokes. Despite the bar's fat-cat image, the Republican Party concludes that attacking lawyers wins votes, prompting one lifelong G.O.P. lawyer, who practices in Dan Quayle's birthplace and serves on "Lawyers for Bush/Quayle," to resign from the group in a huff and vote Democratic for the first time in his life. But for all the knocks against it, the legal profession remains enticing enough for entrepreneurs to launch a summer camp for aspiring lawyers, a place where every camper is a counselor. In the canteen, alongside the sunblock and insect repellent, are legal pads and yellow highlighters.

America can't make up its mind about lawyers. It reviles them, re-lies upon them, respects and ridicules them, feels overwhelmed and intimidated and intrigued and repelled by them. But most of all and now more than ever, it is fascinated by them. Lawyers, long accus-tomed to languishing in the shadows cast by their clients, have be-come personalities in their own right, appearing regularly on the front pages of leading newspapers, in *People* magazine, on *Nightline* and *Larry King Live,* as well as in publications devoted only to them. As our culture produces a seemingly endless supply of marquee de-fendants—William Kennedy Smith, Mike Tyson, the Menendez broth-ers, Lorena Bobbitt, Dr. Kevorkian, O. J. Simpson—so, too, has it made household names of the Dershowitzes doing the defending. And as if 750,000 real lawyers aren't enough, armies of fictional ones, heirs to Bartleby, the Scrivener, and Perry Mason, saturate the movie theaters, the airwaves, and the paperback racks.

Most Fridays over the past seven years, in the "At the Bar" column of *The New York Times,* I have written about these lawyers, real and mythical, heroic and ignoble, and documented America's varied, of-ten contradictory reactions to them. For this volume, I have selected 120 of these 350 columns. They vary greatly in substance and tone, and may delight, outrage, depress, or move, depending on what crossed my mind and desk in any given week. I hope, however, that collectively they chronicle a perpetually fascinating profession in the midst of its greatest upheaval ever.

When "At the Bar" made its debut in November 1987, its mission was vague and its prospects unclear. The *Times* had run columns on sports and foreign affairs, bridge and chess, stamps and coins, doctors and ad men, men and women, but never anything about lawyers. Indeed, with few exceptions, lawyers and law firms had always enjoyed a certain invisibility—and, therefore, immunity—in its pages as well as in those of every other American newspaper. Look up "Cravath, Swaine & Moore" or the names of the most successful personal injury or criminal defense lawyers in the *Times Index* for 1950 or 1960 or 1970 and you'll find almost nothing, except perhaps for a few stray wedding announcements. Only in the early 1980's, prodded by sassy new trade publications like *The American Lawyer* and *The National Law Journal* and the emergence of law graduates who preferred unremunerative careers in noisy newsrooms to more profitable work in cushy law offices, had newspapers like mine hired people like me. Together, we felt like sixteenth-century cartographers surveying uncharted areas of the New World, or perhaps Margaret Mead depicting some exotic tribe.

From the outset, I hoped "At the Bar" would appeal to two distinct constituencies. I wanted lawyers of all pin-stripes to read it, and read it respectfully, knowing that it came from someone who spoke their language and was wise to their ways. But I also sought to engage the far larger population of people interested in lawyers. This has meant many things: that the column had to be accessible, without legal language thick enough to turn off everyone else; that it needed to focus on broader human themes, like valor and venality, rather than on the nuts and bolts of law, a subject covered elsewhere in the paper's pages; that it had to be lively and irreverent, skeptical and detached, going beyond the bar's self-serving pieties and divulging trade secrets about how lawyers behave and misbehave. Above all, it had to be unpredictable. While readers have come to expect Elliott Banfield's distinctive drawings each week, I hope they have never been quite sure what came underneath.

As someone torn about law and lawyering from his first day of law school, who enjoyed cases as much for the characters and stories they contained as for the law they elucidated, who never wanted to practice law but hoped not to stray very far from it, "At the Bar" was a perfect assignment. All that remained was to encapsulate a different facet of the legal world each week, and within the officially prescribed 800 words (though, like any red-blooded reporter, I pushed out that envelope whenever my editors weren't looking). And, seven years later, what remained was to select those columns that most faithfully represent my work and have best held up over time.

It has not been easy to categorize these columns, though I have tried. The first section, a kind of prelude that includes the subjects alluded to above, concerns the ubiquitousness of lawyers and America's ambivalence toward them. Following that are columns on the folkways of the bar: its peculiar organizations, rituals, and language. Lawyers are great joiners, and there are several visits with the group that boasts of being the largest professional organization in the world, the American Bar Association. There is also a side trip to the American College of Trial Lawyers, the self-styled Skull & Bones of the courtroom set. Overall, the language these lawyers speak is pallid, as the surprisingly desiccated last wills of the rich and famous, examined in another column, attest. "Virtually all are the work of lawyers, who can do to language what steam tables do to vegetables," I wrote there. The deflavorizing machine kicks in early, with the student-edited law reviews. But lawyers can occasionally summon something more memorable—an exchange of court papers sprinkled with Yiddish, for instance, and the opinions of a federal appellate judge in Rhode Island, who has tried reintroducing words like "struthious," "neoteric," and "inconcinnate" into the English language.

For all these reflections on the bar's timeless qualities, a second and perhaps more prevailing theme of "At the Bar" has been how dramatically the practice has changed over the past decade. The third group of columns concerns the most compelling of these changes: the newly competitive legal marketplace. Once, corporate law firms were nearly as durable as Ivy League colleges; now, like the famous New York firm of Finley, Kumble et al., they go up in flames, and even onto the auction block. Once, becoming a partner at such places was like winning academic tenure; now, firms jettison unproductive colleagues, loyalties or sentimentality be damned. Once, clients stuck doggedly with firms for decades, rarely second-guessing bills or doing any comparison shopping, and when lawyers hustled business at all, it was discreetly, over tennis matches or golf games; now, newly sophisticated clients hire companies that specialize in scrutinizing legal bills, and even fancy firms must seek out marketing and public relations specialists.

Once, these same firms could sit back demurely, waiting for top graduates to seek them out; now, they compete to produce the fanciest recruitment brochures, though there is a certain sameness to the results. Once, all but a few lawyers, whom their colleagues dismissed as loudmouths, were models of reticence; now, they trade tips on how to be quoted in the press. Once, though most had no demonstrable management skills, corporate lawyers ran their own offices; now, they farm out such tasks to gurus like Brad Hildebrandt. Once, their idea of advertising was boldface lettering in the white pages of phone books; now that some lawyers in the trenches convinced some other lawyers on the United States Supreme Court that the First Amendment protects them, they flog themselves via television, newspapers, matchbooks, Christmas cards, sympathy wreaths, vanity license plates, and even, in the case of one Honolulu maritime lawyer, condoms. ("Saving Seamen the Old-Fashioned Way," his handy, pocket-sized packets declare.) If some lawyer-wary politicians had their way, such advertisements would have to carry warnings akin to those on cigarette packages and Clorox bottles.

The fourth section is devoted to another sea change in the profession: the entry of large numbers of women, and the host of challenges this has presented to the bar's ossified institutions: everything from the need to change traditional standards for promotion to offering day-care facilities to fashioning new codes for dress, conduct with adversaries, and intra-office sexual relations. Just how quickly things changed in only the past few years is apparent from an early column, in which the news of the day—a mother making partner at a prominent Wall Street firm—now seems as quaint as the reference in that column to a "facsimile transmission machine." For the first time, a New York legal newspaper began carrying personal advertisements, with disappointing, though predictable, results. For all their successes, women lawyers have had their comeuppances: consider the tale of Jill Wine-Banks, executive director of the American Bar Association until an obsession with Dalmatians proved her downfall.

A final column in this section—on how a Chicago lawyer threatened to perform a clitoridectomy on the woman opposing him in court—neatly highlights one of several additional trends addressed in Section Five: declining standards of civility and fair play among lawyers, a phenomenon marked by frivolous motions and so-called Rambo tactics. Elsewhere, a profession famed for its paper production is feeling the first stirrings of environmentalism, making the yellow legal pad an endangered species. This concern for the quality of life also extends inward, as illustrated by examinations of the first law firm fitness center, the first law firm shrink, the first twelve-step program for lawyers desperate to break their addiction to the law, and the story of one contented dropout.

Legal ethics, a perennial source of concern to the bar, is also a steady source of material for bar columnists. Columns in Section Six examine the kinds of questions lawyers face at various stages of their work, from the way in which they defend their clients (e.g. by attacking the character of crime victims) to the padded bills some of them submit afterward. Attorneys can sometimes exploit their familiarity with an honorable system for dishonorable ends, like the workers' compensation lawyers in Kansas who collected tens of thousands of dollars for their own alleged injuries, sustained lifting heavy briefcases or reaching for statute books. Other times, lawyers discredit themselves by playing an honorable role in a dishonorable system. The accusation can be made against a historical figure, like a forgotten legal scholar in Nazi-occupied France, or a fictional character like Atticus Finch in *To Kill a Mockingbird*. The profession's efforts to police itself have at times been feeble, as the fates of one twice-victimized client and a legal whistleblower indicate.

The law is filled with subcultures, and the succeeding sections cover three of the most interesting: the plaintiffs' personal injury trial bar, the bench, and the academy.

Tort lawyers like Izzy Halpern and Harry Lipsig, colossi of the Brooklyn and Manhattan trial bars, respectively, have always been among the law's most flamboyant, even outrageous personalities, attorneys who were uninhibited long before it became fashionable. The personal injury bar has been both the birthplace and incubator of legal advertising. And, as any first-year law student quickly learns, the cases these lawyers handle—flowing from the accidents that befall mankind—are both the most bizarre and the most human. One column in Section Seven depicts the professional swap meet offered by one publication, a service through which lawyers can seek out those kindred colleagues who have previously handled lawsuits over defective straitjackets or wart removers. Another describes how a Houston lawyer saw one verdict shrink because jurors caught him driving to court in a Porsche, and were determined not to buy him another.

Learned Hand, the subject of the first of several columns concerning life on the bench in Section Eight, is nearly everyone's model of a judge. But other articles here examine the ways in which judges deviate from Hand's lofty ideal. Judges should be poker-faced, for instance, yet an Indiana judge cries from the bench during one particularly touching trial, thereby posing the question of whether shedding tears is reversible error. Or judges should be wise, but a California court must decide just how stupid some judges can plausibly be. Columns examine the peculiar way in which lawyers treat the judges before whom they appear: obsequious in person, venomous behind their backs. There are tales of people newly arrived on the bench, one by way of the gridiron; of people who never got there, like Herschel Friday of Little Rock; and people who, like Judge Joseph Force Crater, disappeared shortly after they arrived.

Catty-corner from the bar—or, perhaps, the cattiest corner of the bar—are the nation's law schools, the subject of Section Nine. When law professors gather, the topics on the table include Burmese art, the poetry of Adrienne Rich, and Picasso's *Guernica*, but not necessarily much law. When law review editors edit, anal compulsiveness may matter as much as erudition, and the footnotes mount. A column written while the world debated whether Clarence Thomas or Anita Hill was more believable, contemplates the plight of poor Guido Calabresi, Yale Law School's dean and a man famously loyal to alumni, who said he believed them both. Legal academia is extremely competitive; hence, the attention begrudgingly paid to a much-despised poll that annually ranks the nation's law schools, and the rampant professional jealousy of Harvard's famed constitutionalist, Laurence Tribe. Another column set in Cambridge recounts how, following the brutal murder of a law professor, Harvard's best and brightest proved to be its cruelest and crudest. Legal academia has its oddities, like the Reverend Pat Robertson, guiding light at a troubled law school in Virginia. It also has its heroes, including J. Willard Hurst, the man uniformly acknowledged to have been the father of legal history.

Perhaps more than anything else, "At the Bar" has sought to capture the amazing range of America's lawyers. In Section Ten, "Personalities," I attempt to reflect that breadth. In it appear characters fresh out of *The Godfather, The Front Page* and, quite literally, *The Bonfire of the Vanities* and *Woodstock*. As their personalities vary, so does their expertise—e.g. a man who sues Holiday Inn on behalf of persons spied upon through peepholes in hotel mirrors—and their character, ranging from the egomania of a New York lawyer whose collected works, filling three coffee table volumes, includes his 1933 address to the National Fertilizer Association to the courage of an unlettered prison inmate who helped change constitutional law. For every celebrity-lawyer like Alan Dershowitz, there are countless others of instant but ephemeral notoriety, like Howard Diller, one of the defense counsel in the infamous Central Park jogger case. If some lawyers capitalize on events, others—like Hugh Manes, profiled in the final section, who sued brutal Los Angeles policemen long before anyone ever heard of Rodney King—anticipate them.

At times, I must admit, "At the Bar" has been conspicuously quirky, covering the exurbs rather than the downtowns of the law. I confess to having a certain weakness for anti-establishment types, for iconoclasts and oddballs, and even for nonlawyers. Many of the best "At the Bar" columns have been about various laypeople—stenographers, court personnel, baseball players, jury experts—who help shape and enrich legal culture. Their stories, along with other columns too difficult to slot, appear in Section Eleven, "Nooks and Crannies."

As a general matter, lawyers have received "At the Bar" with good humor. There are those, however, who believe it has been too consistently critical of the profession, too snide. In fact, a large number of columns have been devoted to the many lawyers who do God's work: who represent the poor and underprivileged, invariably for low pay, sometimes risking ostracism or their own lives in the process. The high concentration of such people in the law is, in a sense, the highest compliment to the profession one could pay, and I have concluded this volume with some of their stories.

We often view lawyers as alien species. If nothing else, I hope "At the Bar" has helped show that lawyers are, in fact, nothing but mirrors of ourselves: honest and despicable, selfish and generous, free spirits and sticks-in-the-mud, unforgettable and unworthy and everything in between. ❑

I

LOVE,
HATE,
AND
FASCINATION

AMONG LAWYERS, DO LITIGATORS HAVE SOME KIND OF HORMONAL EDGE? SCIENCE MAY DELIVER THE ANSWER.

11/2/90

ATLANTA—IN THE PAST FEW WEEKS, 50 LAWYERS HERE HAVE TAKEN STICKS of Extra sugarless gum, placed them in their mouths, worked up some saliva and expectorated into small plastic vials.

For maximum freshness, each bottle has been whisked into the freezer across the hall from the office of Dr. James M. Dabbs Jr., a psychologist at Georgia State University, where it awaits analysis.

"These are the lawyers," Dr. Dabbs's research assistant, Elizabeth Carriere, recently told a visitor as she opened the freezer. "They've already been centrifuged."

Trial lawyers often say they have more gumption, more guts or more other parts of their anatomy than their paper-pushing partners. What Dr. Dabbs and Ms. Carriere are out to learn is whether these boasts are physiological facts or just self-aggrandizing figures of speech.

In the mini-spittoons of Dr. Dabbs's freezer is the saliva of trial lawyers, of government lawyers, of corporate lawyers, of real estate lawyers, of criminal lawyers, of judges and, as of a few days ago, one lawyer turned newspaper reporter. In the next week or so, all will be tested for their level of testosterone, the principal male sex hormone.

High levels of testosterone have been linked with overly aggressive or antisocial behavior. Juvenile delinquents, substance abusers, rapists, bullies and dropouts tend to have too much of the stuff. It is Dr. Dabbs's hypothesis that trial lawyers, too, are overly endowed in this department, but have learned to harness this primordial force for fun and profit.

"Trial lawyers may have stumbled into this wonderful ecological niche in which they can go out and be aggressive and confrontational and still get a lot of rewards for it," he said. "It may be one of the more primitive ways of making a prestigious living."

Dr. Dabbs tried to include lawyers in a similar study three years ago, which examined doctors, football players, salesmen, actors, ministers, professors, firemen and the unemployed. But no lawyers would cooperate—perhaps, his original research assistant, Denise de La Rue, hypothesized, "out of some underlying fear of failure."

Enter Ms. Carriere, an undergraduate at Georgia State and the daughter and granddaughter of lawyers. She persuaded some of her father's friends to take part in the study and from there, secured toe-holds in some of the city's major law firms. She also solicited volunteers at the DeKalb County Courthouse.

Sure enough, courtroom and boardroom lawyers reacted quite differently when a 22-year-old woman asked to test their testosterone. Ms. Carriere said the trial lawyers seemed to think they had been selected because of their self-evident machismo. One promptly volunteered to recruit some of his fellow "hormonal lawyers," as he put it. When it came time to produce specimens, they spat with gusto.

For these would-be he-men, a low testosterone count could prove far more crushing than a 500 on their Law School Admissions Test. But one of those tested, Robert Katz of Gorby, Reeves, Moraitakis & Whiteman, suggested that for him, at least, the experiment was a no-lose proposition. What if he got a low score? "I don't think a low-level reading means that that attorney is incapable of functioning in court," he said solemnly. And a high one? "Obviously I'll put that in our firm résumé," he said.

Many of the non-litigators, on the other hand, blanched when Ms. Carriere approached them. "They just about crawled under the desk," she said. One real estate lawyer refused to participate. "He acted like I was asking him to donate money," she said. Others insisted on spitting in private.

Dr. Dabbs's research has its skeptics, like former Attorney General Griffin Bell of King & Spalding in Atlanta, two of whose lawyers participated in the study. "It's useless information as I see it," he said.

That may be a bit harsh. The scores could aid career counselors, who might steer poor performers away from courtroom work. It could finally determine whether Wall Street "litigators," who rarely get into courtrooms, are really trial lawyers. It could help elite groups like the American College of Trial Lawyers pick members more scientifically.

Dr. Dabbs has other experiments in mind. To gauge the relative roles of nature and nurture in the making of a trial lawyer, he is considering testing law students. A leading Atlanta criminal-defense lawyer, Bruce Harvey, has agreed to spit periodically while on trial. Dr. Dabbs also dreams of testing the superstar saliva of a Joe Jamail, a Richard (Racehorse) Haynes and/or an Alan Dershowitz.

He could also team up with Dr. Donald Clifford of the Medical College of Ohio in Toledo, who is currently working on another, closely related population. He is testing the testosterone level of pit bulls. ❏

Male litigators really do have more testosterone than most mortals, Dr. Dabbs ultimately concluded, particularly when young. He detected no differences among women who try cases and those who don't. But his findings, he conceded, raise as many questions as they answer: Are trial lawyers higher in testosterone as early as law school, or do their high levels develop over time as a result of job demands? Do levels rise just before they go into court, and do they rise and fall with the winning and losing of cases? Are there subspecialities between which females also differ in testosterone? Clearly, more research—and spittle—is necessary.

IN QUAYLE'S HOME STATE, A LAWYER AND EX-BACKER DOESN'T LIKE THE REPUBLICAN ATTACKS ON THE BAR.

9/25/92

LEBANON, IND.—AMONG THE OTHERWISE FORGETTABLE AD HOC GROUPS supporting this year's presidential tickets, one seems particularly odd. In fact, it could be called "Masochists for Bush-Quayle," for it is made up of what have become the Republicans' favorite whipping boys and girls: lawyers.

On Sept. 15 the Bush campaign unveiled the names of the 100-member steering committee of Lawyers for Bush/Quayle '92. These practitioners are alike in several ways. If, as their favorite candidates contend, America has too many lawyers, none considers himself to be among the surplus. None of them has ever filed a frivolous lawsuit or harmed American competitiveness. All firmly believe that when the President and Vice President chastise lawyers, they are clearly talking about someone else.

But there is a dissenter on the committee, and in the unlikeliest of venues: here where Dan Quayle lived as a young boy.

Earlier this year, when Peter Obremskey of Lebanon was asked to join the steering committee, he casually agreed, then quickly forgot about it. After all, Mr. Obremskey was a lifelong Republican who cast his first vote in a presidential election for Barry Goldwater, liked President Bush all right and knew Mr. Quayle, with whom he had played golf several times at the Ulen Country Club, a stone's throw from the house where Mr. Quayle's grandmother once lived. So his name appears on the list—with Lebanon misspelled.

But the 56-year-old Mr. Obremskey is a trial lawyer—one of the tasseled-shoes set who, after the committee's formation, became a scourge of the Republican National Convention, along with liberals and homosexuals. Much of his livelihood comes from representing accident victims, and he is past president of the Indiana Trial Lawyers Association, which represents those representatives.

So furious is Mr. Obremskey over the Bush-Quayle bar-bashing that on Tuesday, after a reporter's call reminded him of his presence on the list, he quit the steering committee. And come November, he says, he is contemplating something even more radical: casting his first vote ever for a Democratic Presidential candidate.

Mr. Obremskey, a starting forward on the 1958 Hoosier basketball team that won the Big Ten, says his outrage is not a function of hurt feelings, wounded professional pride or economic self-interest. Instead, he says, by making scapegoats of lawyers the Bush-Quayle campaign is poisoning public perceptions of the profession, polluting jury pools and perverting the judicial process, all to score some cheap and ultimately ephemeral political points.

"It's bad for the Republican Party, it's bad for the legal profession and it's bad for the population of the country, because it impacts on the poor bastards I represent," he said.

Truth be told, few on the steering committee actually like the anti-lawyer fulminations. "They were painting with a broader brush than they needed to," said John C. Shepherd of St. Louis, a past president of the American Bar Association.

Another in the association's huge stable of former presidents, Eugene Thomas of Boise, Idaho, said the Republican standard-bearers had been "misadvised."

To Mr. Obremskey, these lawyers represent fat cats—the fat cats at the receiving end of personal injury lawsuits—and can afford to be forgiving. "They don't deal with people who get run over and maimed," he said. "It's the little guy who's affected by this anti-lawyer propaganda."

His partner and fellow trial lawyer, Kent Frandsen, says he feels the same way, though for him the subject is more painful. Mr. Frandsen's late father, G. Kent Frandsen, a onetime judge and director of admissions at the Indiana University Law School in Indianapolis, officiated at the Quayles' wedding ceremony. And it was the senior Mr. Frandsen who had to field the barrage of questions about just how someone with the mediocre grades and low test scores of Mr. Quayle got into law school. The experience was so stressful, his son believes, that it led his father, a healthy 61-year-old, to suffer a fatal heart attack within days of the 1988 election.

He "always had a special place in our hearts," says the handwritten note from the Vice President hanging on Kent Frandsen's office wall. But the younger Mr. Frandsen said his father would be "disappointed" to hear Dan Quayle engaging in anti-lawyer diatribes. Mr. Obremskey was more blunt: "He'd turn over in his grave."

Mr. Obremskey said he still liked Mr. Quayle and did not think he actually believed everything he said. He suggests that the Vice President, like the caddies on the Ulen links, is carrying someone else's clubs.

"By upbringing and because he was born with a silver spoon in his mouth, Dan Quayle's natural inclination is ultra-conservative," Mr. Obremskey said. "But he's just a puppy dog. He's become a tool of the far right and a pawn of big business." ❏

In November 1992, Mr. Obremskey lost his political virginity—and voted Democratic. "I wasn't deserting the Republican Party; the Republican Party had deserted me," he said. Of Mr. Quayle—with whom he has since gone golfing—he added: "He just fundamentally does not understand the legal system, either by choice or because he's never really been involved in it as a practicing attorney. Until he understands the practice of law from a lawyer's perspective, he has no business bashing us."

BASHING THE BAR,
A TREASURED AND STILL THRIVING TRADITION
THAT DATES FROM THE BARD.

1/18/91

"The first thing we do, let's kill all the lawyers."
— *"The Second Part of King
Henry the Sixth," Act 4, Scene 2.*

IN THE PANTHEON OF SHAKESPEAREAN CREATIONS, DICK THE BUTCHER IS
no Othello. But to anyone who follows law or lawyers, his modest proposal has become an overly familiar friend. It is a staple of law school
commencements, momentarily introspective speeches at bar meetings, and legal reporters looking for an erudite and handy way of writing that lawyer-bashing is nothing new.

In their rebuttals, lawyers and lawyerphiles note by rote that Dick is
the lowliest of knaves, a follower of the nefarious insurrectionist Jack
Cade, who heartily seconds Dick's suggestion in his less familiar response: "Is not this a lamentable thing, that of the skin of an innocent
lamb should be made parchment? that parchment, being scribbled
o'er, should undo a man? Some say the bee stings; but I say, 'tis the
bee's wax, for I did but seal once to a thing, and I was never mine own
man since."

But despite these caveats, the Butcher's flock flourishes. His sentiment can now be found in a variety of mediums, including coffee
mugs, T-shirts, pillows and soon, perhaps, at the Cannes Film Festival.

Souvenir plates inscribed "Let's kill all the lawyers" combine the
two passions of Robert van Kluyve of Madison, Va.: English literature
and pottery. For more than 20 years, Mr. van Kluyve has been making
them, along with companion plates for other professions (e.g. "God
heals, and the doctor takes the fee"; "If all the economists were laid
end to end, they would not reach a conclusion").

For a while, Mr. van Kluyve sold his plates through the Folger
Shakespeare Library. More recently, he placed advertisements in The
New Yorker and The National Law Journal. These produced orders
for some 300 plates, placed largely, the artist said, by the mothers and
spouses of either lawyers or those who hate lawyers but have to use
them.

Whether out of humorlessness or hypersensitivity or whatever,
lawyers seem disinclined to buy the plates for themselves; the notice
in the Law Journal netted a grand total of one order. So Mr. van
Kluyve also offers plates with another, more lawyer-friendly message,

from "The Taming of the Shrew": "Do as adversaries do in law, strive mightily, but eat and drink as friends."

Still, one lawyer, Finn M. W. Caspersen of Wilmington, Del., ordered "Kill all the lawyers" plates as Christmas presents for six friends, including Supreme Court Justice David H. Souter and Robert Clark, Dean of the Harvard Law School. Justice Souter would not say whether he had received the plate or if it now hangs in his chambers. Dean Clark acknowledged its arrival but said he would most certainly not display it in his office, even though Mr. Caspersen is a Harvard Law School graduate and fund-raiser.

"I disagree with the sentiment, quite vehemently," he said. "I'm not quite sure what the message was behind it, but I'll talk to him and straighten him out."

This year, Lighten Up Films Inc. of Farmington Hills, Mich., will release "Let's Kill All the Lawyers," a chronicle of a young man's preprofessional angst. In it, the hero rejects a legal career to become a gardener at a retreat for burned-out lawyers.

The story is loosely based on the experiences of Ron Senkowski, the film's director and writer. Mr. Senkowski landed in the 99th percentile when he took the Law School Admissions Test, but his legal career ended prematurely when he devoted the essay portion of the examination to a diatribe on lawyers. It included a quotation from H. L. Mencken worthy, perhaps, of one of Mr. van Kluyve's plates: "If all of the lawyers were hanged tomorrow, and their bones sold to a mah-jongg factory, we'd be freer and safer, and our taxes would be reduced by almost half."

Shannon Hamed, the film's producer, hopes "Let's Kill All the Lawyers" is a sleeper, in the manner of "She's Gotta Have It," and thinks the catchy title might help. "It's our greatest asset," she said.

Though Pamela Du Val embroiders more than 1,000 adages on her pillows, "Let's kill all the lawyers" cushions are perhaps the most popular item in her Manhattan boutique on Lexington Avenue, between 63rd and 64th Streets. She began making them three years ago and since then, she said, they've sold "like wildfire." As disaffection with the bar has grown, sales of "Let's kill" cushions have outstripped those of the previous best-seller: "Old lawyers never die, they just lose their appeals."

"People know that lawyers are brilliant and all that, but too expensive," she said in a telephone interview. But when pressed to explain, she suddenly grew suspicious.

"Why are you asking me all these questions?" she asked. "Are you trying to sue me?" ❑

IN SEARCH OF THE LATEST—
CERTAINLY NOT THE LAST—LAUGH IN
A LONG LINE OF JOKES ABOUT THE PROFESSION.

6/30/89

A MAN ASKED A LAWYER HIS FEE AND WAS TOLD IT WAS $50 FOR THREE QUES-
tions. "Isn't that awfully steep?" he asked. "Yes," the lawyer replied.
"Now, what is your final question?"

A newly deceased lawyer protested to St. Peter that, at the age of
52, he'd been too young to die. "That's strange," St. Peter replied. "According to your time sheets, you're 89 years old."

Why does California have the most lawyers and New Jersey the
most toxic waste dumps? (New Jersey had first choice.) What do you
need when you have three lawyers up to their necks in concrete?
(More concrete.) Why was the shipwrecked lawyer allowed to swim his
way through the piranha-infested waters? (Professional courtesy.)

One might dismiss "legal humor" as an oxymoron, and assume
that collections of the stuff would go alongside what Mad magazine
once described as "extremely thin books," like Nancy Sinatra's "Making It on Your Own" and "Liberals Who Have Been Mugged—and
Are Still Liberals." In fact, lawyers are not only the butt of innumerable jokes but also the target of entire tomes.

Amid the lawyerly decorum, one new book of jokes, "Skid Marks,"
by Michael Rafferty, can be positively nasty. (Q. What is the difference
between a dead skunk and a dead lawyer in the middle of the road?
A. There are skid marks before the skunk.) Still, this tiny book speaks
volumes about the blotted escutcheon of the bar, a problem that led
the American Bar Association recently to create a special image-of-
the-profession task force.

Many of the jokes in "Skid Marks" are juvenile. (Q. What do you
call 2,000 lawyers chained together at the bottom of the sea? A. A
good beginning.) Others are tacky. (Q. Why do medical laboratories
now use lawyers instead of rats? A. They breed faster, are less likeable
and do things rats won't do.) And some of them (What is the difference between a lawyer and a rooster, or a porcupine and two lawyers
in a Porsche?) have X-rated punch lines best left unsaid.

To assemble the collection, Mr. Rafferty solicited friends, placed advertisements in two California newspapers and took jokes over the
phone. He weeded out the truly tasteless—those with ethnic slurs, for
example, or depicting unnatural acts—and sent out review copies to

randomly selected lawyers. Not all were amused. "Most of the jokes really are not funny and are in poor taste," wrote Peter Malkin, of Manhattan. "Perpetuates unfair stereotypes," grumbled John Grillos, of Maplewood, N.J. "So hire a joke writer the next time you are in trouble."

Not everyone agrees. Already the book has sold more than 10,000 copies.

Lawyers have been satirized since the days of Dickens and Daumier. Ambrose Bierce included numerous bar barbs in his "Devil's Dictionary." In his spare time, William Prosser, the great torts scholar, collected catalogues of legal humor. There have been several since, with titles like "It's Legal to Laugh," "Laughter Is Legal" and "Legal Laughs."

The last year, however, has seen an avalanche of anthologies. Cameron Harvey, a law professor at the University of Manitoba with perhaps the world's largest collection of cartoons and comic strips on legal themes—1,100 items at last count—has written "Legal Wit & Whimsy." There's Peter Hay's "The Book of Legal Anecdotes," and Ronald Brown's "Juris-Jocular."

All of the books have their share of lawyers as compulsive pettifoggers, as avaricious, unethical, conniving and ambulance-chasing. Still, most are more benign than bawdy. Collectively, they tend toward that kind of teddibly British humor favored by the same people who hang those colorful "Vanity Fair" prints in their offices.

"I have attempted to counterbalance the sick jokes and the negative images of lawyers by providing the best examples of classic legal humor, which is distinguished by verbal elegance and subtle repartee," explained Mr. Hay, author of such other works as "Theatrical Anecdotes" and "Broadway Anecdotes."

The legal humor books provide some historical perspective on the profession. Lawyers have been likened to sharks for at least two centuries, for instance, and have been scorned as overabundant for at least five.

They are also a rich source of legal aphorisms, suitable for the self-deprecating speeches so common at bar conventions. Oscar Levant once defined "lawyer" as "a man who helps you get what's coming to him." Louis XII of France remarked, "Lawyers use the law as shoemakers use leather: rubbing it, pressing it and stretching it with their teeth, all to the end of making it fit for their purposes." Asked once why he hated lawyers, Samuel Johnson replied, "I don't hate them, sir; neither do I hate frogs, but I don't like to have either hopping about my chamber." ❏

Off to Camp in Search of
a Leg Up on Law School.

7/6/90

MIAMI SHORES, FLA.—IT IS THAT TIME OF YEAR WHEN THOUSANDS OF CHILdren traipse off to summer camp. But the camp here is different. Every camper is here to be a counselor.

Every camper packed not just the usual sneakers and swim trunks, but one set of clothes suitable for court. Instead of stocking sunblock and insect repellent, the canteen here sells legal pads and highlighters. And along with standard camp T-shirts, there are more upscale polo shirts, with the scales of justice embossed where the alligators generally go.

"National Law Camp," the logo on the shirt announces. "Educating America's Future Lawyers."

Once, there were just camp camps. Then there were tennis camps and basketball camps and weight-loss camps. And this week, 28 young pioneers, ages 13 to 22, arrived at the nation's first law camp, beginning what its organizers promised them and their parents would be "a three-week adventure into the legal profession."

"While other kids are practicing tennis this summer," a promotional brochure states, "yours can be practicing law."

Through July 21, anyone who despairs about the glut of lawyers would be well advised to steer clear of Barry University, where this first-of-a-kind camp in this most lawyer-laden of societies is housed. What they would see would make a Boy Scout wince.

Campers here will study torts, evidence, trial advocacy and ethics, as well as how to master the L.S.A.T. They will sit around computers rather than campfires. The field trips are to courthouses and jails. And, like the lawyers they long to be, the campers awaken to alarm clocks rather than to reveille.

For most people, the idea of a Florida camp for would-be lawyers might conjure up images of pathetic children toting briefcases and wearing woolen pin-stripes in the tropical heat. They see youngsters seeking a leg up for law school and pushy parents interested more in Upward than in Outward Bound.

The camp's founding fathers do not exactly discourage that perception. They promise campers "an invaluable chance to gain a competitive edge on the law school admission process," and, having got them in, helping to get them through.

"The National Law Camp may be the edge that separates the students who make it at law school from those that don't," Paul M. Lisnick of Loyola University Law School in Chicago, a member of the program's "faculty," says in the promotional brochure.

But Paul D. Carrington, a professor at Duke Law School now writing a history of legal education, said such a camp gave him "generally negative vibrations," in part because he suspected many of those attending were there "because they have a lawyer parent who's pushing them a bit."

"Most children do not have that developed an interest in law at that stage," he said. "And if they had just a little interest, I'd suggest they be sent to history camp or science camp or English camp, where they could develop their intellects along a somewhat broader dimension. To learn torts at 13 strikes me as premature."

To be sure, there are campers who resisted coming here. "I figured it would be just a bunch of lawyers giving us sermons and lectures," said Craig Goldstein, a 17-year-old from Lexington, Mass.

The youth's father, Jay Goldstein, conceded that it had been "something of a struggle" to persuade Craig to come. "I said to him, 'How bad can it be?' " he recalled at Sunday's orientation. " 'You're going to Florida for three weeks, you'll sit by the pool, you'll play tennis and you'll study a bit.' "

Elena Laguardia, a 16-year-old from Chatham, N.J., admitted that archeology interested her more than law. "If it were my money I'd be on a dig," she said. "But according to my family, I have this big mouth and I should put it to good use."

But most campers needed little coaxing to come here. Gigi Oden, 17, of Westchester, Ill., would be a prosecutor tomorrow if the law would only let her. Unfortunately, she has to endure four years of undergraduate school before she can even begin studying law. For Miss Oden, who called herself a "little yuppie," Law Camp is far more cost-effective than frittering away her July. "I see no point in wasting time," she said. "Reading Danielle Steel all summer just doesn't do it."

For Kenyetta Finley, a 16-year-old from the South Bronx, coming to camp was a family project, with her mother, grandmother and stepfather all chipping in to raise the $2,000 fee. She, too, wants to become a prosecutor, to put drug dealers on her block behind bars, she said. But she has some opposition. "My mother wants me to be a corporate lawyer because they make more money," she explained.

The program pencils in ample recreation time, but includes classes and lectures in the evenings and weekends, including a Fourth of July session on legal ethics. The students have materials hefty enough for a bar review course, and must read and brief cases nightly.

But aside from the usual gripes about camp food—one complained that the only edible item in the cafeteria was the lettuce—they are, well, a bunch of happy campers.

They like the teachers, particularly Steven Friedland and Michael Flynn, both recruited from Nova Law School in Fort Lauderdale. "The professors are amazing," said Heather Brooks, a 16-year-old from North Miami. "I thought they'd be brilliant, but I didn't think they'd be so young or amusing or animated or good-looking."

They like their fellow campers—surprisingly so for some. "I thought they'd be snobs, geeks, idiots and slumheads, but it turned out to be a really nice crowd," said Joelle Lee of Miami, who at 13 is the baby of the group. (Girls, many of them barely graduated from crayons to perfume, outnumber boys here, 17 to 11.)

Most of all, they like the law, at least thus far. During the orientation, they played prosecutor and defense lawyer. They debated whether driving a lawn mower while drunk violated state law. They learned to distinguish between plaintiffs and defendants, appellants and appellees, complaints and indictments. They learned that some questions have no answers. And if they were thinking like lawyers, they were sounding like them, too, with one referring to "the said lawn mower" during a mock trial.

The camp is the brainchild of Chris Salamone, a lawyer in Fort Lauderdale. Mr. Salamone, 28, comes from a camping family; his father, Anthony, who is also on hand here, has run the North Jersey All Sports Camp in Hackettstown for the past 30 years. Its goal, the younger Mr. Salamone said, is to provide a more efficient and less traumatic way to taste the law than the first year of law school.

With parents taking a wait-and-see attitude toward Law Camp, the operation will actually lose money this year, the Salamones concede. But they envision a whole constellation of Law Camps springing up around the country in the next few years.

Making legal education realistic as well as humane is tricky, and the Salamones have erred on the side of humanity. Theirs is a user-friendly, candy-coated law school.

The professors here are encouraging and available, not remote figures off somewhere writing treatises or moonlighting at some law firm. Classes are not torpid recitations of cases but a blend of guerrilla theater, Second City comedy and a Fred Friendly panel.

One of the teachers, Mr. Flynn, said: "If these kids were going to be law junkies for three weeks, I'd be worried, but that's not what this is about. This is to satisfy a curiosity about what it's like to be a lawyer. I am not in the business of producing a bunch of BMW-hungry people at the age of 15."

Within a day, the camp was winning over skeptics like Elena Laguardia and Craig Goldstein. It had also generated a kind of professional esprit, as a Barry University student discovered when he asked one group of campers why in heaven's name they wanted to become lawyers. "There are too many of them already," he added as he walked away.

Robyn Phillips, a 14-year-old from Lee's Summit, Mo., looked at him angrily. "What a weirdo," she said.

"He's probably studying podiatry," Heather Danker, 14, of Fort Lauderdale, added disgustedly. ❑

As the first crop of campers enters law school—camp alumni are now at Harvard, Georgetown and Stanford, among other places—the enterprise has gone bicoastal, with operations in Washington, D.C., and Palo Alto, Calif. In the next five years, Chris Salamone predicts, enrollment will triple or quadruple.

COMING TO A THEATER NEAR YOU: TOM CRUISE, GENE HACKMAN AND SOME THRILLED MEMPHIS LAWYERS.

6/25/93

"THE FIRM" OPENS NEXT WEEK, AND MILLIONS OF AMERICANS WILL NOW BE able to see what they've already read: how a young lawyer named Mitch McDeere outwits the malevolent firm for which he works. But to the lawyers of Memphis, the film promises a kick of another kind: it will be a chance to see themselves and their friends.

All of Memphis was caught up for three months last winter in the filming of the John Grisham novel about a newly minted Harvard lawyer, played by Tom Cruise, who sells himself to the highest bidder, a firm known as Bendini, Lambert & Locke, only to learn that if he sticks around the place too long he will end up as either a criminal or a corpse.

To dozens of local lawyers, however, the film was a chance to go Hollywood. They braved freezing temperatures and interminable waits, sacrificed large fees for paltry pay, eagerly signed contracts filled with small print that they didn't bother to read and elbowed each other out of camera range—all for the chance to mix with Mr. Cruise, Hal Holbrook and Gene Hackman and to immortalize themselves on film.

When McDeere is sworn in to the Tennessee bar—by Judge Frank Crawford of the State Court of Appeals—several genuine lawyers stand nearby. Barbara Zoccola, a local prosecutor, got to play a proctor at a bar exam, even after telling a local newspaper that "Cruise is cute, but not as cute as my husband."

A local judge, George Brown, shoots hoops with Mr. Cruise, though he hits for a considerably higher percentage in his own court. Mike McLaren, who once played basketball for Yale, fared better, at least by his own account. "Every shot that goes in is mine," he said. He received the bulk of his $1,500 fee for saying 14 words, three of them "Oyez!"

Four lawyers named Vescovo—the husband-and-wife teams of Steve and Diana and Chris and Anna—received bit parts, and Steve, for one, thinks he bypassed the cutting room floor. "I was standing right behind Hackman, and I'm about half a foot taller than he is," he said.

Alex Wellford, head of the Memphis Bar Association, and his cousin, Judge Harry W. Wellford of the United States Court of Appeals for the Sixth Circuit, each have parts as well.

But the most unusual cameos went to Mike Williams, Joe Barnwell and Bill Gibbons. Each plays a lawyer whom the firm murders—either for catching on to Bendini, Lambert's mob ties or for merely wanting to leave—then memorializes by hanging their portraits on its rich brown wooden walls. The trio, whom the Memphis Bar Association christened "the Dead Lawyers Society," appear only in those portraits.

"I've got the quintessential non-speaking role," said Mr. Williams, whose picture now hangs in the conference room at his real-life firm. How is it, he was asked, to see the dates of his birth and death under his own portrait? "A little disconcerting, to say the least," he replied.

Whether they are prosecutors or defense lawyers, tax specialists or corporate types, none of the participating lawyers had ever seen a firm like "The Firm." The film's art director, John Willett, set out to create what he called "an unprecedented legal nirvana"—an office spectacular enough to entice a Harvard hotshot to a sleepy Southern city.

Since no existing office, in Memphis or anywhere else, would do, Mr. Willett custom-made his own office inside the old International Harvester plant. It is a world of dark wood molding and marble, of antique furniture and oriental rugs, that exudes money and hints, only ever so slightly, at its tawdry origins.

Topping everything is the firm's library, which is no less spectacular for looking, like Jay Gatsby's, conspicuously unused. Its 40,000 books, which filled three tractor-trailer trucks, came courtesy of the West Publishing Company, purveyors to "The Verdict," "Presumed Innocent," "Other People's Money" and other law-related films. Ten people took two full days simply to put the books on the shelves; the whole set had to be reinforced, Mr. Willett said, to support the 105 tons they weighed.

Mike Cody, a former United States Attorney in Memphis and the Attorney General of Tennessee, also got a small part in the film. But he played another role off-camera: "technical legal adviser," or high commissioner of verisimilitude. Assisted by another lawyer, Kathy Story, he made sure that Tom Cruise's version of criminal law made sense and that the time sheets, case files and clutter at Bendini, Lambert looked legitimate.

Mr. Wellford, the bar president, took issue with at least one scene, in which, he charged, Mr. Holbrook was unconvincingly clad. "I've never seen a Memphis lawyer in an ascot, either at home or at work," he said. "It's a little pretentious."

But Hollywood has time to fix its fix on Memphis. Another Grisham book, "The Client," will soon be filmed there, too. ❑

Raymond Burr's Perry Mason was Fictional, but He Was Surely Relevant and, Oh, So Competent.

9/24/93

DA-DA, DA DA! DA-DA, DA-DUM-DUM!

From the time the opening chords of its familiar theme song first sounded and a pensive figure could be seen sitting alone in an empty courtroom, lawyers have loved to patronize Perry Mason. With all the smugness of the initiated, they have carped about how unrealistic and simpleminded the program was.

No defense lawyer, they would note, won as invariably as the Harlem Globetrotters, just as no district attorney lost as often as the Washington Generals. Mason, they complained, was less a lawyer than a private eye; sometimes the only law books in sight were the volumes of Corpus Juris Secundum shown in the credits. And most murder cases don't end with the guilty party standing up and shouting: "I had to do it! He was laughing at me!"

But when Raymond Burr died last week, he won some praise from surprising quarters. The passing of Corbin Bernsen or Richard Dysart or even Gregory Peck or E. G. Marshall will probably go unnoted by the American Bar Association. But among those grieving for Mr. Burr was R. William Ide 3d, president of the bar group. With bar-bashing at epidemic proportions, all the inaccuracies somehow loom less large.

Mr. Ide saluted the actor for depicting lawyers "in a professional and dignified manner" and helping "to educate many people who previously had not had access to the justice system." He also praised Mr. Burr as a stickler for verisimilitude. "Mr. Burr strove for such authenticity in his courtroom characterizations that we regard his passing as though we lost one of our own," he said.

For a time, some lawyers were not so enthusiastic. Complaining that Mason ran rings around District Attorney Hamilton Burger and Lieut. Arthur Tragg of the Los Angeles Police Department every week, District Attorney Edward Silver of Brooklyn asserted in 1962 that the program was undermining public confidence in law enforcement.

Even then, though, the organized bar knew that Perry Mason had its uses. It was not just that for millions of Americans he made the presumption of innocence real. Incorruptible and ingenious, selfless and serious, Mason also made lawyers look good. He was, as Tim Appelo has written in California Lawyer magazine, "the most influential figure on the public view of lawyers since Abe Lincoln, as incorruptible as Lincoln and more nearly infallible."

Mason continued to make friends for the profession, and for himself, as the original 245 shows, made from 1957 to 1966, were rerun and new ones appeared. When The National Law Journal and the West Publishing Company asked 815 Americans two months ago to name the lawyer, real or fictional, they admired most, he placed second—behind F. Lee Bailey and ahead of Lincoln, Thurgood Marshall, Janet Reno, Matlock and Hillary Rodham Clinton.

When most Americans think of Burr and Hamilton dueling, they think of Mason and Burger on television rather than Aaron and Alexander in Weehawken. And when they think of Mason, they are are more likely to think of Raymond Burr than Erle Stanley Gardner.

This left Mr. Burr feeling professionally hamstrung, but it also made him a favorite of bar groups and law schools. His portrait hangs at the McGeorge School of Law in Sacramento, Calif., to which he made substantial donations, while the Thomas M. Cooley Law School in Lansing, Mich., where he once spoke, has a "Raymond Burr Award for Excellence in Criminal Law."

And if he was the legal profession's greatest friend, he was also, as Steven Stark wrote four years ago in the University of Miami Law Review, its greatest recruiter. As surely as John F. Kennedy called a generation of Americans to public service, Mr. Burr called them to the bar.

Just ask Alan Page, who once starred for the Minnesota Vikings and now sits on the Minnesota Supreme Court. Or Robert Snider, a Deputy State Attorney General in Los Angeles. Or Kenneth Clayman, the chief public defender in Ventura County. Or Mary Binning, a lawyer in Rancho Santa Margarita, Calif. "I try very hard now to be the kind of lawyer Perry would have wanted me to be," she recently wrote to the National Association for the Advancement of Perry Mason, a fan club based in Berkeley. *"He is my idol."*

Mr. Burr did not actually persuade Scott Turow to enter the law, but he helped teach him how to tell tales about it. It was from Perry Mason that Alex Kosinski—now a member of the United States Court of Appeals in California, in the early 1960's a recent émigré from Romania—first learned such English words as "incompetent," "irrelevant" and "immaterial."

Whatever else he was as a lawyer, Mason was old-fashioned. Though he virtually kept Paul Drake, his dashing private investigator, on retainer, he practiced alone. In some episodes a law student named David Gideon worked for him, but Gideon was superfluous and quickly disposed of. So was a law clerk named Jackson. Gertie, his receptionist, was rarely seen, particularly after the actress who played her got married, leaving the faithful Della Street as Mason's only office mate.

According to Jim Davidson, the founder of the N.A.A.P.M., Mason actually lost two murder cases in the original series. But in one, "The Case of the Terrified Typist," he was misled by his client, and in the other, "The Case of the Deadly Verdict," his client was eventually cleared.

Asked why Burger never won a case, William Talman, the actor who played him, sometimes replied, "I'm trying, lady." Asked whether he ever lost, Mr. Burr, too, had a ready reply. "Of course I did," he liked to say. "We just never filmed those." ❏

TESTAMENT TO A LIFE CUT SHORT BRINGS TOGETHER WORLDS OF LITERATURE AND COURTROOMS.

10/2/92

IN THE LAST FEW WEEKS, THERE HAVE BEEN TWO UNVEILINGS FOR JAY WISH-ingrad. One was of his tombstone. The other was of a more enduring testament to his life and work: a collection of short stories on law and lawyers titled "Legal Fictions."

Eight months passed between the time Mr. Wishingrad, a New York lawyer specializing in entertainment law and intellectual property, was told he had leukemia and the time when he died, in October 1991, at 42 years of age.

Chemotherapy was his constant companion in those final days. But so, too, was Kafka, Isaac Bashevis Singer, Louis Auchincloss, Herman Melville and dozens of other writers who portrayed lawyers in their work.

"Legal Fictions" (The Overlook Press) brought together the various intellectual strands that ran through Mr. Wishingrad's career as a practitioner, a professor and a commentator. He was fascinated by the relationship between law and justice; the ways in which lawyers and authors could use the law creatively; and the need for lawyers to communicate effectively.

Mr. Wishingrad loved bookstores at least as much as courtrooms, spent vacations reading all of Solzhenitsyn or Proust, and hoped one day to see several of his own works on the shelf. A labor of love to begin with, "Legal Fictions" became even more important once he realized it would be not just his first book but his only one.

From his hospital bed, between radiation treatments, he read short stories. He fiddled with his introduction until hours before he died. Along with its own intrinsic joys, the effort furnished Mr. Wishingrad with his best defense against the depersonalization of diseases and hospitals.

"Seeing his name on a Supreme Court brief meant a lot to him, but this meant more," his wife, Susan, said in an interview in her apartment, where coffee tables were laden with literary magazines whose subscriptions had yet to expire. "It was what pulled him through all he had to endure that last year."

"Legal Fictions" includes stories by Kafka, Thomas Wolfe and Melville, most notably "Bartleby, the Scrivener." There are also works by Nadine Gordimer, Giuseppe Di Lampedusa and Isabelle Allende, among other foreign writers.

But readers are most likely to be drawn by the works of several contemporary writers whose stories capture the alienation and angst of modern practice—problems to which Mr. Wishingrad, fortified by the breadth of his interests, proved happily immune.

The Bartlebys of the law are long gone, replaced by Xerox machines that do not say, "I would prefer not to," when pressed to copy a document. But Bartleby's successors face dreary work days, broken marriages, lonely lives and dinners cooked in microwaves.

Brad, the hero of Marian Thurm's "Still Life," flees corporate practice after "working for what seemed to be a thousand hours a week on what he was sure were the most unworthy cases in the world." Cynthia Ozick's Puttermesser lands in the back room—"the repository of unmitigated drudgery and therefore of usable youth"—of her fancy law firm. In Margaret Atwood's "Weight," an idealistic feminist lawyer named Molly is murdered by her husband.

"Twenty years ago I was just out of law school," the narrator, one of Molly's law school classmates, writes. "In another 20 I'll be retired, and it will be the 21st century, for whoever's counting. Once a month I wake up in the night, slippery with terror. I'm afraid, not because there's someone in the room, in the dark, in the bed, but because there isn't. I'm afraid of the emptiness, which lies beside me like a corpse."

And, in "The Tender Offer," Valerian Shaw, a prototypically patrician Auchincloss creation, experiences the harsh new world of Wall Street in the 1980's—an era, Mr. Wishingrad writes in his introduction, in which "greenbacks, not bluebloods, reigned." For placing personal loyalty over lucre, his firm orders Shaw to resign. Should he refuse, he is told, the firm will simply dissolve, then reconstitute itself without him.

On the day Mr. Wishingrad died, his wife, Susan Wishingrad, a lawyer herself, promised her husband she would shepherd "Legal Fictions" through to publication. During every stage in the book's gestation she has felt the excitement of two people—three, really, if you consider the pride that four-year-old Mara Wishingrad will someday feel at seeing her father's final achievement.

"What Jay really wanted to do was to get lawyers to read," Susan Wishingrad said. "He felt so many of them spent so little time reading anything other than their briefs and advance sheets, and was hoping to entice them into the world of literature." ❑

What are Law Students Doing Watching Groucho, Bonzo and 'Wanda'? Studying Law, of Course.

12/24/93

Austin, Tex.—As law libraries go, the one at the University of Texas Law School is particularly agreeable. Softening all the usual dreary tomes and tables are innumerable prints, textiles, masks and other objets d'art. Of even greater appeal to bleary-eyed students, however, is a niche on the main floor. It is there that they watch the exploits of Groucho Marx's Thaddeus J. Loophole, Walter Matthau's "Whiplash Willie" Gingrich and hundreds of other fictional lawyers on film.

"This is the part that keeps me sane," one student told a visitor.

The Tarleton Law Library here ranks fifth nationally in volumes, but in videos as well as whodunits, movie posters and, soon, comic books, it is pre-eminent. All are part of the first systematic attempt to collect and catalogue portrayals of lawyers and the legal system on film and in print—media that shape popular perceptions of the law far more than any Supreme Court decision.

They are certainly shaping the perceptions of Texas law students. The school's growing "Law and Popular Culture" collection, the brainchild of its law librarian, Roy Mersky, is not as prestigious as its rare book room, which houses the papers of Tom C. Clark, the former Supreme Court Justice. But it is far more frequented. It constitutes only 2 percent of the library's total holdings but accounts for 10 percent of its circulation. Most popular of all are the films, which can be borrowed free of charge or viewed on the premises.

"I think students are getting a great deal more out of this than from reading a law book," said Marlyn Robinson, the collection's curator. "They're being entertained, but subconsciously they're thinking of the legal issues. They'll watch something and catch procedural errors."

Professors, too, are using the material. Alan Rau shows the famous scene of Chico and Groucho Marx negotiating in "A Night at the Opera"—"There's no such thing as a sanity clause"—in his contracts class. Steven Goode plays "Body Heat," with its conflict over an ill-fated will, while teaching the Rule Against Perpetuities, a notoriously nettlesome part of trusts and estates. He trots out "Miracle on 34th

Street" for his class on evidence—go ahead, prove there is such a thing as a Santa Claus. John Robertson uses the famous bank heist film "Dog Day Afternoon" in criminal law. And Zipporah Wiseman shows "The Good Mother" in her classes on sex and the law.

Though there are works by lawyer-writers like Sir Walter Scott, John Buchan and Louis Auchincloss, most of the collection's 1,800 books are mysteries—many suggested by Otto Penzler, owner of the Mysterious Book Shop in Manhattan, at 129 West 56th Street near the Avenue of the Americas. One prized item is "Counsel for the Defense," a 1912 work by Leroy Scott that, Ms. Robinson contends, features the first female lawyer-detective to appear in popular American fiction. There are also the very nearly complete works of Sara Paretsky, Anthony Gilbert, Sarah Woods and Erle Stanley Gardner.

"We're missing quite a few Gardner books when he wrote under the pseudonym 'A. A. Fair,' " Ms. Robinson lamented.

The collection also boasts a complete set of the Black Bat detective stories, a 1930's pulp novel series featuring a lawyer who dons a disguise to fight crime. Ms. Robinson hopes to add some Daredevil comics in which the lawyer-hero, though blind, is somehow endowed with X-ray vision.

Even more of a draw than the books, or the posters of Glenn Ford and Dorothy McGuire in "Trial," or the scores of movie stills purchased from a New York dealer, Jerry Ohlinger, or even the pilots of "L.A. Law" or "The Defenders," are the films.

Numbering 250 in all, the films fill one side of the room in racks resembling a local Blockbuster video store. They include all the usual suspects, among them "The Verdict," "Anatomy of a Murder" and "To Kill a Mockingbird," along with "Casablanca." (The last named is a bit of a stretch: in the play on which the film was based, it seems that Monsieur Rick was a disillusioned lawyer.)

There are other surprises as well, like "Bedtime for Bonzo," which, along with a former President, features a chimpanzee on trial for burglary. There are also selections for the children of law students, including a Three Stooges short subject titled "Disorder in the Court."

Ms. Robinson said she had seen students watching everything from "Scandal," in which Christine Keeler, a teenage showgirl, nearly brought down British Prime Minister Harold Macmillan's Government in 1963, to "Abe Lincoln in Illinois." But to her surprise, she added, "A Fish Called Wanda," in which the character played by John Cleese was a lawyer, was most popular. "I thought it was going to be 'Body Heat,' " she said.

On Ms. Robinson's Christmas wish list are some science fiction books featuring lawyers. And complete tapes of "Perry Mason." And Clarence Darrow's 1904 novel, "Farmington." And a tape of "The Colored Man Winning His Suit," the first film to feature a black lawyer, and "The Meanest Man in the World," in which Jack Benny plays an obnoxious ambulance chaser. And, for that matter, any of the thousands of other films with lawyer characters that have thus far eluded her.

But you won't catch Ms. Robinson by her home V.C.R., recording away. "It's illegal," she said. "It violates the copyright laws." ❏

AFTER A BEER COMMERCIAL LASSOS LAWYERS, A LAWYER REPLIES IN KIND.

1/21/94

THERE WAS MUCH IRE AMONG LAWYERS LAST SUMMER WHEN THE MILLER Brewing Company tried to prove that bashing one kind of bar could produce business at another. At issue was a beer advertisement depicting "the big lawyer roundup." In it, a porcine man in a three-piece suit, identified as a divorce lawyer who has profited handsomely from human misery, is lassoed at a rodeo.

Lawyers fumed. A few went further, putting together a piecemeal and rather ineffective boycott. The head of the American Academy of Matrimonial Lawyers, Arthur Balbirer of Westport, Conn., went furthest, complaining to Warren H. Dunn of the Miller Brewing Company. Mr. Balbirer wrote, "Miller can certainly come up with advertising that, like its beer, displays great taste while leaving the matrimonial bar less filled with animosity toward your company."

Mr. Dunn, a lawyer himself, replied that it was all supposed to be just good clean fun, and that Miller actually had great respect for the legal profession. That did not placate Mr. Balbirer, who ordered Chicago's Four Seasons Hotel to serve no Miller products at the academy's annual function there.

The company did pull the offending commercial briefly, after a deranged man invaded a San Francisco law firm in July, killing four lawyers. But within weeks the ad was back on the networks.

But while others groused, Neil Kuchinsky, a lawyer in Colonial Heights, Va., went, as they now say, "proactive." He wrote, produced and paid for a parody of the commercial that has lawyers and anti-smoking groups cheering. His target was Miller's parent company, Philip Morris Inc., which has an important factory in Richmond, only a few miles from his home.

With organ music in the background, a solemn, middle-aged woman surfs the television channels with her remote control. The words "Cancer Widow: A Dramatization" appear on the screen. At the woman's side is a photo of her late husband, a cigarette rakishly in his mouth.

Cut to her channel of choice and the scene of a man in a three-piece suit standing wild-eyed in a rodeo chute, pulling feverishly on a cigarette. As fans in cowboy hats cheer, a voice booms out: "Our next champion animal is Mr. Philip Millerd, a major tobacco company executive. His company owns a well-known brewery and produces millions of cigarettes a year, contributing to the untold misery, suffering and deaths of smokers worldwide."

Cut back to the widow, a tear running down her cheek, saying, "Get him!"

As soon as Mr. Millerd comes out of the chute, a mounted, lasso-toting cowgirl gives chase. It is no match. "He can't run very fast because heart disease, emphysema and other medical problems have slowed him up considerably," the announcer says. Clutching at his chest, huffing and puffing, the hapless executive with his briefcase is soon roped.

"If you don't love yourself enough to stop smoking, then think of those who love you," a voice declares. Then this phrase appears: "Paid for as a public service by: Neil Kuchinsky & Associates, P.C. Attorneys."

Mr. Kuchinsky, a 37-year-old non-smoker, said he had been moved to strike back after the Miller commercial came on while he and his nine-year-old daughter, Leah, were watching television together. "She grabbed a hold of my arm and said, 'Oh, Daddy, that's terrible!' " her father recalled.

Then, as Mr. Kuchinsky was on the way to Richmond, he spotted the Philip Morris plant off Interstate 95. "I was thinking to myself, 'Wouldn't I like to rope those bastards,' and then I realized I could," he said.

Within six weeks he found himself a genuine cowgirl, a former smoker named Tereasa Jackson, whose ranch 30 miles from Colonial Heights had horses and a rodeo chute. An actor named David Bridgewater was hired to play the short-winded tobacco executive, and Mr. Kuchinsky corralled a few clients as extras. The cost: $4,000.

No local television station was willing to run it if the name "Philip Morris" appeared; thus, "Philip Millerd" was born. Eventually, the advertisement ran 24 times in Richmond and 10 times in Washington, costing Mr. Kuchinsky another $4,000. Mr. Kuchinsky, a native of Passaic, N.J., hopes to broadcast the advertisement in New York soon.

As word of his handiwork has spread, so has the praise, plus requests for copies. "You are a hero to many of us," said Donald Brown, a lawyer in Torrance, Calif.

Stanley Rosenblatt of Miami, who represents a group of flight attendants now suing the tobacco industry, wrote, "It's so refreshing to see a creative lawyer with some guts rather than the manipulative paper shufflers I am in contact with so often."

Richard Shapiro of Virginia Beach, Va., urged in writing that the

American Bar Association lead a boycott of Miller products. G. E. Borst of Warrenton, Va., suggests that lawyers possess a yet more potent tool. "It has the potential to generate a ground swell of support in the legal community for litigation that might finally force tobacco companies to pay for the devastation their products generate," he wrote.

The public relations manager for Miller Brewing, Scott Epstein, said the company had not seen the parody and would not comment if it had. Actually, Mr. Kuchinsky sent Mr. Dunn what he called "a free, uncomplimentary copy" earlier this month.

"I have just one question," Mr. Kuchinsky wrote in a note accompanying the cassette. "Do you think my commercial is as funny as yours?" ❏

Mr. Kuchinsky continues to receive requests for his advertisement, including one from a man who hopes to translate it into Russian.

II

RITUALS

A.B.A. DONS ALOHA SHIRTS
AND EATS MACADAMIA NUTS IN ITS
ANNUAL FLIRTATION WITH FRIVOLITY.

8/11/89

HONOLULU—THE AMERICAN BAR ASSOCIATION COULD HOLD ITS ANNUAL meeting in Shangri-la—or Beirut, for that matter— and some things wouldn't change. There would still be the office seekers, the glad-handers, the networkers working the crowds. There would be the awards ceremonies and the cocktail parties, the parliamentary debates and the prayer breakfasts.

But one would be hard-pressed to find a venue less suited for seriousness than Waikiki Beach, the site of the association's convention this week. The group seemed to concede as much: "Aloha, Attorneys: 8,000 Practitioners in Paradise," The A.B.A. Journal declared. It offered guides to the best beaches, golf courses and surfing, as well as places to buy coral, pearls and carved ivory. Also listed were the closest cash machines.

No lawyers were actually sighted "hanging 10" on a surfboard. Still, those making the long, expensive trek seemed determined to have a good time, a tax-deductible luau. Or, to put it another way, their minds were more on macadamia than academia. More than most, this year's convention offered the ever-entertaining spectacle of lawyers at leisure.

Spellbinding speakers were few, burning issues (besides burning flags) fewer. This year's panels—on topics like "To Everything There Is a Season: Putting Billable Hours in Perspective," "Evaluating and Retaining the 'Superstars' in Your Firm" and "Why Is My Client Nuts? An Inquiry into the Psychodynamics of Divorce"—were sparsely attended. Even the sexier presentations, like "Heavy Breathing: The Current Status of Dial-A-Porn" or "Law Firm Dissolution: When the Finley Krumbles"—were underpopulated. The press largely stayed home, as shown by the heap of uneaten free doughnuts in the news center.

Instead, the lawyers clustered at places like the Kula Bay Tropical Clothing Company in the Hilton Hawaiian Village, where business in aloha shirts, especially in large and extra-large, was brisk. At one session, 600 judges were wearing them, making each look more like Arthur Godfrey than Arthur Goldberg. Sometimes, it seemed that the only conventioneer not sporting hibiscus flowers, ukuleles, hula girls in grass skirts, pineapples, palm trees, angel fish, Diamond Head by moonlight or bamboo shoots on his back was Robert F. Drinan, chairman-elect of the section on individual rights and responsibilities. But he had an excuse: he's a Roman Catholic priest.

Just about the only lawyers passing up the garish uniform were those who bought the shirts nine years ago when the group met here, and who have not been seen in them since.

As usual, the lawyers wore name tags everywhere—under leis, shopping on Kalakaua Avenue, strolling along Waikiki. Indeed, what made the Supreme Court Justices stand out this week is that they were not wearing them, though whether out of modesty or immodesty is hard to say.

Invariably, the Justices who speak at these gatherings are accorded all the honors of a King Kamehameha. And always, their remarks prompt the same reviews: innocuous, bland, vague, homiletic, hyper-technical, cryptic, cautious—almost as if they can't trust themselves to be real. As one wag once said of the speeches of Dwight Eisenhower, they are continually crossing the 38th platitude.

In his remarks, Justice Anthony M. Kennedy apparently criticized low judicial salaries, but never mentioned the topic by name. As for Justice Antonin Scalia, one unhappy listener grumbled that she'd heard his speech four times before. Justice Byron R. White seemed to promise more, entitling his talk "Some Current Debates." Instead, he waxed nostalgic about other Justices.

Earl Warren, he recalled, was "wise and endearing." John M. Harlan was "wonderful" and "talented." Hugo Black was "unique," but so, too, was "Bill" Douglas. Tom Clark was "engaging" and "skillful," Potter Stewart "cultivated" and "very effective," and Warren Burger "a man of many talents." As for his present colleagues, Justice White said Thurgood Marshall is "a mighty force," called Justice Scalia "very engaging and persuasive" and added: "Bill Brennan fortunately is still with us and as universally liked as ever."

Such remarks appear unexceptionable. Still, the embargo on the advance text was adamant. It could not be released until the speech: 8:30 P.M., Aug. 4, Hawaii standard time.

The A.B.A.'s new president, L. Stanley Chauvin Jr., an affable man of 54, has called the post something he's "lusted after most of my adult life," and that is no lie, for the climb up the bar association's hierarchy is arduous.

His organizational ties would make a Babbitt blush. Moreover, with licenses to practice in 11 states, his résumé resembles the back of a tractor-trailer. All those ties rallied many "Chauvinists." After all, Mr. Chauvin has explained, everyone likes to see a local boy make good. ❑

OF LAW DAY, THE A.B.A. BRAINCHILD
HONORED MOSTLY IN THE BREACH.

4/29/88

WALTER DELLINGER, IRA MILLSTEIN, RAOUL LIONEL FELDER AND NORMAN Dorsen all have at least two things in common. All are lawyers. And all are only dimly aware that this Sunday is Law Day.

Mr. Dorsen, national president of the American Civil Liberties Union, will mark the day by going to the country to play tennis and read. Mr. Felder, the divorce lawyer, will take a long-lost cousin out for blintzes at Ratner's. Mr. Millstein, a leading partner in the New York firm of Weil, Gotshal & Manges, hasn't any special plans.

"I'd be less than honest if I said I had any plans or had ever heard of anyone who did," he said. "I've never given a minute's thought to whether it makes sense to celebrate a thing called Law Day. Someone would have to tell me what it's supposed to achieve."

There have been 30 Law Days dedicated to celebrating the rule of law in the United States, and yet the occasion is observed spottily, more in the South and Midwest than the East and more in smaller communities like Saginaw, Mich., and Hollidaysburg, Pa., than in big cities. Given the multitudes elsewhere who mark May 1, Law Day rather than May Day might well make a more appropriate international distress call.

Officials of the American Bar Association, Law Day's chief boosters, say it is alive and bigger than ever. "It is something that has considerable currency in the country today," said Robert MacCrate, association president. Then why aren't more people aware of it? Theories abound.

Everyone seems to agree most lawyers are lousy salesmen, whether hawking themselves or their holidays. Thus Law Day tends to be an intramural occasion of, by and for lawyers. It is not like National Secretaries Week and other pseudocelebrations. Florists have no stake in it. And some people don't want to celebrate law or lawyers. "We've got laws coming out of our ears," said Bruce Fein, a legal scholar with the Heritage Foundation. "For many, it's not a day for celebration, but for mourning."

Critics say Law Day has become a time for homilies and platitudes rather than introspection. Mr. Dellinger of Duke Law School once used the occasion to speak on slavery. "I thought it was important to recall that the Constitution was based in part on at least one unspeakable compromise," he said.

Law Day was the 1957 brainchild of a Washington, D.C., lawyer, Charles S. Rhyne, president of the A.B.A. It wasn't an easy sell. Sherman Adams told Mr. Rhyne that President Eisenhower wouldn't sign anything glorifying lawyers, largely because of the President's hostility to his brother Edgar, a lawyer. Mr. Rhyne, a backer of civil rights and Earl Warren, feared A.B.A. conservatives might kill the proposal out of spite.

But the President and the bar concurred, and May 1, 1958, was the first Law Day, marked by a Time magazine cover article. Representative James Korman of California called Law Day "America's moral answer to man's most fearful tyranny" and added: "Law Day would counter the Communist image of deceit and tyranny with an affirmation of our own beliefs in truth, fairness and justice."

The bar association spends $100,000 a year promoting Law Day, offering videotapes, brochures and other literature. Also available are model Law Day speeches, feature stories, proclamations, newspaper advertisements and editorials marked "particularly useful as the framework for 'guest editorials' or comments on radio and television." Pamphlets advise on attracting media attention and placing and acknowledging public-service radio announcements: "Thank-you letters may help the station at Federal Communications Commission renewal time," one states.

Adults can compete in the "A.B.A. Judge Edward R. Finch Law Day U.S.A. Speech Awards" competition, or for a "Liberty Bell Award" or an "A.B.A. Law Day Public Service Award" (in that category, past winners included the Cheboygan, Mich., County Bar Association, which sponsored a mock shoplifting trial of rock star Boy George). For children, the group offers mock trial films like "Goldilocks v. The Three Bears."

There are also Law Day trinkets: Law Day bumper stickers, balloons and buttons ($6 per package); Law Day pencils ($6 for 50, unsharpened); Law Day plastic mugs ($1 each); Law Day greeting cards ($15 for a box of 25); and even Law Day litter bags ($6 for 50).

Mr. Rhyne was not invited to a White House ceremony last week where President Reagan signed a Law Day proclamation, but he says his idea has "turned out pretty well." William P. Rogers, who was Attorney General in 1958, speculated his old boss would be "somewhat disappointed" that Law Day is barely noted.

Asked how he planned to mark the occasion, he hesitated. "When is it?" he asked. "I've forgotten which day it is." ❑

IN A NORMALLY GENTEEL BAR
ASSOCIATION CAMPAIGN, TWO VYING FOR
THE PRESIDENCY ARE GOING PHYSICAL.

8/14/92

SAN FRANCISCO—IN THE MATTER OF ITS OWN INSTITUTIONAL POLITICS, THE American Bar Association has always been a citadel of civility. Like patrons at a bakery, lawyers line up politely for the presidency, working their way up through the elective ranks before facing off in genteel personality contests conducted several years in advance, lest any unseemly rancor persist by the time the winner takes office.

But the hot race at the moment, for the 1994 bar presidency, has taken on some of the negative flavor of the national Presidential campaign. Indeed, this contest has lawyers talking about a different kind of corpus, or, to put it another way, lent a new and nasty meaning to the term "body politic."

At issue are the bodies of George Bushnell of Detroit and Anthony Palermo of Rochester, N.Y. Mr. Palermo, the association's current secretary, has suggested that Mr. Bushnell is not up to the job physically, presumably referring to the foot condition that has occasionally incapacitated him. Mr. Bushnell, a past chairman of the bar group's house of delegates, counters that Mr. Palermo is too fat.

Until last February, the 1994 race promised to be a particularly big bore. Once William Paul of Bartlesville, Okla., the also-ran in the 1993 race, bowed out, the affable Mr. Bushnell stood unopposed in the voting next February. To talk bar politics, pundits and gossipmongers had to look to 1995, when either Jerome Shestack of Philadelphia or Blake Tartt of Houston will try to block either Roberta Ramo of Albuquerque or Joanne Garvey of San Francisco from becoming the first woman to head the bar group.

That might have occurred in this "Year of the Woman" were it not for the ridiculously long lead time. When Mr. Bushnell first made presidential noises in the A.B.A., after all, Bruce Babbitt and Pat Robertson were making similar noises nationally.

Then, in February, in what was, by association standards, a burst of spontaneity, Mr. Palermo declared his candidacy for the presidency two years hence. Noting Mr. Bushnell's impending coronation, he wrote, "The A.B.A. is too large, too diverse, and is engaged in too many important areas of activity to allow the presidency to pass by default."

Two years ago, Mr. Palermo led the campaign to keep the A.B.A. neutral on the question of abortion rights, leading some to grumble that when it comes to his own ambitions at least, Mr. Palermo is suddenly pro-choice. (He played no role in the vote this week when the house of delegates endorsed abortion rights.)

But providing the bar group with another option was not the only rationale the 62-year-old Mr. Palermo tendered. There was Mr. Bushnell's health, or as he put it more decorously in a letter to bar brass, "I am mindful of the physical demands which the duties of A.B.A. president exact, and questions have been raised about the health and ability of the other candidate to fulfill all those demands."

The 67-year-old Mr. Bushnell has osteomyelitis in his foot. The condition required him to drive around at one convention in a cart. More recently it sent him to the hospital for a regimen of antibiotics. But aside from that, Mr. Bushnell said between puffs on his cigarette at this week's annual meeting of the association, he is "healthy as a horse, with obscenely low blood pressure."

Though Mr. Palermo's letter, which Mr. Bushnell called "outrageous," caused his blood pressure to rise momentarily, he said his first thought was to ignore it. Then hotter heads—specifically, that of his campaign manager, Dennis Archer of Detroit—prevailed.

Mr. Archer, one of the more ubiquitous personalities at bar functions, is no stranger to the more rancorous brand of politics practiced by James Carville of Gov. Bill Clinton's campaign and the late Lee Atwater of President Bush's in 1988. In November, Mr. Archer is expected to enter the race for Mayor of Detroit. Figuring two terms there, he expects his turn at the bar presidency to come in 2001; there is no word yet on any possible opposition. Mr. Archer said he believed that Mr. Bushnell, having been hit below the belt, should hit back, but above it.

"If Tony will forswear reliance on negative campaigning," he wrote to bar officials, "I promise to try and persuade George, who is a gentleman, not to respond in kind by making an issue of the fact that Tony appears to be somewhat overweight," he wrote. George Bushnell, unlike George Bush, did not disclaim responsibility for the zeal of his surrogate. "I confess that I enjoyed it," he said.

Mr. Palermo took the retort in stride. "It's a fair comment," he said. "My wife says the same thing." And he said there were no hard feelings. He called his relations with Mr. Bushnell "friendly" and described Mr. Bushnell himself as "popular, courageous and talented."

Mr. Bushnell was more elliptical. "Ostensibly we're very courteous and polite and shaking hands and smiling," he said. "That's how it's done." ❑

Mr. Bushnell emerged victorious (so did his campaign manager in the Detroit Mayor's race), by what one might describe as a "slim" margin. Feisty and, apparently, healthy, he now heads the bar association. He will be followed by Ms. Ramo, the bar group's first woman president.

THE WAY OF THE MAVERICK,
OR PUTTING A BURR UNDER PLANS
FOR AN EXOTIC BAR CONVENTION.

3/8/91

FOR 16,000 LAWYERS IN THE STATE OF WASHINGTON, THE DAY OF JUDGMENT is near. This month, in a move costing at least $10,000 in postage, printing costs and apparatchiks' fees, they will vote on a vexing issue: whether to hold their annual convention four years from now in Maui.

Nathan Detroit, goes the song from "Guys and Dolls," ran the "oldest established permanent floating crap game in New York." But on the matter of mobility, the Washington State Bar Association, unlike most bar groups, could give good old reliable Nathan Nathan Nathan some competition. Only once every few years does the Washington bar actually meet in Washington. More often it's in places like British Columbia, San Diego (this year's site) and, in 1980, 1986 and perhaps 1995, Hawaii.

This latest luau was too much for Alva C. Long, a maverick member of the bar group's board of governors. The association lost its Hawaiian shirt when it last went to Waikiki; ferrying all that brass across the Pacific, he charged, forced the members to fork over extra gold and silver. Such junkets are fine for those he disparagingly refers to as "elevator attorneys"—lawyers in large, posh law firms, mostly in Seattle—but not for younger, poorer practitioners on both sides of the Cascades.

Moreover, he asks, what do these conventions accomplish, besides further tarnishing the profession's public image? "I went to one sober 18 years ago and I was shocked by what was really going on," said Mr. Long. "I'd rather contribute $100,000 to the cold and homeless here than the warm and the hip in Hawaii."

But when the issue of the Hawaiian meeting went before the bar governors last fall, Mr. Long was on the short end of a 7-to-2 vote. Undeterred, he collected enough signatures for this month's plebiscite.

"Who is going to believe we go to Maui to take a good C.L.E. or, rather, a tax-free exotic vacation?" asks his statement on the ballot, using the acronym for a continuing legal education course. "What do such conventions do for our public relations, which are none too good anyway? Think about it. Reverse exotic, expensive Maui. Keep us close to home."

In response, Jeff Tolman, another bar governor, insisted that with tax deductions, for most members a Hawaiian convention meant a comparatively cheap trip to an exotic place. Nearly 10 percent of the bar went to the last one, as against less than 4 percent at last year's session in humdrum Spokane. "The 1995 convention in Hawaii is good for you and your family," he declared.

The spokesmen become even more heated in their rebuttals, which appear on the same ballot. Mr. Long concluded with a battle cry: "No Maui Wowie."

Mr. Tolman was unamused. "The rebuttal of my colleague," he said, "exemplifies the professional adage: 'If you have the law, pound the law. If you have the facts, pound the facts. If you have neither, pound the table.' "

The 65-year-old Mr. Long is doing precisely what his backers wanted when they elected him last June. The son of a local judge, he is a self-proclaimed "gorer of sacred cows"—someone who grew marijuana in his father's victory garden, has been divorced five times and once spent time in an Oklahoma jail for urinating his name in wet concrete. He favors psychedelic neckties, fluorescent shoelaces and clothes with colors out of a bowl of Trix. His campaign photograph wasn't one of those funereal portraits from Bachrach but a snapshot of him eating cotton candy at the Puyallup Fair.

"To say Alva Long's presence on the board of governors may make a difference is a bit like suggesting Mount St. Helens could affect the environment," a reporter for The Seattle Times, Peter Lewis, wrote after the election. And sure enough, even before Mr. Long was sworn in last fall, he was challenging the bar's plan to meet in San Diego this year.

"I don't understand this out-of-state garbage," was the way he put it at the time. More recently, he elaborated, "Conventions in far-off, exotic places are obvious tax dodges, but the I.R.S. is not going to do anything about it—probably because it's overpopulated with lawyers itself."

Most offensive to him was the suite rented for the association president at San Diego's Marriott Hotel and Marina, a move costing the group $1,800 a night. "I know some people who are worth $1,800 a night, but none of them are lawyers," he said.

He predicted a "landslide" victory in the referendum, with only what he called "the cigar and cognac set" and those inside the "golden gavel circuit" voting for Maui. But the current bar president,

Lowell Halverson, disagrees. He thinks members will cut themselves a break, particularly since the vote comes in the middle of Seattle's soggy season.

"Those I talk to would like to have a vacation out of town," he said. "We'd like to dry out the moss under our armpits." ❑

Evidently pricking the conscience of the bar, Mr. Long's motion won resoundingly. Ever since, the state bar has not only avoided out-of-state meetings, but has held stripped-down versions at home. Mr. Long is modest about his accomplishment. "You don't need a doctorate in sanitary engineering to lift up the lid of a septic tank and describe its contents," he said.

ENCLAVE OF EXCLUSIVITY TRUMPETS
ITS HIGH PURPOSE IN TRIAL LAW,
THOUGH CRITICS HOLD THEIR NOSES.

3/10/89

BOCA RATON, FLA.—TWENTY-FIVE LAWYERS FORMED A SEMICIRCLE AROUND the lectern, standing solemnly as the famed New York litigator Leon Silverman gave the fraternity's time-honored charge.

"Today the portals of the American College of Trial Lawyers are again opened to receive into fellowship a group of distinguished barristers," he intoned. "You, whose names are freshly inscribed upon our rolls have, by your mastery of the art of advocacy, your high degree of personal integrity, your maturity in practice, your signal triumphs at the bar of justice, earned the honor about to be conferred on you. With pride, we now address you as Fellows of the American College of Trial Lawyers, as sages of our craft. Long and happy may be our years together!"

Pride is never in short supply when trial lawyers congregate. But those assembled here this week are not ordinary litigators. Instead of appending a mere "Esq." after their names, they are "Factl"—Fellows of the American College of Trial Lawyers—members of one of the bar's most prestigious fraternities.

Most bar groups are about as selective as the Book-of-the-Month Club. But the college is more like Skull & Bones: exclusive, mysterious, coveted. Luminaries like Leon Jaworski, Lewis F. Powell Jr. and Mr. Silverman have led it, and 4,400 others, from Cyrus Vance to Arthur Liman to Brendan Sullivan, belong.

"We're more interested in justice than business," said former Attorney General Griffin Bell, another past president. One of the speakers Tuesday, Judge William G. Young of Federal District Court in Boston, who is not a member, went further.

The college, he said, was "the only legal organization I've ever aspired to join," and though campaigning for membership is deemed undignified, his description of the Fellows, using words like "unstinting," "passionate" and "magnificent"—at least sounded aspirational.

At a time when many of his listeners had just returned from playing tennis and golf, Judge Young suggested that one of the principal vices of the members was not taking enough vacations. He then went on to call them "the finest master teachers of the law," "the very mortar that holds society together" and "the very eyes through which blind Justice sees."

"Rise up, my colleagues!' he exclaimed. "Rise up and make her great!"

Despite its Olde English flavor, the college dates back only to 1950. And its short roots are in Southern California. It was the brainchild of a Los Angeles lawyer named Emil Gumpert who, legend has it, hatched the idea over drinks with colleagues on a southbound smoker from Sacramento.

The standard for joining isn't as crass as that of another trial lawyers' group, the Inner Circle of Advocates, which requires at least one million-dollar verdict. Instead, it is, in the words of Sir Francis Bacon, printed in the college's roster, to be "a help and ornament" to the profession.

No more than 1 percent of the bar in a given state can belong. That formula worked in the Gumpert era, but with the bar growing with Malthusian speed, the college has become more of a university.

Selecting members makes the process of choosing Popes seem perfunctory. A candidate must wend his way through a Skinnerian box of nominators, seconders, committees, directors and regents— while pretending to look the other way. All who survive quickly accept—or almost all. Nerves are still frayed from two years ago, when Rudolph W. Giuliani failed to show up for his induction, when he was to have given a speech. (He pleaded the press of business.)

Like most clubs the college has its critics. They consider it silly and snooty, the trial bar's "Mystic Knights of the Sea." Worse, they charge that it is loaded with pin-striped poseurs more familiar with conference rooms than courthouses, and discriminates against more street-smart, rough-and-tumble types like Gerry Spence, F. Lee Bailey and Richard (Racehorse) Haynes.

With 15 years of trial experience required for membership, women and blacks remain scarce. (All of those inducted this week were white men.) So, too, are public-interest and criminal-defense types. If the college is supposed to be a demographic portrait of the trial bar, it is a faded Kodachrome.

But in this court, at least, one hears few dissents on that, or any other issue. Speaking for the new inductees, William R. Jentes of Kirkland & Ellis in Chicago quarreled with the Carl Sandburg poem that hails the good works of the bricklayer and plasterer, but asks why "a hearse horse snickers" when "hauling a lawyer's bones."

"Our work is upon the cathedral of the law," Mr. Jentes declared. "We fashion the small stones that support the towering arch of justice." ❏

A PROBATE LAWYER'S OBSESSION WITH WILLS
OFFERS YET ANOTHER PEEK AT THE WORLD
OF THE RICH AND FAMOUS.

3/22/91

THE GRAVEDIGGERS AT THE WESTWOOD VILLAGE MEMORIAL PARK SAY THAT for a mere $50,000 one can buy the still-vacant crypt next to Marilyn Monroe. Groucho Marx, who once said he would not want to join any club that would let him in, considered his membership in the Hillcrest Country Club in Beverly Hills precious enough to pass on to his son. Calvin Coolidge, not unexpectedly, was a model of testamentary taciturnity: his will was but one sentence long.

These are among the gems in what could be called the last word on last words: "Wills of the Rich and Famous" (Warner Books, $9.95), a compilation of the wills of 68 writers, actors, politicians and plutocrats assembled by Herbert E. Nass.

Mr. Nass, a New York probate lawyer in real life, has a thing about wills. "I would guess I have the largest collection in the world," he said of the 250-document collection he maintains in a fireproof safe in his basement. "I can't imagine anyone who is as obsessed with this as I am."

Over the past few years he has tracked down the wills of Norman Rockwell (in Stockbridge, Mass.), Elvis Presley (in Memphis) and Mark Twain (in Redding, Conn.). For history buffs, he includes the testaments of George Washington and Franklin Delano Roosevelt; for comedy fans, the wills of those who portrayed Egbert Sousè, Ralph Kramden and Sgt. Ernest Bilko.

Others include Tennessee Williams (Mr. Nass calls that chapter "Here Today, Iguana Tomorrow"); Gloria Swanson ("Sunset on Sunset Boulevard"); George M. Cohan ("Born on the Fourth of July, Dead on the Fifth"); and Harry S. Truman ("The Buck Stopped in Independence").

So what do these wills say? Malcolm Forbes left $1,000 each to the owners of nine of New York's most famous restaurants, including Lutèce, the Four Seasons and Mortimer's, "as a token of gratitude for the joys their skills and genius added to the lives of those who've been lucky and sensible enough" to dine in them, as well as to some 30 different motorcycle clubs. Bob Fosse specified that $25,000 be divided among 66 friends, including Dustin Hoffman, Liza Minnelli, Neil Simon and E. L. Doctorow, "to go out and have dinner on me."

Cole Porter left a diamond stud pin to Douglas Fairbanks Jr. and his clothing to the Salvation Army. Albert Einstein and Jack Benny made separate bequests of their violins, and Edward G. Robinson of his autographed piano. Lillian Hellman gave her Toulouse-Lautrec poster to Mike Nichols, and Jim Morrison, lead singer of the Doors, left everything to his wife, Pamela Courson. (She died three years later, and the Morrison estate's considerable income now goes to his father-in-law.)

Some wills are notable for being dated: John F. Kennedy never changed the one he signed six years before he was elected President. Some are significant for what they do not say: W. C. Fields never did request, at least in writing, that "On the whole, I'd rather be in Philadelphia" be carved on his tombstone, but he did leave some bottles of liquor to his brother and of Shalimar perfume to his sister.

Some are significant for their signatures. Joan Crawford's, affixed shortly after she had disowned her daughter, Christina, is defiant, almost John Hancockian, in its proportions; the 96-year-old Georgia O'Keeffe's looks like something off a child's Etch-A-Sketch. And some have revealing instructions. Bing Crosby asked that his funeral be modest, while Jackie Gleason ("And Away We Go") told his executors to spend whatever they wanted.

Mr. Nass has been unable to learn the whereabouts of the wills of either Lucille Ball or Babe Ruth. Ernest Hemingway's will is missing from the files in Ketchum, Idaho. Humphrey Bogart's, in Los Angeles, is minus a signature, apparently torn off by a collector, but still includes a bequest for cancer research. William Randolph Hearst's will was sealed in San Francisco after his granddaughter was kidnapped. For reasons that are not quite so clear, Bette Davis's will remain under seal, in Manhattan Surrogate's Court.

Mr. Nass tries mightily to vivify these documents. But what is most striking is not how exotic they are, but how pedestrian. Few display any panache or style or individuality; there are almost no parting shots, literary flourishes or wisecracks. Liberace was never dull, but his will certainly is.

Perhaps wills are not for gushing. One must also consider their authors: virtually all are the work of lawyers, who can do to language what steam tables do to vegetables. Only where the testators labored on their own behalf does any passion or pathos come through.

"The last years were painful but made bearable by friends I made through the years," Phil Silvers wrote in a shaky hand a year before his death. "I go to my God knowing at least as a comedian I was one of a kind." ❏

OY! ONE MISUSED YIDDISH WORD IN COURT,
AND JUST LISTEN TO ALL THE KVETCHING GOING ON.

6/26/92

MONICA SANTIAGO V. SHERWIN-WILLIAMS ET AL. HAD ALREADY DRONED ON for four years when counsel for the defense filed its umpteenth otherwise unmemorable motion in the case last August. "It is unfortunate," it declared, "that this court must wade through the *dreck* of plaintiff's statement of undisputed facts."

Jonathan Shapiro of Stern, Shapiro, Rosenfeld & Weissberg in Boston, one of the plaintiff's four lawyers, was startled by the choice of words. "Dreck," he knew from his grandparents, was Yiddish for doo-doo, though a tad more tart. Even by the standards of the *nareshkaytn* [1] normally filed by opposing lawyers, he thought such *chuzpah* [2] intolerable. So last September he and a co-counsel, Neil Leifer of Boston, resolved to talk *takhles* [3] with Judge Joseph L. Tauro, the *tsadik* [4] hearing the case.

"For almost four years now, plaintiff and her attorneys have been subjected to constant *kvetching* [5] by defendants' counsel, who have made a big *tsimis* [6] about the quantity and quality of plaintiff's responses to discovery requests," it stated. "This has been the source of much *tsores* [7] among plaintiff's counsel and a big *megillah* [8] for the court."

It was hardly *balebatish* [9], the lawyers complained, to call a fellow lawyer's work "dreck," particularly "in view of the *khazeray* [10] which they have filed." Finally, "since not all of plaintiff's lawyers are *yeshiva bokhers* [11], it was presumptuous as well. "Plaintiff prays that the court

---

1. Foolishness; triviality.
2. Gall, brazen nerve; effrontery.
3. The point, heart, nub of the matter.
4. A most righteous man.
5. Complaining, griping, fretting.
6. A prolonged procedure.
7. Troubles, woes, worries.
8. Anything very long; a rigmarole.
9. Quiet, respectable, well-mannered.
10. Food that is awful; junk, trash.
11. Students of the Talmud.

put an end to this *mishugas* [12] and strike "dreck," he concluded.

Ever since the motion was filed, *yentes* [13] at law firms have been photocopying and faxing the Shapiro-Leifer broadside throughout the country. In a way, the memo has challenged all of the *bobe mayses* [14] about the death of Yiddish.

The offending memo was written by Karen DeSantis, an associate at the Washington office of Kirkland & Ellis of Chicago. But it was signed by *makhers* [15] from three other firms—Goodwin, Proctor & Hoar and Bingham, Dana & Gould in Boston and Popham, Haik, Schnobrich & Kaufman in Minneapolis. And, Mr. Shapiro asserts, the word "dreck" was retained at the specific insistence of lawyers at Bingham, Dana.

Lawyers at Bingham, Dana at first tried to make Mr. Shapiro's request sound like *bobkes* [16]. "We find it difficult to believe you would seriously have us all *shlep* [17] to court to argue such a *meshugganah* [18] motion," Meghan Magruder, a partner, wrote to Mr. Shapiro. Had he called only to *kibitz* [19], she continued, he would have learned that the scriveners of the offensive motion "are all *goyim* [20]" who innocently misused the word.

Were Mr. Shapiro enough of a *mentsh* [21] to withdraw the motion, she went on, the defense would happily stipulate that "dreck" be changed to "morass." "As the taxpayers must ultimately pay to resolve such a motion, it would be a *mitzvah* [22]," she concluded. "Moreover, your *shtik* [23] may be lost on the court."

But when he ruled on the motion last December, Judge Tauro showed the defense lawyers no *rakhmones* [24]. "Any further use of inappropriate language in any proceeding before this court will result in the imposition of sanctions," he wrote in stern and unadulterated English.

---

12. A wacky, irrational, absurd belief.
13. Scandal-spreaders; rumormongers.
14. Old wives' tale; nonsense.
15. Big wheels; operators.
16. Something trivial, worthless.
17. To drag oneself, pull, or lag behind.
18. Crazy, nuts, absurd.
19. To comment, joke, tease.
20. Gentiles.
21. An upright, honorable person.
22. A meritorious act.
23. A piece of misconduct.
24. Pity, compassion.

In the meantime the authors of the memo continue to get *nakhes* [25]. Stanley G. Feldman, vice chief justice of the Supreme Judicial Court of Arizona, awarded the Shapiro-Leifer collaboration his prestigious "motion of the year award." And in an article entitled "Plain Yiddish for Lawyers and Judges," in Trial magazine, Ralph Slovenko of Wayne State University Law School in Detroit quotes the memo at length.

"With the almost complete extermination of European Jews during World War II, many scholars prophesied the end of the Yiddish language," he noted. Instead, he continued, with its "peculiar mix of toughness and compassion," Yiddish is "finding new and unprecedented application in American law."

He might just as easily have said that Yiddish is supplanting Latin as the *mame loshn* [26] of the law. ❑

---

25. Proud pleasure; special joy.
26. Mother language.

Yiddish spellings by Dina Abramowicz, Yivo Institute. Definitions from Leo Rosten, "The Joys of Yiddish" (McGraw-Hill Book Company).

SUSTAINED BY DICTIONARIES, A JUDGE RULES THAT NO WORD, OR WORD PLAY, IS INADMISSIBLE.

3/27/92

WHEN BRUCE M. SELYA BECAME A JUDGE A DECADE AGO, HE VOWED THAT HIS opinions would not be the bromidic, otiose, etiolated, jejune, desiccated tomes that had put him to sleep as a practitioner. He would forge at his judicial smithy a gleaming alloy of wit and erudition rather than the leaden dross pounded out on lesser legal anvils.

In other words, Judge Selya, who sits on the United States Court of Appeals for the First Circuit in Boston, would forsake the usual boring legalisms for lively, polysyllabic words of the sort found only in the unabridged Oxford English Dictionary, puns of the sort once found in the headlines of Barron's and The Sporting News, and figures of speech found primarily in the "Block That Metaphor!" department of The New Yorker magazine.

In Judge Selya's linguistic armamentarium, various entities may be described exiguous (meager), struthious (ostrich-like), neoteric (modern, recent) or inconcinnate (unsuitable, awkward). His world is populated with people who are forever repastinating (digging again), resupinating (turning upside down), prescsinding (withdrawing attention from), perfricating (rubbing thoroughly) or vaticinating (prophesizing).

Woe betide the litigant with an unusual name or occupation and thin skin. Consider, for instance, his 1987 opinion in a case involving Brad Foote Gear Works Inc. Judge Selya used phrases like "Foote's stance sidesteps the established principle" and "does not toe the mark"; Foote "stumbled" and "put its best foot forward"; and the trial court had not allowed Foote "to slip free of his laces." Not surprisingly, he kicked Foote out of court. "The shoe, fitting, must be worn," he concluded.

Similarly, a Selya opinion involving the International Ladies' Garment Workers Union uses phrases like "a lingerie manufacturer made a slip," "plaintiffs' own filings place them in the tightest of corsets" and the union had "played pantywaist." In another case, he wrote that the Boston Edison Company had "blown a fuse" and that its legal "surges" were "of low voltage." A prisoner complaining about poor meals provided Judge Selya with "scant food for judicial thought." Such persons, he said, were "receiving their just desserts."

Judge Selya has spoken of his eagerness "to desert the long line of solemnity which stretches from Blackstone to Burger and beyond." But in the manner of Ralph Kramden, some critics greet his attempts at humor with a jeering "ha-ha-hardee-har-har." One is Bryan Garner of Dallas, author of "A Dictionary of Modern Legal Usage" and editor of The Scribes Journal of Legal Writing.

In an article in the most recent issue of Scribes, Mr. Garner faults the judge's use of words that, while arguably more precise than more commonplace synonyms, send even a professional wordsmith like him to the dictionary. He compared Judge Selya to Holofernes, the pedantic schoolmaster who spouts Latinisms throughout Shakespeare's "Love's Labor's Lost."

"Many of his words are not in most dictionaries and have been obsolete for a long time," he said. "To say 'perscrutation' instead of 'examination' is ludicrous." But deep down, he was asked, wasn't he impressed by Judge Selya's word power?

"I might have been when I was 17," Mr. Garner replied.

He is even more agitated by Judge Selya's puns. In an article entitled "Cruel and Unusual English: When Judges Play with Words," which appeared in the Dallas Bar Association's newsletter, he asserted that the judge's jokes demeaned litigants and the legal process.

Take the Foote case. "Behind the company name, one assumes, is a person named Brad Foote, who probably had to put up with sophomoric jokes about his name throughout adolescence," he wrote. "Judge Selya allowed Mr. Foote to revisit those years." As for the Garment Workers case, "one wonders whether the other judges on the panel felt perfectly comfortable in joining in the opinion," Mr. Garner wrote.

"I think he thinks he's very funny, but to me it's the worst example of a judge's abusing his position rhetorically," Mr. Garner said in an interview. "To me, the puns are mean-spirited and the big words are pompous."

Judge Selya, whose spoken language is surprisingly normal, has no apologies for his vocabulary. "I don't go looking for unusual words to use, but if it pops in my mind I don't withhold it simply because it may not be in common usage," he said. "There are worse things than forcing people to go occasionally to the dictionary, which is one of the most under-used books in the library."

And though conceding there were a few phrases in his opinions he would, in retrospect, like to strike, he said he had no intention of muzzling himself.

"Legal humor has got to be used, no pun intended, judiciously," he said. ❏

Judge Selya remains an unregenerate sesquipedalianist. In the past year, he has sent lawyers and litigants scurrying to their dictionaries to plumb the meanings of, inter alia, "uxoricide," "gadarene" and "philotheoparoptesism."

III

COMPETITION

When a Park Avenue Firm
Goes on the Auction Block,
Canal Street Wields the Gavel.

10/28/88

THERE HAS BEEN A BRISK TRADE IN FINLEY, KUMBLE DESKS AND CHAIRS, AL-
though Finley, Kumble matchbooks and Finley, Kumble neckties
aren't in such demand. As for the Finley, Kumble art collection, the
results are mixed. The bucolic English sporting scenes have sold well;
not so the portraits of Hugh L. Carey, Robert F. Wagner and other former partners that once graced its halls.

Finley, Kumble, Wagner, Heine, Underberg, Manley, Myerson &
Casey, once the nation's fourth-largest law firm, went up in the flames
of bankruptcy last January, but the ritualistic scattering of its ashes
goes on—and on and on. It is the work not only of bankruptcy lawyers
but also of auctioneers and art dealers, who are channeling the chat-
tels to souvenir hunters, collectors, used furniture stores, warehouses
and law offices throughout the country.

Supervising the grim task is Francis Musselman of Milbank, Tweed,
Hadley & McCloy, the court-appointed trustee. Before apportioning
Finley, Kumble's $150 million debt among its former partners, he
must first seek to reduce it. Mr. Musselman's wares are Park Avenue,
Finley, Kumble's last address. But his methods are strictly Canal
Street, as is his motto: "Everything Must Go."

Much of it went in June, when Mr. Musselman held an auction at
the late firm's offices. On the block was office furniture, typewriters,
sofas, rugs, garbage pails, copying machines, law books, trays and
other assorted gewgaws. Prices ranged from $210,000 for two Wang
computers to $2 for an electric pencil sharpener, complete with
eraserless pencil.

The sale netted nearly $2 million, with at least some of that value
attributable to the novelty of the seller; in some sadistic circles, "Finley, Kumble" now has the panache of "Edsel" or "Titanic." "The name
made the sale, that's for sure," said Robert Strauss, the auctioneer.

The purchasers were a varied lot. A reporter for Manhattan Lawyer
magazine paid $75 for a Finley, Kumble filing cabinet, not so much
for storage space as for a scoop; it seemed someone neglected to
empty it. (The contents: unnewsworthy check stubs.) The firm of
Mudge, Rose, Guthrie, Alexander & Ferdon bought some Finley,
Kumble desks and chairs, apparently unconcerned that they were
jinxed; then again Mudge, Rose, the firm where Richard M. Nixon,

John N. Mitchell and Rose Mary Woods once worked, cannot let itself be haunted by history.

Some of the buyers were from Finley, Kumble itself. One partner bought back his old desk set. And Peggy Vandervoort, wife of one of the firm's founders, Steven Kumble, thought she had bought a four-drawer cabinet for $40. In fact, because the item was sold in lots, she unwittingly bought three, for $120. Now Ms. Vandervoort, like everyone else in the Finley fiasco, is in litigation—but hers is with the auctioneer.

Most alumni weren't remotely interested in mementos. "To tell you the truth," one said, "I was so disgusted walking out of there I wasn't even interested in stealing anything."

Finley, Kumble's most valuable assets weren't sitting on its floors but hanging from its walls. In the firm's brief history Mr. Kumble assembled a large art collection. The earliest acquisitions were 19th-century English portraits and nautical scenes; after he married Ms. Vandervoort, a dealer in thoroughbred horses, it became more equestrian, with occasional cocker spaniels, foxes and pheasants thrown in. One need not have wandered the halls to view the "Finley Collection"; Mr. Kumble had it reproduced in leather-bound books placed in the firm's reception area.

At first blush, the Anglophilic flavor of the artwork may seem odd, given the provenance of Finley, Kumble's founders. Both Leon Finley, né Finkelstein, and Mr. Kumble hail from the New York area. But former partners say the selection typified an enterprise that craved not only cash but also cachet. One sensed it in the firm cafeteria, where bagels were briefly banned. It was apparent, too, in the formal attire favored by some Finley, Kumble lawyers. As Mr. Kumble once put it, "Think Yiddish, Dress British."

In a sale coinciding with the running of the Belmont Stakes last June, Christie's sold 20 Finley, Kumble hunting scenes for $170,000. A week ago, it sold four of its remaining 32 "old masters" for $82,000. And yesterday a Scottish late-Georgian mahogany longcase clock for $1,760.

More problematical are the matchbooks, the monogrammed cocktail glasses and the more than 100 Finley, Kumble neckties now sitting in Mr. Musselman's office. Made by Chipp & Company of Madison Avenue, they are maroon, with "FKWHUMC" printed on a scales-of-justice motif. One thing is certain: no Milbank lawyer will ever be seen with one of them. "Anyone caught wearing one will be fired," Mr. Musselman said firmly. "That would be making fun of the situation, and this is not a very funny case." ❏

WHEN THE BOTTOM LINE IS THE BOTTOM LINE, NOT EVEN A PARTNER IS SAFE.

5/13/88

THE MAN WAS 58 YEARS OLD, OUT OF WORK AND BROKE. SO, DESPITE DEgrees from Dartmouth and New York University Law School, he found himself driving a limousine. But as much as he hated the work, things could always be worse: the next passenger could be one of his former partners.

The man's predicament was quite unusual. How many people could say they spent 15 years as a partner at a major Wall Street law firm, only to end up in a dial-a-cab? But the story is also increasingly familiar. It is the saga of the cashiered partner.

Even in a more genteel era, corporate law firms were hardly eleemosynary institutions. Under the system devised by the legal pioneer Paul D. Cravath, young lawyers spent eight years of drudgery, then either moved "up" or, more frequently, "out." The reward was nonetheless worth the risk; the select few were set for life.

Every firm, of course, has always had its deadwood. The Cravath system, which supposedly works with Mendelian predictability, nonetheless produces mutations. Unproductive partners were stuck in back offices until they retired. Partners were dismissed as often as Presidents were impeached, and only for high crimes or misdemeanors, like the Cravath partner who regularly shipped his associate away on assignment, then hopped over to Brooklyn Heights to visit the young man's wife.

Nowadays, life tenure is a quaint anachronism. With firms monitoring partner productivity the way dairy farmers scrutinize Guernseys, no one is entirely safe. After decisions by management committees or partnership votes, firms like Rosenman & Colin; Willkie, Farr & Gallagher; and the driver's own alma mater, Brown & Wood, have sacked partners. And in law firms, as New York goes, so, too, eventually goes the nation.

"It has its unfortunate aspects but it's a competitive world and you have to come to grips with life as it exists," said George A. Sears of Pillsbury, Madison & Sutro, San Francisco's largest firm, which dismissed three partners last fall.

Because the case is in litigation, Brown & Wood will not discuss the lawyer who turned limousine driver. The man insists it was not for poor work but poor "rainmaking," the vital knack of fetching new business. The firm gave him $120,000 severance pay and promised to help him find work.

Five hundred letters, 2,000 telephone calls and numerous headhunters later, he remained unemployed. Eventually, he landed a job as an associate at a midtown firm. "They made a shambles of my life and my career without giving it a second thought and now I'm trying to rebuild things," he said. Two weeks ago a New York judge dismissed most of the man's case. Herbert Deutsch, his lawyer, plans an appeal.

"This lawsuit demonstrates another of the economic misadventures involving New York law firms—and one approach at revitalization," Judge Harold Baer Jr. wrote in his opinion. "Many believe that the last decade has seen the bar move from a profession to a business. In some firms we find that profits have replaced pro bono; production has undercut professionalism and compensation has overtaken collegiality."

In the Orwellian language of the law business, few are ever actually "fired." An article entitled "When Firing Partners, Most Firms Revert to Gentlemanly Approach," in Of Counsel magazine, includes the latest fig leaves, consolation prizes and state-of-the-art euphemisms to camouflage reality. The issue is no longer whether such executions are proper, but how to perform them with the least bloodshed.

John Wagner of Omaha's Kutak, Rock & Campbell talks of partners being "encouraged to find a practice elsewhere." Others become "emeritus" long before they're gray. But the most popular device is to call them "resignations." This is what two former Milbank partners did in recent interviews, even as Alexander Forger, the firm's head, matter-of-factly told Of Counsel how the firm handles those it asks to leave.

Edward J. Reilly of Milbank, who opposed his firm's recent dismissals, said: "Partners are more than just the people down the hall handling S.E.C. filings. I went to their weddings, their parents' funerals, watched their children grow up. As long as they were doing their best, they deserved to stay."

Donald Shack of New York's Golenbock & Barrell agrees. A decade ago, his firm let five partners go after the loss of a key client. But the dismissals had other costs: friendships and a certain professional joy. The firm's good deeds in the community matter little, he has concluded, if charity does not begin at home.

"We would not do it again" he said. "We'd try to create some livable space for the partners affected, then roll up our sleeves and replace the client. And in the interim, we'd perhaps make a little less money." ❑

Things only got worse for our cashiered friend. After a traffic accident he stopped driving his limousine and took a menial construction job, all the while sending out hundreds of résumés to law firms. None landed him so much as an interview. He worked briefly as an associate in a small firm, but lost that job when the firm disintegrated. Now, at age 65, he works part time for a business on Long Island. "I always figured that if you worked hard and stayed late at night and got your job done, you'd get ahead—that if I treated everybody right, they'd treat me right—but that seems naive in retrospect," he said. "The moral of the story is that things have changed in this country. If you're not a business-getter, you don't belong in this business."

AMID COMPETITION FOR CLIENTS,
LAW FIRMS HOLD THEIR NOSES
AS THEY TRY PUBLIC RELATIONS.

5/27/88

HE WAS THE MANAGING PARTNER AT A MAJOR WALL STREET LAW FIRM, AC-customed to making hard decisions daily for a multimillion-dollar enterprise. But when he began to talk to a marketing consultant he lost all his aplomb. Suddenly, the lawyer was acting like an accessory to a crime—a crime against his profession.

"We've taken, ah, the traditional law firm view that the least publicity is the best," the consultant recalled hearing over the phone. "But there's ah, ah, a growing feeling that perhaps, that maybe that's not the best, might not be the best approach. There's some concern here, among some of the partners here that we ought to be, that maybe we should be doing some—" He paused, gulped, then uttered the dreaded words, "some public relations."

The consultant felt he should cut him off simply as an act of mercy. "In other words, you don't have to like it, but you may have to do it?" he asked. The partner confessed that this was so.

In the hierarchy of hype, the assistance the firm was seeking was the most genteel. It didn't want the television spots Chief Justice Warren E. Burger once likened to dog food commercials, nor did it seek matchbook covers or the shrill solicitations for the maimed and bankrupt that appear in the classified advertising section, alongside pitches for high-school equivalency courses and bartender schools. All it sought was an occasional mention in the press.

A decade after Bates v. Arizona, the case in which the Supreme Court invalidated bans on advertising for legal services, even the most innocent forms of public relations remain a hard sell on Wall Street, particularly among top firms. "I can't imagine having any need for a P.R. firm, period," said Thomas Barr of Cravath, Swaine & Moore.

But while a few elite firms can ignore it, Madison Avenue has come to Wall Street. Firms like White & Case; Willkie, Farr & Gallagher; Curtis, Mallet-Prevost, Colt & Mosle; and Winthrop, Stimson, Putnam & Roberts now use public relations consultants. Others seem certain to follow, their disgust for promoting themselves overcome by their fear of losing their competitive edge with clients.

Aided by their publicists, law firms like Milbank, Tweed, Hadley & McCloy and Fried, Frank, Harris, Shriver & Jacobson have planted articles about themselves in The National Law Journal, Manhattan,inc. and other publications. Costly brochures, like one for the normally staid Shearman & Sterling depicting all its lawyers in shirtsleeves, are commonplace. Press releases clog the mails.

Some are sober, like the announcement that Stroock & Stroock & Levan has hired a refugee from the demised Finley, Kumble firm for its Los Angeles branch. Similarly, Phillips, Nizer, Benjamin, Krim & Ballon details how it recently won $960,498 for a chemical company suing a copy machine manufacturer. Its release, however, includes some of the Churchillian rhetoric that a firm partner, Jay F. Gordon, used to dazzle the jury: "Without blood, the human heart doesn't beat; without ink, a pen doesn't write; without toner, copiers don't copy."

Some appeals try a more user-friendly approach. "What's it like to be Mickey's lawyer?" one asks. "Frank Ioppolo, head of the real estate department at the New York law firm Donovan, Leisure, Newton & Irvine can tell you." Mr. Ioppolo, it seems, represented the Walt Disney Company in an "incredibly complex" hotel deal at Epcot Center.

And some speak in the breathless parlance of the legal press. Jack Nusbaum of Willkie, Farr is one of the "hottest" lawyers in mergers and acquisitions, with Donald Trump among his clients, the firm's publicist proclaims. "How and why he has become a 'superstar' would make an interesting story," he adds. A recent Fried, Frank release describes how a partner, Jean Hanson, has metamorphosed from "comer" to "heavy hitter." "Based on 1987, Ms. Hanson is clearly someone to speak with in 1988," it declares.

If the announcements seem amateurish, it's easy to see why. Firms want their public relations cheap, and they're generally getting what they pay for—$5,000 a month or so.

The most tasty tidbits—sensitive cases, internal wrangles—will never make it onto press releases. And with all that off limits, what's left? The Chicago law firm of Mayer, Brown & Platt may use the same publicist as StarKist tuna and 9-Lives cat food—Daniel Edelman Public Relations—but Mayer, Brown's managing partners, Leo Herzel and Robert Helman, aren't exactly Morris the Cat and Charlie the Tuna.

Ultimately, the problem is really one of attitude. Wall Street firms may be more insecure than ever among themselves, but to the outside world, much of the old arrogance remains. Publicity, though necessary, is still viewed with abhorrence, and publicists, even one's own, are considered almost a lower order of primate.

"Lawyers are used to giving advice, not taking it," said Loren Wittner of Edelman. "They hire public relations people, but they don't want to deal with them." ❏

As the much criticized general counsel to the Treasury Department during the Whitewater affair in 1994, Ms. Hanson no longer had to reach for publicity.

'IN' IMAGE IN RECRUITING:
SNORKELING, WINE-TASTING, JOGGERS
WHO PROVIDE 'FULL-SERVICE.'

12/23/88

One might expect the picture on the cover of the O'Melveny & Myers recruiting brochure to be of, well, Mr. O'Melveny and Mr. Myers. But the photograph is not of the two lawyers but of two rocks: "Moon and Half Dome," Ansel Adams's famous shot of Yosemite National Park.

Inside there are more of Mr. Adams's photographs and on the inside cover a portrait of Mr. Adams himself that is far more impressive than the fuzzy picture of the firm's chairman, Warren M. Christopher, appearing three pages later.

What has Ansel Adams to do with the third-largest law firm in Los Angeles? It seems the firm owns 82 of his works, carefully selected by Mr. Adams himself. But more than that, photographer and firm share a credo. "Creativity, persistence, integrity, discipline," the brochure states. "There is much we can learn from Ansel Adams."

Large law firms do not hawk themselves on bus posters alongside blurbs for hemorrhoid potions. But advertising for recruits is a different story. Once, when top graduates beat down their doors, firms got by with grim, uninformative prospectuses. Now, with competition for talent keen, they're choosing glossier presentations with a bullish look and tone that belies their underlying anxiety.

Changes like this always come more slowly to New York, where some firms still consider it unseemly to use telephone listings in darker type. But even mighty Cravath, Swaine & Moore recently produced a booklet, in which it calls itself "one of the pre-eminent law firms in America."

A few years ago, Shearman & Sterling produced a video. To a tune from the "Royal Fireworks Music," youthful voices sing of utopian lives there. "There's room for all kinds of people here," one says. "There's no dress code, there's no uniform, there's no back-stabbing." After the occasional all-nighter, a second notes in legalese, "there's generally a celebratory party." (The scene shifts to Windows on the World. In the background, the pop of a champagne cork can be heard.) This is a place where even the equipment prompts euphoria. "I really think our Xerox department is the best," one woman gushes.

The firms face a problem already familiar to anyone pushing aspirin or cigarettes: how to distinguish the indistinguishable. For although the firms are not the same, the image they covet is. The description offered by Houston's Vinson & Elkins comes closest to the generic: "A diverse collection of talented individuals engaged in innovative legal work across a broad spectrum of practice areas."

All are "full-service"; that is, if there's anything they can't do, they don't admit it. All are "cutting edge." All throw their young lawyers immediately into the fray. (Mackall, Crounse & Moore of Minneapolis makes this point with a picture of six legs in a puddle to show how its young lawyers "get their feet wet fast.")

All are both old-fashioned and forward-looking. All have mushroomed, but without compromising quality. All have top clients, but aren't dependent on any of them. All are public-spirited. All are meritocratic. Judging from the pictures, suit coats are superfluous. So are doors, since they are always open.

In other words, all are unique, and in precisely the same way.

Once, the dominant images were of earnest lawyers on telephones and hard-hat lawyers at construction sites. Now emerging is a second-generation cliché: "lawyers at their leisure." Just as Newport advertisements no longer show people smoking, lawyers are shown snorkeling, jogging, sailing, wine-tasting, theater-going, ball-playing, hang-gliding, rock-climbing, rafting, surfing, golfing—anything but practicing law.

How, then, can the firms stand apart? Some stress their clients. An associate at Shearman & Sterling, Ford Holbrook, appears to represent the Kramdens and Nortons, since they appear with him on page 19 of the firm's brochure. (In reality, he helped National Amusements take over Viacom, which syndicates "The Honeymooners.") Others note blockbuster deals. Vinson & Elkins actually boasts of helping the nation's largest cemetery concern acquire the second-largest casket manufacturer.

Along with the growing sophistication of the propaganda, however, something else has changed. Law firms no longer hold a monopoly on information about themselves. There are alternative sources like The American Lawyer's annual survey of young lawyers, which recently ranked O'Melveny & Myers last in Los Angeles in quality of work, knowledge of partnership chances and the likelihood of lasting two more years. That might exhaust the "creativity, persistence, integrity and discipline" of even an Ansel Adams. ❑

Even Warren Christopher eventually left O'Melveny & Myers, albeit to become Bill Clinton's Secretary of State.

NOW ENTER THE 'MEDIA ADVISER,'
A NEW LINE OF DEFENSE
FOR THE SOPHISTICATED LAW FIRM.

2/24/89

THE PRIMERS TELL LAWYERS HOW TO DEAL WITH THE WILIEST OF ADVERsaries: how to anticipate their stratagems, exploit their weaknesses, protect their clients and themselves. But the enemy they are speaking of is not opposing counsel. It's the press.

Much has changed since the time when lawyers, asked for comment on pending cases, reflexively zipped their lips. Many formerly reticent firms, in fact, now have their very own "media advisers," whose principal task it is to get their names in print.

Donald J. Bingle, a lawyer at Chicago's Bell, Boyd & Lloyd, "is an experienced and articulate resource on takeover strategy and defense," Priscilla Whittier, the firm's director of marketing and public affairs, wrote reporters recently. "If you require further information don't hesitate to call me or Don Bingle directly." Or, should you be considering an article on public-interest law, "I'd like to suggest that you solicit the opinion of Harold 'Ace' Tyler," wrote Alan Quinby of Doremus Public Relations, which represents Patterson, Belknap, Webb & Tyler of New York.

Beneath the bonhomie, however, an age-old, visceral antagonism remains. Not so deep down, many lawyers view journalists with a mixture of fear and loathing, resentment and anxiety. "Lawyers are by nature boosters, company men who respect the party line, while journalists have little respect for anything but what's interesting," explained Edward J. Burke of Hildebrandt Inc., a legal consulting firm.

But now the question is not whether to talk to the press, but how. And that is where the primers come in. "The words 'A reporter's on the line' shouldn't panic legal professionals," wrote Donald Blohowiak, a legal publishing executive, in The National Law Journal. "But it should snap them to attention."

These are some of the cardinal rules for dealing with the press suggested by advisers:

❡ Say something. "Defending one's firm or client in the press may seem distasteful but the alternative might be far worse," advises Mr. Blohowiak, author of "NO COMMENT! An Executive's Essential Guide to the News Media." The most diplomatic way to duck is to be dull. Constance Belfiore and Frank Trotta, authors of "Lois Lane Is on Hold," a pamphlet issued by the American Bar Association, suggest using clichés like "The story will come out in court."

¶ But don't gush. Even when you're available, don't take a call immediately. Waiting gives you time to weigh—and mouth aloud—your responses beforehand (as well as putting a call in to make sure the reporter is who he says he is). "Pause before each answer, even if the question is 'What is the spelling of your name?' " the A.B.A. booklet suggests.

¶ Do your homework. "Prepare for your interview as you would for a client meeting, deposition, or speaking engagement," a legal consultant, Wendeen H. Eolis, urged recently in The New York Law Journal. Expect tough questions ("Every firm has a skeleton or two in its mahogany closet," Mr. Blohowiak says) and, like politicians, say what you want, regardless of whatever was asked.

¶ Speak English. Whereas "whereas" may trip off a lawyer's tongue, omit what Fred Rodell of Yale Law School once called the "streamlined voodoo and chromium-plated theology" if you want to be quoted. Skip the legalese and Latinisms; hold the semicolons. Or, as Nancy Boles and Katherine Heaviside put it in the A.B.A. Journal, "distill your arguments into a few sentences, even if it took you umpteen pages to say it in your brief."

¶ Garnish with stories or puns, analogies, similes and metaphors. Media hounds, it seems, are just as predictable as Pavlov's dogs. "Journalists, accustomed to interviewing unimaginative spokespersons, quickly latch on to colorful or memorable language," Mr. Blohowiak advises.

¶ Don't be greedy. Given space constraints, don't expect both you and your firm to be mentioned in an article, particularly if you work at a place with such cumbersome names as Sirote, Permutt, McDermott, Slepian, Friend, Friedman, Held & Apolisky of Birmingham, Ala.

¶ Stroke the reporter's ego. Never ask one to read back a quotation or, worse, to show you an article before publication, Mr. Blohowiak says. Instead, tape the conversation, and say you're doing so.

¶ Never pull rank. "A lawyer shouldn't remind a reporter of the advertising dollars the firm's clients spend with the publication, or of the firm's close relationship to the reporter's publisher," Mr. Blohowiak says.

And finally, plead ignorance where appropriate. Though it may sully their carefully cultivated image of omniscience, lawyers should say "I don't know" if they really don't. Or as Larry Smith, managing editor of the legal newsletter Of Counsel, wrote recently, "Saying something stupid in print is a lot worse than having some reporter simply think you're stupid." ❏

A TRENDMEISTER FOR LAW FIRMS
FINDS HIS COUNSEL IS HIGHLY COVETED
AS TIMES TURN TOUGH.

11/30/90

SOMERVILLE, N.J.—ON THE AFTERNOON OF OCT. 17, 1989, BRADFORD Hildebrandt sat in a San Francisco law office, preaching his message of the coming shakeout in the legal industry. And sure enough, the earth shook.

Even Mr. Hildebrandt could not foresee the California earthquake. But given his seer-like status in the legal profession, one wouldn't be surprised if he had.

Mr. Hildebrandt, who is 49 years old, presides over Hildebrandt Inc., the nation's largest, most successful and certainly most visible law firm consultants. Along with his flock in eight American cities plus London, Mr. Hildebrandt tells lawyers at more than half the nation's 500 largest law firms how to run themselves, pay themselves, train themselves, sell themselves and save themselves—things they have little aptitude or stomach for unassisted. As firms grew like the national debt in the 1980's, Hildebrandt grew with them. Now, as times turn tough, its counsel may be even more coveted.

Mr. Hildebrandt is an unlikely guru to credentials-conscious lawyers. He has no graduate degrees in law, accounting, business or anything else. Indeed, for a time he dabbled in law enforcement, a fact The Times of London seemed to savor earlier this year when Hildebrandt Inc. opened on Chancery Lane. It described him simply as "a former policeman in New Jersey."

Mr. Hildebrandt does have a Middle American, Rodgers & Hammerstein feel to him. He is the type to place his "world headquarters" in this horsey Somerset County town, who calls Washington "Warshington" and who has hung a stuffed tuna and a ship's wheel on his office wall. "The trouble with Brad Hildebrandt is that he looks as if he's from Ohio," a law firm maven in New York once noted.

But far from bothering the Brahmins, they seem to find this meat-and-potatoes personality refreshing. Mr. Hildebrandt has no religious training. But at one time or another, for one law firm or another, he has performed most of the sacraments.

As the broker behind several megamergers, he has officiated at both marriages and baptisms. Lawyers with problems come to him for confession. He decrees the ordination of new partners. A few years ago he gave extreme unction to one firm that had retained him, Herrick & Smith of Boston. For that he won The American Lawyer's coveted "Undertaker of the Year" award.

Mr. Hildebrandt is also a missionary. Once he spread the gospel of growth. More recently, he has amassed millions of frequent-flier miles evangelizing a creed of leanness-is-meanness, spreading apocalyptic visions of smaller profits or worse to firms that fail to tighten their money belts.

Not long ago, Hildebrandt Inc. issued what it called an "unprecedented advisory" to its clients. Roughly akin to a hurricane watch from the National Weather Service, it warned of the blood, sweat, tears and toil on tap, urged firms to "weed out" unproductive underlings, dismiss "under-utilized" partners or get them busy, and to warn even rainmakers that "their compensation expectations may be over-inflated."

If the "king of the road," Roger Miller, knows every engineer on every train, Mr. Hildebrandt knows every concierge at every conference center where law firms hold retreats. When he is not spreading the creed of efficiency, his disciples are. Recently, people around the globe could listen, by means of international satellite broadcast, to Hildebrandt Inc.'s Joel F. Henning expound on "Managing and Motivating Lawyers."

Mostly, Mr. Hildebrandt makes his name in the press—as oracle, soothsayer, trendmeister. His pronunciamentos, uttered in the peculiar Esperanto of law firm management ("bottom-line," "midsized," "full-service," "two-tiered") pop up regularly in everything from The Financial Times of London to The Puget Sound Business Journal. In legal periodicals, his name appears more often than some bylines.

There are Hildebrandt sound bites, which range from the catchy ("Sabbaticals and hot tubs seem to go together—they're West Coast phenomena for the most part.") to the clunky ("The two-tier concept is not a blanket medicine that will cure all law firm ills.").

"We spend hours on this stuff," said Edward J. Burke, the man Mr. Hildebrandt calls his "media consultant." Mr. Burke added, "I get sick of reading about him myself."

As if that's not enough, in a column each month in The New York Law Journal, beneath one of those airbrushed photographs from the Dear Abby school of perpetual portraiture, Mr. Hildebrandt opines on all facets of law firm life. "The circulation desk should be near the main entrance of the library," he counseled recently.

And there are Hildebrandt advertisements. "The best time to choose us," one declared ominously, "is while you still have a choice." ❑

In one of the greatest law firm burials ever, Rev. Hildebrandt presided over the 1994 funeral of Shea & Gould. "I think he's Dr. Death, our own little Kevorkian," a partner at the soon-to-be-defunct firm told New York magazine.

SOME TIPS, TRICKS AND TRADE
SECRETS FOR LASSOING GOOD CLIENTS.

11/24/89

LEARN HOW TO SAY "LAWYER" IN SERBO-CROATIAN OR FARSI. PRACTICE AT an address like Park Avenue or Wilshire Boulevard, or, if you cannot afford that, at least have a mail drop there. If you are toiling weekends or nights for a client, find an excuse to call him because martyrdom can be good business.

In today's saturated legal market, hustling clients is "a never-ending, 24-hour-a-day task," says Jay G. Foonberg, a Beverly Hills, Calif., lawyer and author of "How to Get and Keep Good Clients." His tome, about to enter its second printing, is to "legal marketing" what Heloise is to household hints: a huge collection of aphorisms, tips, tricks and trade secrets.

From it, one learns the intricacies of lassoing clients—from the proper chairs for reception rooms to whether clients prefer clean or cluttered desks to how to dispose of the impoverished clients your richer clients may dump on you. For those seeking to drum up business in parking lots, the book includes a compilation of 200 possible vanity license plates, ranging from WHIPLSH to ARBITR8 and LAWYR4U to SUE4FUN. And for anyone handling international work, there is a handy list of how to say "lawyer" in 36 languages, including Swahili, Bulgarian and Vietnamese.

If good marketing boils down to aggressiveness and self-confidence, Mr. Foonberg is People's Exhibit No. 1. He boasts that his last work, "How to Start and Build a Law Practice," is the "book most stolen from law libraries in America," and that based on innumerable lectures and two million miles of travel, "no other person in America is as qualified as I" to write this book.

Mr. Foonberg insists that the price of the book, $96 in hardcover and $85 in paperback, is fair given what lawyers stand to learn and how much they themselves charge. At the rate most lawyers bill, he writes, his book would take them 20 to 40 minutes to recoup.

Herewith is a sampler of Mr. Foonberg's suggestions:

❡ For finding clients, bar groups sounding elitist and exclusive are better than "animal clubs" like Moose, Elks, Lions or Eagles, even though the seemingly elite organizations rarely require anything more than a law license and dues to join.

❡ When choosing periodicals for your waiting room, select whatever projects the right image, not what might actually be read. Because they suggest expertise, stupifyingly dull bar journals may be preferable to National Geographic. Anything, he says, is better than magazines suggesting to clients that when they need you, you are out playing tennis or golf.

¶ Always dress, travel and sleep first-class, even if you cannot really afford it. Clients, he says, "will be more favorably impressed when you tell them you can be reached at the Ritz rather than at the Happy Cockroach motel."

¶ Christmas cards bring sugarplums. Each year, Mr. Foonberg says, his holiday greetings more than cover costs. A typical response from a recipient? "Jay, I just got your Christmas card and it reminded me that I have to update my will because I have a new grandchild." Many cards represent two potential clients, he says, since couples with children generally wait until just after the holidays to break up. If they divide their property, you may get a house closing along with a divorce.

¶ To get referrals, butter up old clients. "Remind your friends of your long-standing relationship," he says. "There must be 100 people who think they were one of my first clients."

¶ A fictitious address does not matter if it is fancy. "There are many communities where lawyers rent mailing addresses to give the appearance of being where they are not," he writes. Among them: Cambridge, Mass., Princeton, N.J., and Newport Beach, Calif.

¶ Nice lawyers may finish last. When a client is out for blood, any lawyer coming across as too likable is a sap and a fool, he writes in a chapter entitled "When to Be a Mean, Rotten S.O.B. with a Potential Client."

¶ Do not say you have forgotten your business cards. Instead, say you are "out of them," thereby making yourself seem in demand.

¶ Ply potential customers with drinks. "Clients have a high anxiety level and often are nervous and/or thirsty. The drink may wet a dry mouth and give the client something to do with their hands." And, he suggests, do not forget the breath mints yourself. "Lawyers talk a lot, which dries out their mouths and is conducive to mouth odor. An occasional mint may help."

Talking about bad breath, when to wear jewelry or whether to attend funerals may discomfort some lawyers, particularly those who do not need to hustle for work. But such aloofness is becoming a luxury as the lawyer count mounts. As of July 1989, it stood at 725,574, with 35,000 more each year.

In this sense, Mr. Foonberg is more than a maven. He may also be a seer. ❏

A FIRM WITH MOSTLY SEAFARING
CLIENTS DISPENSES COUNSEL,
AND SOMETHING ELSE, FOR PORTS OF CALL.

12/17/93

JAY LAWRENCE FRIEDHEIM AND JOE MOSS, A PAIR OF ADMIRALTY LAWYERS IN Honolulu, have never vied for the American Bar Association's annual "dignity in advertising" award. But if the bar group offered a prize for originality or ingenuity or outrageousness, they would probably win hands down.

Their firm, which caters primarily to sailors and fishermen, is surely the only one that hands out customized condoms. They come in packages of one shaped like oversized matchbooks. "Friedheim & Moss," each package declares. "Saving Seamen the Old-Fashioned Way."

With all purveyors of legal services tending to sound the same, it is hard for lawyers to differentiate themselves. But Mr. Friedheim and Mr. Moss believe they have come up with the most effective calling card ever, something that serves clients, saves lives, produces laughs and generates business, all at once, and for only 35 cents apiece. Having gone through the first order of 2,000 condoms in the past eight months, they are about to order that many more.

Sailors, merchant marines, fishermen, ship passengers—unlike more landlubbing clients—are elusive prey. "There are no ambulances at sea," said Mr. Friedheim, a former stand-up comic who was an extra in the movie "The Blues Brothers." He and his partner decided they needed something that potential clients would carry with them, something more useful than the usual baseball caps or key chains or cheap ballpoint pens, something healthier than liquor and less quickly tossed in the nearest trash bin than business cards.

The inspiration was Mr. Moss's, coming to him several bottles of wine into a dinner party. "When we got done laughing and picked ourselves off the floor, we thought, this is a great idea," Mr. Friedheim recalled. It was unconventional, memorable and, coming from two lawyers, endearingly self-deprecating.

"Lawyers have spent many centuries taking themselves entirely too seriously, when they're really just the equivalent of auto mechanics with words," he said.

The giveaway also happened to be socially responsible. "My clients are in fact a high-risk group for H.I.V.," the virus that causes AIDS, Mr. Friedheim said. "These are guys who go to whorehouses for fun." With even the President urging that condoms be distributed to school-children, he reasoned, who could quibble about handing them out to sailors?

Their only fear was the bar, and whether unamused disciplinary officials could possibly bring charges of unprofessional conduct against them. It hasn't happened, leaving Mr. Friedheim, who was born on the Lower East Side of Manhattan, grateful for politically liberal Hawaii. "There are places on the mainland where I would have been burned at the stake," he said.

Mr. Friedheim came up with the motto, then found a medical supply house in California offering tailor-made packaging. The finished product arrived in April. Since then the two lawyers have handed out their giveaways wherever their clients congregate: in harbors, union halls and the offices of local shipping lines.

It is hard to know just how many have chosen Friedheim & Moss because of them; no one has come right out and said so. But sailors are only one target audience. Mr. Friedheim estimates that 8 of every 10 condoms end up with other lawyers, and that's no accident, for it is from them that he and Mr. Moss receive some 70 percent of their business. Thus, the two men distribute the condoms to their peers, in person and by mail. "Every time I go to court I take another handful," Mr. Friedheim said.

Some lawyers have politely declined the freebies. An 86-year-old judge recently told Mr. Friedheim that he did not need them. Others, including four people at a meeting last Tuesday of the Hawaii Bar Association's section on admiralty law, have taken to approaching Mr. Friedheim for handouts rather than the other way around.

And many recipients, men and women alike, have actually come back for more. So did a reporter for "Lawyer Advertising News," a newsletter published by the A.B.A.'s Commission on Advertising. She asked Mr. Friedheim for a dozen, explaining that various members of the commission wanted packages of their own.

There have been rumblings and grumblings from some local lawyers, though none of them, at least so far, has said anything to the perpetrators themselves. At least one person complained to the Hawaii State Bar Association, though judging from the sentiments of the man heading the state bar's committee on advertising and solicitation, Mark S. Davis, the matter seems unlikely to go anywhere.

"Dignity, taste and humor cannot be regulated by our bar association," Mr. Davis told the A.B.A.'s advertising newsletter. "It is only in the area of factual misrepresentation to the public that we are obligated to get involved and impose appropriate prophylactic measures." ❏

Demand for Mr. Friedheim's freebies has been so great—including requests from disciplinary officials in Indiana, Florida and Maryland—that he recently ordered 3,000 more. Though colleagues like the condoms, their wives (some of whom have happened upon them while going through their husbands' pockets) have not, at least until told who Mr. Friedheim is and what he's up to. The reaction at his alma mater, Tulane Law School, has also been mixed. "There's a split over whether I'm a local hero or a guy who went off the deep end," he said. Thus far, Mr. Friedheim said, there have been no copycats. "I think we really reached the cutting edge of bad taste," he said.

KEEPING TABS ON LEGAL FEES MEANS
GOING AFTER THE PEOPLE WHO
ARE HIRED TO GO AFTER PEOPLE.

3/20/92

"IF A CLIENT DOES NOT COMPLAIN ABOUT A BILL, IT ISN'T HIGH ENOUGH." This aphorism was part of the lawyerly wit and wisdom John J. Mc-Cloy, the former diplomat and New York lawyer, gave each year to the tenderfoots in his law firm.

But such an attitude was by no means limited to Milbank, Tweed, Hadley & McCloy. Reluctant to dirty themselves on such unseemly matters, lawyers long set their fees arbitrarily, often erring on the side of extravagance. Conversely, clients, either intimidated by counsel or unduly deferential to them or too rich to care, rarely kept close tabs.

In the last few years, though, as the economy has slumped, belts have tightened and sentimental traditions have yielded to hard-headed pragmatism, all this has begun to change. For a fee, a number of companies will now monitor legal bills. The oldest and busiest, it seems, is Legalgard Inc. of Philadelphia.

In its promotional literature, the company describes its mission euphemistically. "Legalgard conducts an objective and detailed review of in-force attorney billing and utilization practices to determine a baseline for billing and case management problems and to identify opportunities for savings," it states. Translated into English, that means investigating rip-offs.

The growth of Legalgard, which primarily serves insurance companies and corporations, reflects the fertility of the territory. Begun only five years ago, it has expanded 300 percent annually ever since. It has opened branch offices in Woodland Hills, Calif., Tampa, Fla., and Chicago and now employs 80 people. Most are lawyers-turned-investigators, presumably familiar with all the fine points of padding.

"Lawyers were the last of the sacred cows, the last people on the face of the earth to be held accountable to anyone," said Legalgard's chairman, John J. Marquess. He recalled how, only a few years ago, a potential client of his balked at second-guessing his lawyer. "He told me, 'If you can't trust your lawyer, it's like not being able to trust your wife,' " Mr. Marquess said. "I told him, 'Based on what your legal costs have looked like for the last five years, maybe you should go home and check what your wife is doing.' "

Mr. Marquess, who practiced law for 15 years himself, said his investigators found irregularities on four of every five legal bills, ranging between 10 and 30 percent of the total. With legal fees in the United States totaling $100 billion a year, he said, "The target market is gigantic."

Since 1987, Mr. Marquess's minions have found all manner of machinations, including these:

❡ A lawyer in Century City, Calif., who, on three occasions, billed a client for 50-hour workdays. "I don't care what you say, nobody has an excuse for billing more than 24 hours a day," Mr. Marquess indignantly declared.

❡ A Los Angeles lawyer who charged a client in 135 separate cases for the same piece of legal research: the meaning of a "collapsed" condominium.

❡ A San Francisco law firm that passed on to clients the $17,000 cost of its program for summer law clerks—all under the guise of "legal research." "It was really devious," Mr. Marquess said.

❡ Boston lawyers who billed their clients for the cost of either heating and air-conditioning their offices and commuting between their homes and offices.

❡ A lawyer in Cleveland who charged his client for the suit, shirts and underwear he purchased in the midst of a long trial.

❡ A Chicago law firm that put 79 of its 82 lawyers, along with all of its paralegals, on a single products-liability case, racking up a $6 million tab for work which, Mr. Marquess estimates, should have cost no more than $200,000. Another Chicago lawyer, he said, charged $25,000 for "ground transportation" during an assignment in San Francisco. "Either the attorney was renting a limousine on top of a rental car or was renting an escort," Mr. Marquess said.

❡ A firm in New Orleans that routinely billed four hours of work for letters that were one sentence long.

Since he signs confidentiality agreements with his clients, Mr. Marquess would not identify any of the malefactors. But he offered some clues.

Abuses, he said, tended initially to be more novel on the West Coast. But the worst offenders, he said, were the largest and ostensibly the most prestigious law firms, a fact he attributed to a combination of bureaucracy and arrogance.

"The big firms on Wall Street are having it both ways: they're billing $400 an hour and massaging the billings on top of that," he said. Their preferred modus operandi: overstaffing. "A matter that takes 10 lawyers and 3 paralegals in one firm will typically take 25 lawyers and 12 paralegals in New York," he said. ❑

WARNING (FROM LAWMAKERS):
NEVER JUDGE A LAWYER
BY HIS MATCHBOOK COVER.

3/16/90

BALTIMORE—UNTIL NOW, PERHAPS THE MOST MALIGNED ENTREPRENEURS IN this city were its "tin men," the fast-talking aluminum-siding salesmen depicted in a 1987 Barry Levinson movie of the same name. But if some newly proposed legislation is enacted, the tin men may be displaced by lawyers.

This month the Maryland State Senate voted overwhelmingly to require lawyers to include disclaimers in their advertisements, whether in newspapers, on television or matchbook covers. If lawyers sell themselves like cigarettes, the legislators seemed to say, their pitches should also carry appropriate warnings.

The proposed disclaimers mention nothing about heart disease, cancer or emphysema. Instead, they would simply state, "The decision to seek legal services and choose a lawyer is extremely important and should not be based solely upon advertisements or self-proclaimed expertise."

The bill, which now goes to the State House of Delegates, provides that the warnings be printed in at least 9-point type—slightly smaller than what you're reading. On television the disclaimer must appear continuously on the screen.

Maryland would not be the first state to enact such rules. They have been on the books in Iowa since the infancy of lawyer advertising, and a similar measure is pending in Florida. But in the hotly contested market of Baltimore, where lawyers fight for cases the way Gunning's and Bo Brooks vie for lovers of steamed crabs, the proposal has generated a vicious debate, including charges of elitism and anti-Semitism.

The bill is the brainchild of State Senator George W. Della Jr. of South Baltimore. None of his constituents has ever complained about the ads, except perhaps over how often they interrupt their late-night movies. To listen to Mr. Della, it's more a matter of theoretics and esthetics.

For instance, there is a commercial run by the firm of Saiontz & Kirk. It shows an accident scene with flashing lights and crashing sounds and sirens. "If you have a phone, you have a lawyer," the ad declares.

That "leaves the impression that you should call a lawyer before you should call an ambulance for your loved ones in the car," Mr. Della said.

Then there are the ads of Stephen L. Miles, who is to Baltimore's personal injury bar what Victor Kiam is to electric razors: the most aggressive advertiser of them all, spending more than $1 million a year. His most recent ad focuses on his feet, showing them emerging from a car. "Is that him?" a voice asks breathlessly. "Look, that's him!" another says in wonder. The feet are shown walking into a courtroom, where a judge asks sternly, "Are you ready to proceed, Counsel?" In fact, he's raring to go.

"Don't just call a lawyer," the announcer declares. "Call former Assistant State's Attorney Stephen L. Miles."

That last line, Mr. Della contends, hints that Mr. Miles can push buttons with his old cronies.

Mr. Miles takes the legislation personally. "The bill is designed to put me out of business," he says. He told The Baltimore Sun that the bill was "total bull." And noting that virtually all of the leading lawyer advertisers are Jewish, he accused Mr. Della of anti-Semitism. "If the nine biggest lawyers advertising in Baltimore weren't Jewish, I don't think this bill would have been introduced," Mr. Miles said.

Mr. Della called that charge "way out of line" and said Mr. Miles had made it "out of total desperation." Seconding him was the president of the Maryland State Bar Association, Herbert S. Garten. "Anyone who interprets the action as an act of anti-Semitism is guilty of reckless and baseless accusations that are a disservice to the lawyers of this state," he wrote Mr. Della.

Both Mr. Miles and Donald Saiontz, of Saiontz & Kirk, hint darkly that Mr. Della is a pawn of the plaintiffs' lawyers-hating insurance industry, a charge he denies. But they also see the paw prints of their fellow lawyers, notably those who don't advertise and don't like losing business to those who do. Ten of the 13 lawyers in the state Senate supported the Della bill.

"If you were Joe Chevrolet, and Jerry Chevrolet down the street was on television every night, you would ask your favorite state senator to undercut him by loading them down with baggage," said Mr. Saiontz, a onetime classmate of Mr. Levinson and, he says, the model for a character in the filmmaker's earlier Baltimore movie, "Diner."

Asked about that, the Senator equivocated. Well, he doesn't advertise on television, he said. How about disclaimers in his print ads? He would, he said, if the law required him to. But would he do it voluntarily? He paused, then said he had no such plans now. ❑

As of mid-1994, eight states now require such disclaimers. Thus far, Maryland is not among them.

IV

THE FEMINIZATION
OF THE LAW

BEATING THE ODDS AND JUMPING THE 'MOMMY TRACK' ON A CROOKED PATH TO PARTNERSHIP.

11/11/88

FEW PEOPLE WHO KNEW CAROLYN PARIS AT STANFORD LAW SCHOOL WOULD have pegged her as a future partner in a major Wall Street law firm. It was a matter not of her intellect, which was obvious, but of her sensibilities. For her, as for many others, the transition from studying liberal arts to law was painful enough; the further step into mainstream law practice was almost inconceivable.

That, however, was where the jobs were, and in 1978 she joined Davis, Polk & Wardwell, one of New York's most illustrious firms. The work itself she found surprisingly satisfying. But other obstacles appeared. For one thing, she got married. Worse, when her husband was transferred to Singapore, she went with him. Since Davis, Polk had no office there, she joined New York's Coudert Bros., which did—an act most firms viewed as treason.

When she returned to New York in July 1983, Davis, Polk nonetheless took her back despite another complication that many firms would view as crippling: she was four months pregnant. Within a few months, then, she was briefly gone again. Earlier this year, the same year she was to come up for partnership, she took a second maternity leave.

Ms. Paris was, in short, the perfect candidate for the "mommy track," the second-class status to which women who want to lead balanced lives are often relegated at large firms. But last week, when she was summoned to what she thought was a routine meeting, Ms. Paris was greeted by handshakes and applause. She had been named a partner.

Clearly, the path toward partnership remains steeper for women, particularly mothers, than for men. But Ms. Paris's story shows that when a resourceful woman and an innovative law firm join hands, the situation need not be so bleak. Young mothers have also been promoted at Lord, Day & Lord, Barrett, Smith and Simpson, Thacher & Bartlett.

Innovation is not a word one would have historically associated with Davis, Polk, which is in Wall Street's blue-chip triumvirate along with Sullivan & Cromwell and Cravath, Swaine & Moore.

While none of these institutions embraced change, Davis, Polk was arguably the most conservative of all. Old-timers invariably describe the firm in decades past as "white shoe": that is, a place where social connections were paramount. It was populated by Social Register types who had attended not only Yale or Harvard, but Groton or Hotchkiss.

The firm did not name its first Jewish partner, Henry King, until 1961. (Mr. King is now the firm's managing partner and president of the New York State Bar Association.) Its record on women was no better.

But in the early 1960's the situation began to change. On issues like recruitment, promotion and computers, Davis, Polk was more progressive than its two rivals. What remained taboo at Cravath or S. & C.—detours for government service, intra-office marriages, permanent places for those passed over for partnership—was permitted, and the sky did not fall in. On the contrary, the firm grew and diversified.

In 1971 it named its first female partner, an observant Jew and the mother of four. The firm developed a liberal policy on maternity leave and permitted part-time work during early child-rearing years. To make that easier, it agreed to install personal computers and facsimile transmission machines in the home of anyone wanting them.

However competitive the three firms are privately, even the most pallid public puffery remains bad form among them. Thus, after Sullivan & Cromwell's managing partner, John Merow, was quoted recently in The American Lawyer as saying, "We really don't think that all in all Cravath or Davis, Polk has quite the range of strengths we do," he felt compelled to apologize to both Mr. King and Samuel Butler, Cravath's managing partner. (Mr. Merow says he was misquoted.)

But while avoiding direct comparisons, Mr. King says the firm's flexibility has borne fruit in both recruiting and retaining talent. Davis, Polk now has more former Supreme Court clerks than any other New York firm. And, with Ms. Paris and two other women promoted with her, it will have eight female partners on Jan. 1—not many in a 98-partner firm, but twice as many as S. & C. and four times as many as Cravath.

Ms. Paris has had to make plenty of adjustments herself. Many of them—living near her office, skipping most social engagements, minimizing what she stuffs into her briefcase each night—have been planned with one goal in mind: to be with her children when she's not working.

"There were people here who went out of their way to encourage me at very difficult points, when I was tempted to throw in the towel," she said. "Without them I'd have left some time ago. I doubt I'd even still be practicing law." ❑

A WOMAN MAKES PARTNER THE HARD WAY:
PRACTICING LAW ONLY THREE DAYS A WEEK.

11/20/92

IN THE LAST DECADE WOMEN HAVE MADE NUMEROUS INROADS INTO THE LEgal profession. Now Millie Kalik has pulled off the latest, and perhaps one of the last, firsts.

Ms. Kalik, a 44-year-old mother of two, has spent the last 12 of her 20 years in the law practicing only three day a week. Not so long ago, large law firms, whose profit margin and culture hinge on 50-, 60- or 70-hour work weeks, considered such arrangements subversive. But earlier this month Ms. Kalik's professional home, Simpson, Thacher & Bartlett of Manhattan, made Millie Kalik a partner. No one can think of a precedent.

Mainstream law firms are adjusting to the demands of female lawyers, but slowly, painfully and, at times, begrudgingly. In the seven years that Working Mother magazine has ranked the top 100 companies for working women, only one law firm, Morrison & Foerster in San Francisco, has ever made the list.

But as women rise through the ranks and competition for talent intensifies, some firms are fiddling with their rules, surprising even themselves in the process. "Law practice in New York City can be brutal, particularly for women," said Richard Beattie, chairman of Simpson, Thacher's executive committee. "If we want to continue to attract really terrific women to the firm, we've got to be more flexible."

Mr. Beattie said he was amazed Ms. Kalik's elevation did not encounter any opposition, particularly from the 100 other partners, 7 of them women, who endured an average of six workdays a week for eight years for the privilege. But if any of them felt that Ms. Kalik, however sterling her qualifications, had not paid her dues, they did not make their opposition known.

He conceded that Ms. Kalik's case will be, at least in the short run, unusual. She practices probate law, a field generally thought to be more sedate and, therefore, more amenable to unorthodox arrangements. Will litigators or bankruptcy lawyers follow suit? How about men? He has his doubts.

Ms. Kalik, a 1972 graduate of George Washington University Law School, worked full time at White & Case, where her husband is a partner, for eight years. In July 1981, when her first daughter, Melanie, was 5 months old, she moved to Weil, Gotshal & Manges, where she began her three-day-a-week routine. Seven years and another daughter later, she relocated to Simpson, Thacher. Her status there was "counsel," a kind of professional limbo in which her partnership chances seemed slim.

Just how she has apportioned her time has varied. Initially, she found that three long days at the office—generally Mondays, Tuesdays and Thursdays—allowed her to discuss codicils with clients and play Candyland with her children. Now, with her children in school, she comes into work more often but works shorter days in order to be home, whenever possible, for dinner.

Never, she said, had she been tempted to go full time. "I find that the older my children get, the more they need me," she said.

Asked a few Mother's Days ago why she loved her mother, Ms. Kalik's younger daughter, 8-year-old Juliana, replied, "Because she doesn't work on Wednesdays." But if Ms. Kalik's most recent Wednesday is any indication, Juliana must be a very frustrated girl.

Ms. Kalik rose at 6 and made breakfast, which, with two working parents, constitutes the closet thing to the day's family meal. At 8:30 she began her 45-minute, head-clearing walk to her office. From 9:30 to 11 she worked at her desk; from 11 to noon she met with a client.

There were more phone calls, then lunch with the investment banker handling some client portfolios, then another meeting with another client. This one lasted until 4, when it was time to pick up Juliana at the Ethical Culture School. While waiting, she snuck in a return call to a reporter. At 6, after dropping Juliana at home, she attended a party for the women practicing at Simpson, Thacher, by now 100 or so strong. After that, she attended her monthly discussion group with her fellow estates lawyers. She returned home in time to talk to Melanie about her homework.

To Mr. Beattie and other Simpson, Thacher executives, Millie Kalik's principal utility lies in drafting wills and trusts. But she performs another function for them which, while unsalaried, may be just as important: she places things, notably about the relative importance of work and family, in perspective.

Ms. Kalik's claims for herself are more modest. "Sometimes I think I have the perfect mix, other times I fear I'm shortchanging either my kids or my career," she said, nursing her daily can of diet Coke. "I'm doing what works for me, but I don't necessarily advocate it for anyone else. Each person has to find his or her way." ❑

WHO SHOULD WEAR THE PANTS IN COURT?
A FASHIONABLY CORRECT QUESTION.

1/17/92

JUDGES MANQUÉS ENJOY SERVING ON BAR ASSOCIATION ETHICS COMMITTEES, where they get to pronounce on the mores of the legal profession. For the most part, though, what they ponder are not crowd pleasers but less-than-scintillating technical matters like questions about client confidences or conflicts of interest.

The ethics committee of the New York County Lawyers' Association, however, recently received a cri de coeur from a Manhattan law firm that raised what the panel's chairman called "needlesome" questions about fashion, popular culture and sexual politics: Is it acceptable for female lawyers to wear pants suits in court?

"There is apparently some opinion that women in pants or slacks are undignified (not too long ago such attire was barred in some restaurants), while others suggest that such attire is much less diverting and permits much freer movement than skirts or dresses," a lawyer at the firm wrote to the committee, apparently referring to recent expressions of disfavor from the bench. He—though his identity, as well as his firm's, are unknown, he is said to be a he—feared that women wearing pants suits in court runs afoul of provisions of the Code of Professional Responsibility that lawyers be "dignified," "refrain from morally reprehensible conduct" and "not engage in conduct that offends the dignity and decorum" of court proceedings.

The first question facing Marjorie E. Gross, a vice president at Chemical Bank and the ethics panel's chairman, was whether its 26 members should deal with such a problem at all. Some thought the question either insufficiently dignified or overabundantly sexist: It should be considered, one member suggested, only if at the same time the panel weighed the propriety of male lawyers' arguing cases in kilts.

Ms. Gross's compromise was to investigate the question, but with a bit of whimsy. "We hesitate to invade the territory of Mr. Blackwell," she wrote boldly, referring to the fashion maven who compiles annual lists of the world's best- and worst-dressed people. But "while attempting to avoid all manner of puns on what constitutes 'suitable' attire," she continued, "we will not skirt the issue."

There is nothing inherently disrespectful about pants suits, she quickly concluded. As an authority, she cited no less an arbiter of popular culture than TV Guide, which asserted recently that Sharon Gless, the star of the television program "The Trials of Rosie O'Neill," had once and for all established that there was "a place for casual chic in the courtroom."

As is often the case on committees, particularly lawyers' committees, less humorous heads—stuffed shirts, one might call them—prevailed. The opinion that emerged is the editorial equivalent of the gray flannel suit, with none of the wit or indignation the question probably deserves. "We find it difficult," it states, "to see how an appropriately tailored pants outfit could diminish the order and decorum of the tribunal, affect the rights of parties or witnesses, or impair the administration of justice."

Along with the pompous verbiage, however, the opinion offers some threads and patches of courtroom sartorial history.

In New York State, it seems, the Amelia Earhart of women's courtroom dress was one Carolyn Peck of Syracuse. In October 1968 she represented her client while wearing a skirt with a hemline that was some five inches above her knees—a level, according to court documents, that was "extremely and excessively short" and that "revealed substantially more of the human frame than is customarily displayed in a courtroom." She was held in contempt and ordered never to appear in court so attired again.

The 27-year-old Ms. Peck got herself a lawyer. Then Faith Seidenberg, the lawyer who broke down the sex barrier at McSorley's Old Ale House in Manhattan, joined Ms. Peck in an appeal supported by the American Civil Liberties Union. Together they persuaded an appellate court to overturn the judge's order.

"Whatever may be one's personal judgment as to the propriety of petitioner's dress, we are compelled to conclude that it has become an accepted mode of dress, not only in places of business or recreation, but, to the consternation of some, in places of worship," wrote Justice Domenick Gabrielli, later of the New York Court of Appeals.

Ms. Peck had her moment of fame, being quoted in Time magazine and appearing on "What's My Line?" She later moved to Cambridge, Mass., where she was prosecuted on lewdness charges for walking around her property naked. Here, too, she eventually prevailed, convincing a jury that, as she put it, "nudeness is not lewdness." ❏

As Cravath shifts to new quarters, it is boldly moving into the world of Crayola.

6/23/89

THE MOST COMMONLY SEEN CONSUMER ITEMS IN LAW OFFICES HAVE BRAND names like Lexis or West. But the current shopping list at Cravath, Swaine & Moore contains some more unusual trademarks: Fisher-Price, PlaySkool, Child Craft and Crayola.

Over the next few months, in an operation worthy of the Allied Expeditionary Forces, a convoy of 300 trailer trucks will move Cravath from the financial district to Worldwide Plaza, the neo-Woolworthian skyscraper at 825 Eighth Avenue between 49th and 50th Streets. The firm's new stake on the site of an old Madison Square Garden will be for the bar what the Dakotas were to homesteaders and the Dakota was to homes: a bold leap to the frontier.

But Cravath, a firm that has blended the old and the new more successfully than most, is doing more than changing venue. It is changing cultures. When it opens around Labor Day, it will become the first major New York law firm with its own on-premises emergency child-care service. Or, to put it in street language, Sesame has come to Wall.

Cravath's operation, which will cost $100,000 to install and $75,000 a year to operate, will not provide classic "day care." It will be a more modest fail-safe service, designed to be used only when other child-care arrangements fall through. Thus it will accommodate only 15 of the 225 eligible children, from the age of 6 months to 12 years, at one time.

Still, as modest as it is in a firm of 300 lawyers, the center marks a dramatic departure. Since it is open to the children of all the firm's employees, partners to paralegals to custodians, it will instantly become the most egalitarian facet of a traditionally stratified, hierarchical operation, a place where, not so long ago, partners and associates used separate toilets and desks were said to have "partners' legs."

More importantly, like so much of what Cravath does, the concept is sure to be emulated. Cravath lawyers have already received anxious inquiries about the center from the firm's archrival, Sullivan & Cromwell.

The Cravath project is largely the brainchild of Christine Beshar, a mother of four who is the first woman to become a partner in the firm. Cravath was free to innovate in part because it is suddenly awash in space: at 370,000 square feet, its new home is twice as large as its cramped current quarters.

Nowadays, a city of mahogany—1,285,000 square feet of it along with 50 tons of marble—is rising from the 38th to 49th floors. The lawyers' offices—small parallelograms for associates, larger polygons for partners—have spectacular panoramas of New York; from the 46th-floor perch of the presiding partner, Sam Butler, for instance, one can see the East and Hudson Rivers and the Central Park Reservoir.

Forty-four floors below, in the room where the kiddie pictures and toys will soon go, there remains mostly rubble. But Cravath has already hired the center's first director, Tara Greaney of Manhattan's Caedmon School, and has issued its first regulations.

Initially, the center will be open from 9 A.M. to 6 P.M. each day, with shorter weekend hours. But at a firm where hard work is legendary—it was a bicoastal Cravath associate who logged the first 27-hour day—that may well be extended. Children may not use the center for more than five consecutive days, nor, ideally, more than 15 days a year. The operation is B.Y.O.D.D.—bring your own disposable diapers—but will limit other imports. "Bring a teddy bear or cuddle toy if you'd like, but no other toys," they advise.

The first emergency child-care center at a law firm opened nearly three years ago at Wilmer, Cutler & Pickering in Washington. Unable to make other arrangements after a hurricane shut down local schools, an associate, Jane Sherburne, brought her young son into her office, where all went well until he began singing "Rudolph the Red-Nosed Reindeer."

Such centers, the firms have learned, reduce absenteeism and turnover and increase billable hours. Having children around is good for morale and ambiance. And in the tweedledum and tweedledee world of law firm recruiting, firms with day care have a distinct edge. At Wilmer, Cutler, the same people who first opposed the idea—complaining that the firm should not be child-tending or that the regulations were too onerous or the insurance too costly—are now among its biggest boosters.

Emergency day care makes so much sense that one wonders why it's caught on so slowly. Anne Marie Smith, who started the Wilmer center and has since moved to Hogan & Hartson, offered one explanation: On matters of personnel, she says, law firms are still in the 1950's. "That kind of 'Leave It to Beaver' world no longer exists," she said, "but at many law firms, Ward Cleaver is still in charge." ❏

So many parents have availed themselves of Cravath's day-care center that the firm has had to expand its hours. At lunchtime, many of the children dine at the firm's cafeteria, 46 flights up, which now has its own high chairs and children's menu.

LEGAL PRESERVE OPENING ITS DOORS TO PERSONAL ADS AS SEARCH FOR ROMANCE (AND PROFITS) BEGINS.

9/29/89

CAN A YOUNG PROSECUTOR SLIP AND FALL FOR A PERSONAL INJURY LAWYER? Can a conservative corporate lawyer find romance with a public defender? Can a mergers and acquisitions specialist make a tender offer to a law professor? Soon some answers to these questions may emerge.

In the last two weeks, an incongruous notice has begun appearing in The New York Law Journal, the staid, buttoned-down publication perused each morning by thousands of local lawyers. There it peeks out, amid more traditional advertisements—for title search companies, legal seminars and the Big Apple Pothole and Sidewalk Protection Corporation. "Personals for Professionals," it declares.

"Your work may be rewarding, but is your life fulfilling? Or is it incomplete?" it asks, in an empathetic tone uncharacteristic for the journal. It goes on to relate how, in response to numerous requests, The Law Journal will go the way of New York magazine, The Village Voice and The New York Review of Books and offer what it calls "a unique opportunity to create meaningful long-term relationships."

For the last few years, the century-old Law Journal has tried to freshen up its stuffy image and brighten its look. It recently redesigned its front page, whose antediluvian graphics had seemed better suited for dispatches from the Crimean War. It also runs more features, photographs and profiles, regularly reviews movies and plays, and even rates restaurants—predictably, on a scale of one to four gavels. Still, by the time the journal examined relationships, in columns or court opinions on divorce law, equitable distribution or custody, those relationships had already gone bust. Anyone doing a computer search of its archives would rarely come up with the word "love."

But come Oct. 11, The Law Journal will run personals each Wednesday, behind more traditional classifieds for office space, termite inspectors, lie detection services and experts in swimming pool accidents. In the process, a new, more lawyerly shorthand may emerge, to supplement abbreviations for single (S), male (M), female (F), white (W), black (B) or Jewish (J) already appearing in lay publications. They might include "L" (for "litigator"), "C" (corporate lawyer), "ADA" (assistant district attorney), "P" (partner), "A" (associate), "PD" (public defender) and LA (Legal Aid Society lawyer).

Already, the first few advertisements are trickling in. Two-thirds are being placed by women, though most of the telephone inquiries come from men. "Striking blonde blue-eyed attorney (Italian), 27, enjoys film, theater, country weekends, zoos, travel, museums, seeks male counterpart for lasting relationship," one states.

James Finkelstein, The Law Journal's publisher, said that given the newspaper's well-deserved reputation for seriousness, he had instituted the new policy with "reluctant enthusiasm." At least one irate reader has written to complain that the idea of such ads is unbecoming, although Veronica McDonald, who wrote the initial announcement, strove valiantly to phrase it decorously. "My effort," she explained, "was to make it uplifting, to take earthiness out of it, shall we say."

But Mr. Finkelstein is a shrewd businessman and knows a potential market when he sees one. To paraphrase the old cigarette commercial, lawyers these days are working more and enjoying it less. Already, the journal profits handsomely from attorney angst, with ample ads for placement services, career counselors and agencies employing lawyers wishing to work only part time.

Part of that unhappiness is undoubtedly social. At a time when lawyers at big firms are expected to bill 2,200 hours a year, there is not a lot of time left over for singles bars.

At $15 a line, the ads are $14 cheaper than those in New York magazine. Aside from price, there are pluses and minuses. The average household income of the journal's 85,000 readers, Mr. Finkelstein says, is $239,630, the highest of any daily in the country. But his demographics are a bit skewed. At last count, 84 percent of them were men, and, with an average age of 45, many of them are a bit long in the tooth.

One might wonder why personal ads are necessary in an era when record numbers of women practice law alongside men. But as matchmakers already know, many lawyers recoil at the idea of dating other lawyers, particularly in their own firms. Among single lawyers, "at least he/she is not a lawyer" is a line repeated like a mantra.

If The Law Journal's ads don't produce results, customers will soon have an alternative. Apparently inspired by its example, Manhattan Lawyer magazine has announced that it, too, is starting a personals column—five days later. ❑

The advertisements bombed, and the feature was quickly canceled. "It was a terrible idea," said James Finkelstein, The Law Journal's publisher. "Lawyers are too sophisticated or too discreet to have used the service in a major way. And perhaps they see enough of lawyers during the day to want to see more of them at night."

IN RETROSPECT, FATHER DIDN'T KNOW BEST
IN THE CASE OF A DAUGHTER
WITH A HABIT OF MAKING HISTORY.

5/14/93

FIORELLO LA GUARDIA MAY HAVE KNOWN HE WAS MAKING HISTORY THAT Saturday when he summoned Jane Bolin to the New York City building at the 1939 World's Fair. But Ms. Bolin, then a 31-year-old lawyer in the Corporation Counsel's office, thought she was in for a reprimand, though for what she could not fathom.

"I was very apprehensive," she recalled the other day. "I couldn't think of anything that I had done."

Shortly after she and her husband arrived in Flushing Meadow, "the Mayor breezed in and just ignored me," she continued. "He said to my husband, 'I want to speak with you,' and took him in another room. I couldn't imagine what was going on. When they came out, my husband was smiling, and the Mayor said to me: 'I'm going to make you a judge. Raise your right hand.'

"I was in a state of shock. I did what he told me. I raised my right hand." And when she did, she became the first black woman in the nation to be sworn in as a judge.

Her appointment, to New York's Domestic Relations Court, was news around the world. But neither then nor now, as the Corporation Counsel's office prepares to present its award for distinguished service to Judge Bolin on Monday night, was it a big deal to her. After all, she had already had her fair share of firsts as a black woman: first to graduate from Yale Law School; first to join the New York City Bar Association; first in the Corporation Counsel's office.

When Judge Bolin, who is now 85, decided to become a lawyer, she was only following precedent. Her father, Gaius Bolin, the first black graduate of Williams College, practiced law in Poughkeepsie, N.Y., for more than half a century and was president of the Dutchess County Bar Association. As a child, she would hang around his law office after school, soaking up the ambiance. "Those leather-bound books just intrigued me," she said.

Judge Bolin took the path, later followed by Hillary Rodham Clinton, from Wellesley College to Yale Law School. When she told her father that she had been admitted to Yale and needed tuition money, he looked at her askance; he did not think women should see all the misery that crosses a lawyer's desk. She ignored his warning, though she had many occasions to consider it during the 40 years she spent in what was to become Family Court, hearing tales of violence in the home, child abuse and neglect.

At Yale Law School, she was one of three women in her class, and the only black. "We were the lone pepper pods in all that sea of salt," said Edward Morrow, a former reporter for The Chicago Defender who was Yale's sole black undergraduate part of that time.

Judge Bolin recalled that a few Southerners at the law school had taken pleasure in letting the swinging classroom doors hit her in the face. One of those Southerners later became active in the American Bar Association and invited her to appear before the bar group in Texas. She declined.

There was more unpleasantness when she looked for law work in New York after a six-month apprenticeship with her father. When she applied to a few local firms, she found the climate frosty. "I was rejected on account of being a woman, but I'm sure that race also played a part," she said. "The reception I got was very, very business-like, and I was disposed of rather rapidly."

She spent five years practicing law with her husband, Ralph Mizelle, then two years in the Corporation Counsel's office, an appointment that itself made the newspapers. She was assigned to the Domestic Relations Court—a tribunal, The New York Times reported at the time, that "handles many cases involving members of her race."

On July 22, 1939, in the shadow of the Trylon and Perisphere, Mayor La Guardia administered the oath. When she informed her father of the appointment, he was once again chagrined. "He told me, 'Judges have so much tension in their lives, they die early of heart attacks,' " she said. On this point he was less prescient.

Judge Bolin said she relished the work of the court. "I loved trying to help children and families," she said. "I never would have to go to any other court and deal with property rights." She stepped down from the bench quite reluctantly in 1978, when she reached the mandatory retirement age of 70. Judge Bolin has recently curbed her charitable activities, but still works, mainly reviewing disciplinary cases for the New York State Board of Regents.

Sojourner Truth. Marian Anderson. Fannie Lou Hamer. Rosa Parks. Charlayne Hunter-Gault. The list of women who were trailblazers in civil rights is well known. Modest and matter-of-fact, Judge Bolin has kept herself off the roster.

"Everyone else makes a fuss about it, but I didn't think about it, and I still don't," she said about her role. "I wasn't concerned about first, second or last. My work was my primary concern." ❑

HIGH BAR OFFICER DRAWS FIRE OVER
DISMISSALS, FLAMBOYANCE AND DALMATIANS.

3/31/89

CHICAGO—THE CAREER OF JILL WINE-BANKS HAS BEEN A SERIES OF FIRSTS. At 44 years of age, she has already been the first woman to be a Watergate prosecutor, general counsel to the Army and now executive director of the American Bar Association.

A year and a half ago, Ms. Wine-Banks was chosen to succeed Thomas Gonser as head of the vast bureaucracy of the bar group, which picks women as leaders as often as the College of Cardinals picks Polish popes.

Then there was her bar pedigree (almost non-existent); her age (youngish); her religion (Jewish); her style (aggressive, visible); and her politics (liberal Democratic), all atypical for the association. And Ms. Wine-Banks boycotted the bar group for her first 10 years of practice. Her selection marked a stark change from Mr. Gonser, a laconic computer type known around bar headquarters as "the big walking silent giant."

Today Ms. Wine-Banks is experiencing a less festive first: criticism. The complaints are many. But the most painful involves her Dalmatian.

Dogs might seem as irrelevant to Ms. Wine-Banks's job as the miniskirts that made her famous in 1973, when, as the prosecutor Jill Wine Volner, she questioned Rose Mary Woods about an 18½-minute gap in a White House tape. But Dalmatians are not ordinary creatures to her and her husband, Michael Banks, an antique dealer.

Until recently, her office was decorated with Dalmatian posters, Dalmatian figurines, Dalmatian cutouts, Dalmatian pencils, Dalmatian flowerpots, Dalmatian book bags, Dalmatian stationery. And yes, there was a copy of "101 Dalmatians" on the shelf. Her 1987 A.B.A. Christmas card showed the Bankses' two Dalmatians, Finnegan and Samantha.

Shortly after the card was mailed Finnegan died, apparently from swallowing a tampon. He was 7 years old. Convinced that a veterinarian, Dr. Mell Wostoupal, had bungled the dog's treatment, the grieving Bankses struck back. Ms. Wine-Banks helped persuade the Illinois Attorney General's office, of which she had once been second in command, to assign a special prosecutor to the case. That prosecutor happened to be the lawyer she had retained to sue Dr. Wostoupal.

She insists she only asserted her rights as a citizen. But to the image-conscious A.B.A., what was left in Finnegan's wake, the appearance of a bar leader manipulating the legal system, was serious business—particularly when the press pounced on the story. "Grieving Dog Owner Unleashes Clout with State," The Chicago Tribune declared. A former bar association president, Eugene Thomas, charged in a letter to four bar leaders that the episode showed that Ms. Wine-Banks "does not understand the use of power and lacks a sense of decorum and propriety in professional matters."

"It is time to replace her," he said.

The Finnegan episode was not Ms. Wine-Banks's first imbroglio. Bar types eager to shed their fat-cat image deplored her use of a chauffeur-driven, cabernet-colored 1988 stretch Lincoln Continental with bar, telephone and pop-up television. With its view of Lake Michigan, her office was already the most luxurious in the building, but she enlarged and festooned it with photographs of herself. She summarily dismissed longtime bar association employees without the due process for which the bar stands. She was already receiving $210,000 a year but she put in for $65,000 more.

She dismisses complaints as the work of "a very minuscule minority."

"I am a strong person and I have made changes," she said. "This job requires that you make waves if you're going to do it right."

One hears enough cracks about her lunchtime shopping sprees at Water Tower Place and her pink jogging suits and polka-dot dresses to detect the hyperscrutiny of sexism. References to her liberalism suggest that politics has played a part. Why else would the dogs on her Christmas cards generate more ridicule than the doggerel on Tom Gonser's?

"Look, I hate dogs," said one of her strongest backers, Llewelyn Pritchard, a Seattle lawyer, "but this lady is bonkers about animals. And she's entitled to vindicate her rights."

Robert Raven, the current bar president, said Ms. Wine-Banks had "gotten off to a very good start." He said she had done nothing wrong in the Finnegan affair, though he conceded he had not looked into it. But he added, "I imagine that if Jill had it to do over again she would do it differently." ❑

By August, Ms. Wine-Banks had resigned, and is now an executive at Motorola. There has been no further noise from her Dalmatians.

In Connecticut, an Empathic Advocate for Scores of Women Suing Over Breast Implants.

7/31/92

BRIDGEPORT, CONN.—OVER THE LAST YEAR THE EVIDENCE LOCKER AT Koskoff, Koskoff & Bieder has come to resemble a refrigerator. Its shelves are filled with Ziploc bags, cottage-cheese containers, plastic salad-bar boxes and those large white buckets in which restaurants buy potato salad and cole slaw in bulk.

But what each of these items contains is a tragedy made of polyurethane, silicone, polymers and glue. Until very recently, their contents were inside women's breasts.

Earlier this week, Karen Koskoff, Esq., gave a guided tour of the locker's contents to a visitor. In a shoe box, the bottom of which has rotted out from the seepage of silicone, are the implants of Mrs. J. W., a photographer from eastern Connecticut. Nearby, in a plastic container that once held peanut-butter cups, are the Dow Corning implants of Ms. G. W. of Norwalk, who said she believes her implants caused doctors to detect her breast cancer belatedly.

In one of the buckets, surrounded by a crumpled surgical garb, are the implants of Mrs. B. M. of New Haven, which ruptured, releasing silicone throughout her body. Floating in formaldehyde are the implants of Mrs. J. S. of Stamford, a housewife now suffering memory and hair loss, fatigue and other conditions. Next to that, in two Ziploc bags, are the pouches that, until eight months ago, were inside Ms. Koskoff. In one, she can see some of her own tissue.

At last count, about 700 lawyers were handling thousands of lawsuits against those who made and installed breast implants, and the number is growing. But of them all, only Ms. Koskoff, a 37-year-old divorced mother of a 10-year-old son, has publicly acknowledged having had implants herself, after a bout with breast cancer, and having had them removed.

That ordeal helps account for Ms. Koskoff's current conspicuousness. She represents more than 130 plaintiffs in Connecticut state courts who have sued breast-implant manufacturers and plastic surgeons. As co-chairwoman of the Association of Trial Lawyers of America's breast-implant litigation group, she has been active in helping to determine what shape the mass litigation will take. That role, in turn, led to a recent profile on the cover of The National Law Journal.

All Federal cases are now before Judge Sam C. Pointer Jr. of the United States District Court in Birmingham, Ala. The arrangement is a hybrid: that is, both a class action and multidistrict litigation in which cases will be tried separately throughout the country but with centralized exchange of information. Ms. Koskoff has assailed the class action, contending it will enrich a few lawyers at the expense of victims.

Throughout their discussions, she has impressed colleagues with her fervor, tenacity and modesty. She neither hides nor flaunts her own emotional stake in these cases. "She does not go around saying: 'I know more. I feel more. No one else has the right to talk,' " said Robert Gordon of Weitz & Luxenberg of New York, which is handling 800 breast-implant cases.

Ms. Koskoff, a graduate of Goddard College and Antioch Law School, is heir to a family tradition of social activism. Her late father, a neurosurgeon in Pittsburgh, was among the first hospital chiefs of staff to hire a black resident. Her aunt was a supporter of Paul Robeson during the McCarthy era. Her uncle was a famed plaintiffs' trial lawyer in Bridgeport. Since joining his firm, Ms. Koskoff has specialized in psychiatric malpractice cases.

Her career came to a halt in February 1990 when she learned that she had breast cancer. Within a month her right breast had been removed, and a silicone gel implant had been inserted in its place. In the fall, her left breast was removed to prevent the cancer's spread.

In December, a nationally televised report on the dangers of implants sent some women scurrying to their lawyers. Among the first was Diane Caulfield of Madison, Conn., who sought out Ms. Koskoff, an old friend. With Ms. Koskoff doing the drafting, Ms. Caulfield filed suit against the manufacturer of her device, a subsidiary of Bristol-Myers Squibb.

The resulting publicity brought a steady stream of women with implants into Ms. Koskoff's office, some limping, some chronically fatigued, some out of commission, some simply terrified. Sensing that in these clients she was seeing herself several years down the road, Ms. Koskoff had her own implants removed.

Ms. Koskoff expects to spend virtually all her working time over the next five years on these cases, in court, in her office or at the evidence locker. "For the last 30 years, manufacturers and plastic surgeons have conducted an uncontrolled experiment on American women, including me," she said. "Now they will pay the consequences." ❑

A LAWYER SAYS HIS LETTER TO A RIVAL
WAS MEANT TO BE FUNNY,
BUT THE RIVAL SAYS SHE ISN'T LAUGHING.

4/16/93

CHICAGO—DAVID CWIK TRIED TO GET A LAUGH OUT OF HIS OPPOSING counsel. Instead, he said something stupid and, as he puts it, he "saw a mushroom cloud erupt."

In 1989 Mr. Cwik (pronounced swik) and Marilee Clausing, both Chicago lawyers, were facing each other in a garden-variety personal injury case. At one point Ms. Clausing, representing the defendant hospital, had moved to dismiss the case, contending that Mr. Cwik, the plaintiff's counsel, had taken too long to produce his expert witness.

The motion, which he deemed foot-dragging typical of defense counsel, made Mr. Cwik angry and, as he later described it, rambunctious. So one Friday afternoon that August, in an otherwise sober letter to Ms. Clausing, he slipped in a zinger.

"Should you succeed on your motion," he wrote, "we would merely dismiss the case, refile it shortly thereafter, and in the interim send somebody over to perform a clitorectomy on you." (The procedure, actually called a clitoridectomy, is a ritualistic practice in some traditional societies involving the removal of the clitoris and inner labia.)

To Mr. Cwik, 38, it was "nothing more and nothing less than my attempt to be funny." His goal, he said, "was merely to inject humor" into his relationship with Ms. Clausing.

Ms. Clausing read the letter, then read it again, first incredulously, then indignantly. She then fired off a response in which she called it "offensive, unprofessional and beyond the bounds of human decency," adding: "No apology you could give me would be sufficient. You can rest assured that the Attorney Registration and Disciplinary Commission will be advised of the matter."

Since then the Cwik case has bobbed up and down the disciplinary process, stretching four accordion-like legal folders, the disciplinary panel's resources, Ms. Clausing's patience and Mr. Cwik's finances.

Perhaps the oddest thing about Mr. Cwik's predicament is that it was not entirely of his own making. The offending reference originated with his secretary, Gregory Vince, who thought that sticking something outrageous into the innocuous letter Mr. Cwik had given him to type would get his all-too-serious boss to loosen up. It worked, but only after Mr. Cwik, who had never heard the word, looked up "clitoridectomy" in a medical dictionary. Thinking that Ms. Clausing would "get a kick out of it," he signed the letter and sent it off.

Upon receiving Ms. Clausing's response, Mr. Vince drafted an apology. "I am not only startled by the vulgar, insensitive nature of my action, I'm embarrassed and ashamed," he wrote. A "long, disordered and hectic week," he explained, had left him in a "giddy and warped state."

Mr. Cwik also signed the letter. All told, he said, he has tried to apologize to Ms. Clausing at least half a dozen times. But while pleading guilty to stupidity, he suggested that Ms. Clausing was thinskinned. Nor, he said, did he violate disciplinary rules barring conduct compromising the administration of justice or casting lawyers in a bad light, as she and the commission lawyer handling her case had charged. Those rules, his lawyer argued, regulate morals, not manners.

"Lack of courtesy or consideration are not fit subjects for regulatory oversight because (unfortunately) they occur too frequently to regulate," Mr. Cwik's lawyer, Aram Hartunian of Chicago, argued. "The standards for measuring rudeness and bad taste in the way lawyers treat each other are as elusive as the standards for measuring good and bad taste in art and literature."

In June 1990, the panel of lawyers considering the case agreed. While Ms. Clausing's opinion of Mr. Cwik had "unquestionably and understandably changed for the worse," the panel decided, the profession had not been sullied. But an appeals panel reversed the decision and sent the case back to a new panel. After an extensive hearing, the second panel recommended that Mr. Cwik be reprimanded, the mildest possible sanction. And in March, the appeals board upheld the reprimand.

"The nature of the comment here, in its reference to mutilation of opposing counsel's body, makes this more than a simple discourtesy or vulgarity," the board held. Mr. Cwik has opted not to appeal the ruling to the Illinois Supreme Court.

Ms. Clausing declined to comment about the case. As for Mr. Cwik, he said there was a bright side to what he called "four years of absolute aggravation" and legal fees, which he placed "in the low five figures." Most notable, he said, were offers of support from dozens of other lawyers, men and women alike.

"I tried something off the wall, and I just picked the wrong person, and the world exploded," he said. "But my career and my personal life have done nothing but prosper since this happened. It doesn't repel people from asking me to be their lawyer. I don't know what that means, but I find it interesting." ❏

V

OF RAMBOISM
AND RECYCLING

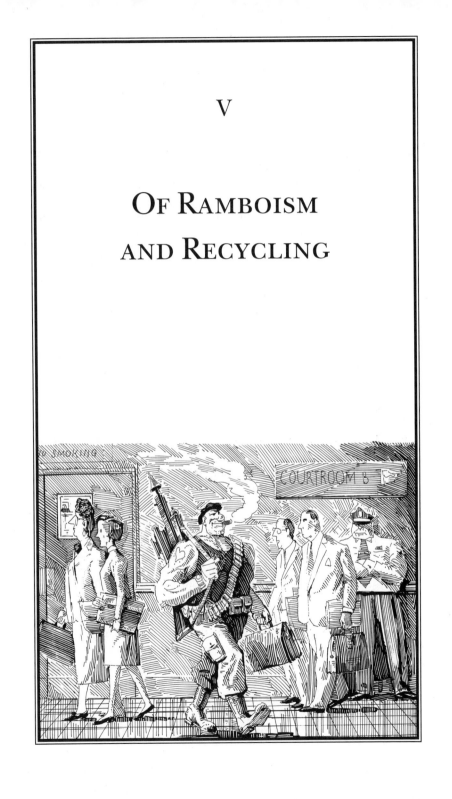

Has the Profession's Attempt
to Curb Ludicrous Litigation
Actually Boomeranged?

3/11/88

COMPLAINTS ABOUT INCOMPETENT LAWYERS AND FRIVOLOUS LITIGATION are perennial. But they reached a peak in the early 1980's, with the nation's top lawyer, Chief Justice Warren E. Burger, leading the assault. Indeed, along with his attacks on advertising by lawyers and his scuffles with television photographers, Chief Justice Burger's acidic comments on silly lawsuits were as much a ritual at bar gatherings as cocktail parties.

Largely at his prompting, an advisory committee began exploring ways to curb spurious lawsuits, to penalize those bringing them and generally to make lawyers more accountable to the courts and less to their angry, and at times irrational, clients. Rule 11 of the Federal Code of Civil Procedure, which defines what a lawyer must do to ascertain the merit of a claim, was revised.

In its initial incarnation, circa 1938, Rule 11 was toothless and largely ignored. It allowed lawyers to make the most dubious or irresponsible claims as long as they believed they had good grounds. But this subjective, "pure heart-empty head" standard was jettisoned in 1983.

Under the rule now, lawyers can make only those claims an average attorney would deem reasonable. Before filing any pleading, they must be sure of its soundness factually and legally. Failing that, opposing parties may ask the court to sanction the counsel, the client or both.

Under the revised rule, lawyers have paid for their frivolity, like the attorney-softball player who was penalized for contending that his free speech and equal protection rights were violated when he was kicked off a diamond reserved for hardball games. San Francisco's former Mayor, Joseph Alioto, drew the heavy fine of $294,141.10 for inadequate case preparation.

Other sanctions are more imaginative. An Atlanta lawyer was forced to run a printed mea culpa in the local law journal. A California attorney had to give his partners copies of an opinion criticizing his conduct. Others were sent to ethics classes.

In a profession where peer pressure and reputation are so important, sanctions need not be severe to hurt. Only this could explain why Kirkland & Ellis of Chicago spent thousands of dollars to overturn a very modest fine for violating Rule 11.

Some authorities, like Michael Silberberg of Golenbock & Barell in New York, say the change has made some lawyers more careful. But who can say how many ludicrous motions have not appeared? The rule's ill-effects are more obvious. Critics warned early that in its own rickety, imperfect way, the adversary system worked reasonably well, and tinkering was perilous. In some ways the new rule, designed to purge the courts of far-fetched or redundant litigation, has become the courts' version of Super Tuesday in the presidential primary season, a reform with results just the opposite of those intended.

Several people, among them Chief Judge Jack B. Weinstein of the Federal District Court in Brooklyn, charge that by encouraging intralegal battles, the new rule poisons relations between lawyers, thereby discouraging settlements. More importantly it has generated a whole universe of "satellite" litigation as courts grapple with what duties it imposes on lawyers and what powers it gives the courts.

According to Prof. Georgene Vairo of Fordham Law School, the amended Rule 11 has been explored in more than 700 court decisions. Still, some judges are avoiding the rule until, as Judge Gerard Goettel of the Southern District of New York once put it, "the line between creativity and frivolity" is clarified.

But perhaps most disturbingly, a tool designed to temper the adversary system has become one more weapon in it. Instead of seeking sanctions only in cases of truly egregious conduct, many defendants seek Rule 11 penalties almost reflexively. They do not cost a dime and, if successful, may foist expenses on the other side.

That has had a particularly adverse effect on plaintiffs in civil rights and employment discrimination cases. Because their cases are harder to prove and their lawyers less well-heeled, they are vulnerable to charges that their lawsuits are not "reasonable." Last December, for instance, a Federal judge in North Carolina assessed nearly $54,000 in sanctions against Julius Chambers, director of the N.A.A.C.P. Legal Defense and Educational Fund Inc., along with several associates.

The spectacle of Rule 11 motions flying back and forth has vindicated those with visions of a Kafkaesque system so inundated with complaints of lawyer misconduct that case merits are never reached. In several instances, lawyers have charged that by filing improper Rule 11 motions, their adversaries have themselves violated the rule. Will there come a case in which counsel files a Rule 11 motion against another Rule 11 motion that he violated Rule 11? It seems only a matter of time. ❏

RAMBOS INVADE THE COURTROOM, AND THE PROFESSION, AGHAST, FIRES BACK WITH ETIQUETTE.

8/5/88

HE HAS ALREADY VANQUISHED THE NORTH VIETNAMESE AND CRUSHED THE Russians in Afghanistan and now Rambo has landed on another kind of battlefield. Rambo-style litigators are running rampant in the legal profession and bench and bar alike are mobilizing to combat them.

The practice is "hardball," and the practitioners talk of "scorched earth" or "taking no prisoners" or "giving no quarter" in advocating a client's cause. "When I go into the courtroom, I come in to do battle—I'm not there to do a minuet," was how Wyoming lawyer Gerry Spence explained his philosophy in The American Bar Association Journal. Increasingly, said Marvin Karp, president of the Cleveland Bar Association, the courtroom ethic has become "litigation is war, the lawyer is a gladiator, and the object is to wipe out the other side."

Critics say there is nothing wrong with fighting hard for a client, but they also say hardball usually amounts to petty obstruction. Sometimes, they concede, it can grind an adversary into submission. Far more often it makes a case slower, more expensive and more unpleasant.

Why has it proliferated? There are so many lawyers now that professional bonds between them have broken. With competition stiff and clients looking to be dazzled, some attorneys think it pays to play the junkyard dog, even in sectors of the profession that once prided themselves on their civility. And for lavishly paid younger lawyers anxious to impress superiors, dragging things out means more hours to bill for.

Now the legal establishment is fighting back. In June the Cleveland Bar Association promulgated a "lawyer's creed of professionalism," an effort to reduce "uncivil, counterproductive and unprofessional conduct." It was developed with the American Bar Association's tort and insurance practice section and will be debated at the annual bar convention in Toronto next week.

The creed calls for 33 separate pledges. They include: "I will advise my client that civility and courtesy are not to be equated with weakness." "I will advise my client against pursuing litigation that is without merit and against insisting on tactics which are intended to delay resolution of the matter or to harass or drain the financial resources of the opposing party." "I will conduct myself with dignity, avoid making groundless objections and refrain from engaging in acts of rudeness or disrespect."

The Cleveland group has printed 5,000 copies of the creed, "on fine paper in a decorative format, suitable for framing," according to an accompanying promotional letter. The gold-leaf-and-filigree document has the wholesome look of the "Seal of Good Practice" that broadcasters once displayed after programs like "Lassie." Bar leaders hope lawyers and judges throughout the city will frame it, hang it and heed it.

As usual, what is a disease elsewhere is an epidemic in New York. A report issued last week by the Federal courts committee of the New York City Bar Association chastised lawyers for such things as serving papers the day before Christmas, piling briefs on top of affidavits on top of letters in an effort to get in the last legal word, acting belligerently to impress clients and directing personal attacks at adversaries. It also proposed a code. "Written submissions should not disparage the intelligence, ethics, morals, integrity or personal behavior of one's adversaries," one provision says. "Counsel should at all times be both civil and courteous," says another.

All this can sound a bit like Amy Vanderbilt or the Boy Scout oath. Moreover, since they contain explicit disclaimers insisting that violations may not be considered in disciplinary proceedings or malpractice actions, they are toothless as well.

Lawyers in Amarillo, Wichita Falls and Lubbock are more likely to be impressed by a recent ruling by the Federal District Court in northern Texas, which actually threatens them with sanctions for improper or dilatory conduct.

"With alarming frequency, we find that valuable judicial and attorney time is consumed in resolving unnecessary contention and sharp practices between lawyers," the court stated in its 20-page order that approved guidelines prepared by the Dallas Bar Association. "Litigators who persist in viewing themselves solely as combatants retained to win at all costs will find their conduct does not square with the practices we expect of them."

Ultimately, the best disincentive of all is money. Robert N. Saylor of Washington's Covington & Burling, director of the A.B.A.'s litigation section, has argued that far from cleaning up, legal Rambos don't get referrals from other lawyers, are rarely picked to lead multiparty litigation teams and may not live as long as their peers.

They do succeed in irking rivals and judges alike, and sometimes that may be cathartic, Mr. Saylor said. But how satisfying can it ever be to hear one's lawyer say something like "We lost—but boy, did we leave that sucker a bloody pulp!" ❏

The attempt to replace screeds with creeds has met with mixed results. The certificates, which are now sent to every new member of the Cleveland Bar Association, have gone into a second printing, and Mr. Karp sees some signs of increased civility in the bar. But attempts to put some teeth into the standards foundered at the Ohio Supreme Court, which appointed a commission to look into the problem. "The damned commission has not done a blessed thing; it's gone off and just disappeared," Mr. Karp complained. Gently, of course.

WITH VIOLENCE INVADING THE COURTROOMS, OKLAHOMA WEIGHS LETTING JUDGES PACK PISTOLS.

4/23/93

SOME JUDGES UNDOUBTEDLY CARRIED GUNS WHEN OKLAHOMA WAS A TERRI-tory. Now the Oklahoma House of Representatives has passed a bill that would let them pack pistols again.

But this is not a story about the Wild West revisited. It is about how the Wild West has come to encompass the entire country. Once upon a time, the thought of judges with pistols under their robes would have been shocking. Any proposal authorizing it would have been hotly debated and intensely publicized.

But the Oklahoma House devoted all of five minutes to the mea-sure before passing it this month, and the local press paid scant atten-tion. That judges are quite literally under fire, and want to be able to protect themselves, is apparently no longer news. "It's kind of a weird situation," said Representative Bill Paulk, a Democrat from Oklahoma City who opposes the measure. "I say 'weird.' It's really sad."

The bill's sponsor, Raymond Vaughn, a Republican from Ed-monds, said Oklahoma is no different from other states, only more practical and prescient. "I know Oklahoma has the reputation some-times as being a gun-on-your-hip, cowboy-type of state," he said in an interview, "but I don't think the problem is worse here than anywhere else."

Paul Banner, a criminologist with the South Carolina Criminal Jus-tice Academy in Columbia who instructs court personnel throughout the country on how to improve security, concurred. "I've been to a lot of courtrooms, and it's not uncommon for me to see judges take off those robes and see shoulder holsters," he said.

The impetus for the Oklahoma bill was a letter sent last fall by the Federal Drug Enforcement Administration to Sam Gonzalez, chief of the Oklahoma City Police Department. The D.E.A. informed Mr. Gonzalez that the Medellín drug cartel had begun a "bloody retalia-tion campaign" against American law-enforcement personnel, includ-ing judges, and urged him to pass the word. The police chief then told Richard Freeman, presiding administrative judge of the state courts in Oklahoma City, and Judge Freeman told Mr. Vaughn.

To Judge Freeman, the threat comes not only from drug barons but from disgruntled litigants. In the last few months, four people, none of them judges, have been killed in courthouse shootings in California, Dallas and Brooklyn. Judge Freeman said he had polled his judicial colleagues, and they unanimously favored arming themselves.

"We're not frantically trying to grab guns and shoot everyone in sight," he said. "We're just wanting to provide an element of caution to the thing. It's a sign of the times. There used to be respect for the law, and even criminals would not think of causing trouble in the courthouse. Those days are gone."

Mr. Vaughn's bill would require judges seeking to carry a gun to undergo the same training—at their own expense—as police officers. That was not enough to satisfy Mr. Paulk. Even death threats, he said, did not justify arming the judiciary.

"I think we're deluded by the John Wayne macho cowboy-type image, that all we need to do is strap on a six-gun and we can handle it," he said in an interview. But judges as much as anyone else, he warned, are liable to swagger dangerously when in possession of a gun. "Just carrying a gun makes you a whole lot taller and a whole lot tougher than you really are," he said.

Mr. Paulk invoked another Hollywood icon to suggest that the guns were likely to afford the judges little real protection. "It's not like Judge Roy Bean or the shootout at the O.K. Corral," he said. "If your life has been threatened, the person isn't going to face you down at high noon like Gary Cooper. They would tend to sneak up behind you and blow your head off." He said he hoped Gov. David Walters would veto the legislation, which is now in the State Senate. The Governor would not comment.

The measure passed, 58 to 38, perhaps because of Mr. Vaughn's closing point. "I said I thought judges ought to be equally as well armed as the people appearing in front of them," Mr. Vaughn recalled.

Such reasoning did not convince The Tulsa World. The newspaper noted in an editorial that Oklahoma chooses its judges by popular vote. "It doesn't happen very often, but sometimes a flake gets elected," the editorial said. "It's one thing to have a flake sitting on the bench; it's quite another to have an armed flake." ❏

While the Oklahoma House of Representatives ratified the measure twice, it has never made it through the State Senate. "Unfortunately, I expect it may pass only as the result of some tragedy," said Mr. Vaughn. "I hope that's not the case."

THE GREEN MOVEMENT REACHES
THE LAW OFFICE AS FIRMS GIVE UP
YELLOW LEGAL PADS.

9/28/90

LAWYER, SPARE THAT TREE!

Environmental law may be a hot area of practice these days, but for the most part, even environmental lawyers are more lawyers than environmentalists. Now, though, a few firms have concluded that conservation begins at home—that is, in their paper-guzzling offices.

They are photocopying on both sides of the page and using botched photocopies for memos. They are recycling briefs, memorandums, writing samples and résumés of rejected applicants. At coffee breaks, they are trading plastic cups for china. Some are even re-examining that most cherished talisman of the profession, the yellow legal pad.

Among those firms leading the way is Cravath, Swaine & Moore of New York, which consumes 70 million sheets of bond paper, and nearly 16,000 legal pads, every year. Some people keep running tabs of the national debt; Cravath counts the number of trees it says it has saved since July, when its recycling program began. By Sept. 20, the number had grown to a veritable forest of 680.

Over the summer, Cravath, which also serves "dolphin-safe" tuna in its cafeteria, distributed 1,500 (non-recyclable) plastic recycling trays to its staff. Items once tossed reflexively into the trash—file cards, visitors' passes, envelopes, all manner of papers except newsprint, magazines, carbon paper and cardboard—now go into the trays instead.

From there, they are dumped into the 55-gallon drums placed near crucial pit stops: bathrooms, photocopying machines and coffee stations. Then they are carted off to the Rapid Recycling Paper Corporation in Brooklyn. (Instead of paying someone to shlep away its waste, Cravath now collects $12 to $15 a ton for it.)

The papers are sorted, baled and shipped to the four corners of the earth, where, according to a recent issue of the biweekly Cravath Chronicle, they are "poured into a paper beater, treated with chemicals, dissolved, pulverized, macerated and so physically transformed as to lose all identity as paper." (The Cravath Chronicle continues to be printed, like all Cravath materials, on "virgin" rather than recycled paper.)

Nuala Ramirez, Cravath's office manager, says higher-quality white paper is reprocessed into something similar; cheaper or colored varieties are reincarnated as napkins, tissues or toilet paper. Theoretically at least, then, the high-priced notes a lawyer produces one month could be the White Cloud or Charmin he uses the next.

In recycling colored paper, Cravath is a step ahead of another trailblazer, Hannoch, Weisman of Roseland, N.J. Last month the firm, which has 20 environmental lawyers, issued a solemn edict: henceforth, all legal pads are to have the more ecologically congenial undyed white paper. "From now on, it will be easy to spot Hannoch Weisman attorneys in the courtroom," The New Jersey Law Journal reported last month.

The transition is already under way, said the head of the firm's environmental law department, Sanders Chattman. "I was concerned that the fluorescent lights might cause a glare problem with the white paper, but that hasn't been the case," Mr. Chattman reported reassuringly. And what is environmentally responsible is also fiscally prudent: the white pads are cheaper by $4 a dozen.

At Manko, Gold & Katcher, an environmental law firm in Bala Cynwyd, Pa., the change is still more dramatic. There, the changes involve not just color (from yellow to white) but kind of paper (original to recycled) and size (8½ by 14 inches to 8½ by 11). There, however, the transition has been a bit bumpier.

"The arguments against ranged from 'lawyers have always used 8½-by-14 yellow pads' to 'sure, we're a progressive firm, but let's not get carried away,' " said the office's director of administration, Mary McCullough. Weaning lawyers off something so familiar proved "the turning point" of the entire recycling program. "Once we convinced the attorneys to use 8 ½ -by-11 white paper, everything else sort of fell into place," she said.

As part of Earth Day celebrations in April, a committee of Philadelphia lawyers distributed a recycling and conservation manual to 200 local law firms. Taking the lead, Manko, Gold now uses only recycled paper for bond paper, brochures, stationery and business cards. "Our firm thought it was important to close the loop, to create a market for recycled products," said Jonathan E. Rinde, who led the effort.

Meanwhile, Ms. Ramirez and Lorraine Winheim, Cravath's director of operations, are carrying out the next stage of the firm's program: porcelain coffee mugs. Alas, this change has proved more problematic: the first prototype, showing the firm's new headquarters at Worldwide Plaza, left out the comma between Cravath and Swaine. Worse, it lacks the firm's custom ampersand. ❏

Cravath is now using recycled legal pads (both yellow and white), pencils, envelopes and desk calendars, and has cracked down on the use of paper and cardboard in the firm's cafeteria. It has, however, lost track of the number of spared trees.

FITNESS, ESQ., WHERE THE FLABBY
CAN BECOME FIRM—
AND THE FIRM PICKS UP A HEAVY TAB.

4/28/89

THE TIME IS 8:15 A.M., THE SETTING A MANHATTAN GYM CRAMMED WITH space-age, calorie-consuming contraptions. The players are sweating middle-aged men. In the background is a cacophony of news programs, clanging metal and the agony of heavy lifting, the sounds of the chain gang once sung of by the late Sam Cooke: "Uh!" "Ah!" "Uh!" "Ah!"

It could be any exclusive health club, except for the jumble of letters, looking like a bad hand in a Scrabble game, stitched into the T-shirts and shorts: SASM&F. That's short for Skadden, Arps, Slate, Meagher & Flom, New York's largest law firm—and, at least for now, the only one with its own "fitness center."

A bankruptcy lawyer, Dennis Drevsky, is on the rowing machine. Michael Goldberg and Michael Gizang are on treadmills but not the metaphorical kind they live on as merger and acquisition lawyers. Nearby lies Mitchell Gitin, a corporate finance partner, exercising on a sit-up board.

Of the many trails Skadden, Arps has blazed, the fitness center—none dare call it a "club"—is surely the most novel. A year and a half ago the firm brought in half a million dollars' worth of mechanical masochism, along with 12 full-time trainers, who chart the heart rates, blood pressure and fat content of 533 overweight, overstressed, sedentary lawyers in the New York office.

Lawyers are usually stationary creatures, wedded to their work, welded to their desks, better known for posturing than posture. Many firms, convinced that leaner is meaner, cover health club costs. So, once, did Skadden, Arps, which favored the Vertical Club for associates and the Cardio-Fitness Center for their more arteriosclerotic elders.

Some time ago White & Case bought a few exercise machines. But its spread is piddling next to Skadden's, which includes innumerable Exercycles, pairs of Concept II rowing ergometers and StairMaster 6000 imitation escalators, 11 Eagle and 4 Nautilus strength machines—what a corporate associate, Les Nelkin, called the "Marquis de Sade line of training equipment." Within a radius of 10 feet, lawyers can simulate swimming in the Caribbean, cross-country skiing in the Alps or mountain climbing in the Andes.

Collectively, the devices have helped turn 199-pound weaklings into jocks. Consider Mr. Gitin, whose peripatetic practice regularly takes him to places like Bangkok and Sydney: he will now stay only at hotels with training facilities. The devices have also helped tame the Type A types who congregate at the firm. "Exercise has the effect of diffusion of anger and rage, fear and anxiety," a notice on the bulletin board states. "Like music, it soothes the savage in us. It is the ultimate tranquilizer."

From 6:30 A.M. to 10 each night, Skadden, Arps lawyers—the place is off-limits to secretaries, paralegals and other underlings—can exercise on their own or have personalized appointments with trainers. Patrons run from the most junior associate to Peter Mullen, Skadden, Arps's executive partner, and the firm's patriarch, Joseph Flom, who stopped by periodically until a neck problem kicked up. All undergo a brutal initiation, a battery of exams to measure such metabolic minutiae as cardio-respiratory efficiency and hamstring flexibility (as well as to protect the firm from catastrophic liability).

The lawyers supply their own Reeboks and Nikes, but the firm furnishes freshly laundered, all-cotton SASM&F T-shirts (in five sizes), shorts (also in five sizes) and jock straps (only in four sizes). There are magazines to help relieve the drudgery.

The shower rooms are stocked with Johnson & Johnson baby oil and powder, Q-Tips, Desenex, Arrid Extra Dry, Right Guard, Curel moisturizing lotion, Tresemme European styling mousse, AquaNet, Scope, Gillette Foamy, Vitalis and other greasy kid's stuff, as well as several Conair Grand Champion II hair dryers. In the larder are bowls of bananas and Granny Smith apples, along with jugs of fresh-squeezed orange and grapefruit juice.

John Amberge of the Sports Training Institute, who manages the club, says the Skadden, Arps lawyers have already shed at least a ton, with one litigator accounting for 5 percent of the total. Less quantifiable but equally apparent are gains in pep, stamina, morale and collegiality. The club has proved a unifying force in a firm with 900-odd lawyers, 7 of whom are Schwartzes.

Other firms, like Simpson, Thacher & Bartlett and Milbank, Tweed, Hadley & McCloy, have checked out the place but have yet to emulate it. For one thing, the annual expense—$350,000—comes out of the partners' hide. Perhaps, too, there is something vaguely threatening about it. After all, locker rooms, unlike law firms, are democratic. In them one is constantly reminded that all men and women—even partners and associates—are created equal. ❏

The grunting goes on, but in a concession to the cost-conscious 1990's, Skadden lawyers desiring personal trainers must now pay for them themselves.

When a Law Firm Hires a Psychiatrist for Treatment of Its Institutional Psyche.

5/18/90

WHAT DO YOU HAVE WHEN YOU HAVE 50 LAWYERS TOGETHER ON A COUCH? It sounds like yet another lawyer joke. In fact, what you have is a partnership retreat of Morrison, Cohen, Singer & Weinstein in New York, and there is nothing funny about it.

In each of the last four years, usually in some rustic setting far from their telephones and Tagamet bottles, the firm's partners have met with Dr. Edward Shapiro, a psychoanalyst and family researcher at Harvard Medical School. Together they have drawn trees, devised baseball teams, impersonated college deans and South American dictators—the better to know themselves and, they hope, to serve their joint enterprise.

In the process, they have taken the art of running a law firm into a brave new psychological world. Another New York firm, Kramer, Levin, Kamin, Nessen & Frankel, has a psychiatrist on retainer who consults occasionally with individual lawyers. But Dr. Shapiro, who was recently named medical director of the Austen Riggs Center in Stockbridge, Mass., is not paid to hear about bad marriages or tortured childhoods. Instead, he treats the psyche of the institution.

"Every lawyer in New York City either goes to a shrink or has someone in his family who does," said Robert Stephan Cohen, the managing partner of Morrison, Cohen. "It is simply going the next step for a firm to consult one.

"I don't think it's saying 'we're sick,' but that 'we want to be better.' It's a concession that we're swimming upstream, that we want to get to where we're going, and we need all the help we can get."

Like the short-lived World Journal Tribune of New York newspaper fame, Morrison, Cohen is the product of an awkward tripartite marriage, with three separate sets of folkways, loyalties and egos. It is also a midsize firm in formation when many such operations are disintegrating. And it faces the problems of all law firms, regardless of size: battles over authority, autonomy, money, power and perks.

Pragmatic lawyers (the term may well be redundant) may scoff at the "touchy-feely" approach. But Morrison, Cohen partners say the group therapy, though awkward and occasionally even brutal, has helped a firm of disparate parts survive, cohere and grow—from 18 lawyers six years ago to 46 today. The treatment has even helped the firm develop a subspeciality: handling schisms at other offices.

When Morrison, Cohen was assembled in 1984, it brought in Hildebrandt Inc., the Somerville, N.J., consultants who are to running law firms what Walt Hriniak is to the science of hitting baseballs.

On nuts and bolts Hildebrandt was fine, but the firm was still unable to make a partnership of strangers gel. That was when Jay Seeman, another Morrison, Cohen partner, suggested Dr. Shapiro.

Dr. Shapiro, who had no prior contact with law firms, conducted his first weekend retreat in October 1986. To simulate the tensions of mergers, he designed a scenario in which two colleges in a university consolidate, and one of them must lose its beloved dining room. He divided the partnership in two, and watched them negotiate, compete and haggle over who would make the sacrifice.

At the next retreat, he divided the group again and asked each to draw a metaphorical picture of a hearty, stable institution. One drew a baseball team, but minus the fans or umpires—a sign, Dr. Shapiro said, of institutional myopia. The other group did better, drawing a tree with roots, branches and bark, more in harmony with its environment.

Always, discussions of nitty-gritty issues begin at the same level of abstraction, where defenses do not come into play. The issue of compensation was approached, for example, via an elaborate game involving a South American country called Perlibia, a military junta, some inhabitants of platinum-rich land and hostile neighbors.

For Dr. Shapiro, the work has been so interesting that he is devoting a chapter in his new book, "Lost in Familiar Places," to his experiences at Morrison, Cohen—with the permission of the patient (which he refers to as "Abe, Bingstrom & Cabot"), of course. The study, co-written by Dr. A. Wesley Carr, an Anglican priest and dean of Bristol (England) Cathedral, will be published next year by Yale University Press.

"Lawyers are not accustomed to thinking psychologically, which makes this an unusual opportunity for us," Dr. Shapiro said. "They really are a very brave group of people. This process takes them from the familiar to a never-never land, where they don't know what they're doing."

And the travel costs are, at least comparatively speaking, cheap. Dr. Shapiro charges less per hour than most Morrison, Cohen partners. And only a little more than a good Park Avenue shrink. ❑

ALIENATED LAWYERS SEEKING—
AND GETTING—COUNSEL IN MAKING
THE TRANSITION TO OTHER CAREERS.

2/10/89

FIDEL CASTRO DID IT. FRANCIS SCOTT KEY AND TONY LARUSSA DID IT. PAUL Robeson and Peter Ilyich Tchaikovsky did it. Even Cole Porter did it. Let's do it. Let's leave the law.

It's a song many seem to be singing these days. And Celia Paul, a 44-year-old career counselor to disaffected lawyers, is leading the chorus.

There is no doubt that many lawyers, particularly young ones, are alienated labor. Whatever prompted them to enter the profession—idealism, status, intellectual curiosity, skills training, the lack of a clear alternative—many are appalled by what they've found. As many people are now abandoning the law annually—roughly 40,000—as entering it.

More than anyone else, Ms. Paul guides such lawyers along the underground railroad to other careers. She has discovered that not only is disillusionment widespread, but also it is lucrative. In the last year, she advised nearly 1,000 disgruntled lawyers, many of whom paid her $1,200 for her wisdom.

This week, nearly 100 of them attended her "Lawyers in Transition" workshops in New Jersey, Long Island and New York. They had seen her advertisement in The Manhattan Lawyer—"Take Control of Your Career," it urged—and were finally facing up to the reckoning so many of them had put off for so long.

The phenomenon is not confined to New York. Foundering, floundering lawyers have established self-help groups in San Francisco and Seattle. The founder of the Seattle program, Deborah Arron, lapsed lawyer, author of "Running from the Law: Why Good Lawyers Are Getting Out of the Legal System," soon to be published, said 10 percent of the local bar had participated in her seminars and workshops.

Ms. Paul, who first taught a course called "Lawyers, You're Not Stuck" at the Learning Annex five years ago, will soon take her show to Tampa, Miami and Albuquerque. She foresees a mushrooming market for videos and other materials. She is even registering the phrase "Lawyers in Transition" with the United States Patents and Trademarks Office, giving it the same protection as "Put a Tiger in Your Tank."

As they filed into the Princeton Club Wednesday night, Ms. Paul's latest crop of clients were somber and tense, befitting people coming from jobs they could not abide. But like anyone trying to shed a noxious habit, they quickly discovered the cathartic power of communal confession.

As they introduced themselves, first names only, they talked of professional stagnation, personal stultification, pressure to bill long hours, tedium, sexism, degradation, infantilization and gamesmanship.

"Quite honestly, I feel guilty charging clients $185 an hour," Tom said. "Half of what I do is very silly. I get to the point of saying 'lawyers are ridiculous,' and then I realize I'm one of them." Nancy lamented about how she was "just making rich people richer."

They then filled out forms, listing their skills, values and job preferences. "Write several metaphors that express your feelings about law," one exercise directs. "Example: Working in law is like a nightmare: you'd like to get out of it but you need the sleep."

Most of the lawyers had been out of school only a few years. Few were from very top firms, where unhappy associates usually fend for themselves. The most agitated were the litigators—some of whom, Ms. Paul says, throw up nearly every morning before coming to work—while bored corporate lawyers were more prevalent. More than half were women. All have other loves.

"People ask me: 'How can you work with lawyers all day? They're so boring,' " Ms. Paul said. "But my clients are into a lot of different things."

Next month, the lawyers will hear from others who have already made the transition, like Craig Davidson, who directs the Gay and Lesbian Alliance Against Defamation; Martin Stone, an originator of television's "Howdy Doody"; and Andrea Lachman, co-owner of Mike's American Bar & Grill in Manhattan.

Ms. Lachman endured seven years at three law firms, including one of Ms. Paul's most fertile spawning grounds, New York's Rosenman & Colin. Now she spends her days serving up "killer-hot chili" and "arugula and cucumber salad with frizzled corn tortillas."

"A month after I stopped practicing law, I realize I'd had a knot in my stomach all those years, and that it had suddenly gone," she said, as Patsy Cline crooned "I Go to Pieces" in the background.

"Financially I'm not as well off now, but emotionally I'm far ahead," she continued. "I got married and had a child. And I felt tremendous professional satisfaction. Everything just fell into place." Patsy Cline was still on the jukebox. Only now she was singing "Sweet Dreams." ❑

Enrollment in Ms. Paul's workshops has doubled in the past five years. Increasingly, participating lawyers tend to be older and, as the employment market has tightened, driven less by existential angst than economic necessity: that is, having been told to leave, they're being forced to find something else.

A HARVARD GRAD FOUND
THAT LYRICS, NOT BRIEFS, BROUGHT
FULFILLMENT (MONETARILY AS WELL).

3/9/90

AMID THE RUN-OF-THE-MILL PUFFERY IN THE PAGES OF PLAYBILL, DAVID ZIP-pel's autobiography stands out. True, it lists his theater credits, most recently as lyricist for the Broadway musical comedy "City of Angels." But instead of the usual nods to coaches, God and family, it ends with a bit of educational editorializing.

"A graduate of Harvard Law School," it states, "he is delighted not to practice law."

It is a sentiment many lawyers understand. Surveys show that as a group, lawyers are even unhappier with their career choices than doctors; 85 percent of lawyers under the age of 30 in the State of Washington say that if given the chance, they would not re-enter the profession.

In most leading law schools, one need not look very long to find some ambivalent protolawyer who prefers Lerner & Loewe to Sullivan & Cromwell, who scribbles songs when he should be writing briefs. But while most just dream of escape, Mr. Zippel actually did.

The 35-year-old Mr. Zippel, a native of Easton, Pa., didn't hang around the law long enough to become disappointed with it. Even in his third year at Harvard, he spent more time studying Preston Sturges, Alfred Hitchcock and Billy Wilder at local movie revival houses than he did antitrust. Even then—to cannibalize the title of one of his songs—he knew his life would be "better with a band."

As most in the class of 1979 set out for Wall Street, he headed for Tin Pan Alley. What followed sounds glitzy: writing songs for Barbara Cook and Michael Feinstein; writing shows at Carnegie Hall and Radio City.

The process of making it on Broadway was far more perilous—and considerably less lucrative—than of making partner at a place like Cravath, Swaine & Moore. While classmates grew fat, Mr. Zippel barely scraped by. He did so only by writing the occasional jingle—for one Uncle Ben's commercial he turned the memorable phrase "We're talking twice the rice at half the price."

But all that has changed with "City of Angels," the spoof he wrote with Cy Coleman and Larry Gelbart about the Los Angeles of the 1940's, its movie tycoons and its private eyes.

Mr. Zippel's career path is not, as lawyers like to say, sui generis—a law school Latinism for "unique." He noted that Arthur Schwartz, composer of "Dancing in the Dark," was once a lawyer, and that both

Oscar Hammerstein Jr. and Cole Porter attended law school, albeit briefly. While at college, Mr. Zippel worked summers at a hometown law firm. Then he headed to Harvard, though always the master plan, he said, was "to write a hit Broadway musical and not practice law at all."

Why, then, did he bother going to law school? It is a question he is often asked, and for which he has a ready reply: "Planning a career as a lyricist is a bit like wanting to be shepherd," he said. "There's not a lot of call for that kind of work."

His choice of law schools was just as pragmatic. Above all, it had to be big. "Harvard is the best place to go if you're not going to be a lawyer," he said. "I figured that the larger the law school, the more likely there would be someone I liked there."

He was a good student, and an efficient one, too, after making a crucial discovery. "At Harvard you can kill yourself to get an 'A' and not get one, and you can do nothing and get a 'B,' " he said.

By his own count, he saw 120 movies in his last semester, including soon-to-be-useful classics like "The Big Sleep," "Double Indemnity" and "Sunset Boulevard."

"I saw every 30's and 40's film they showed," he said. "That's when I did a lot of the research for 'City of Angels,' but that was before I knew I had the job."

Mr. Zippel did have a brief taste of practice, enduring one summer at the late Manhattan firm of Marshall, Bratter, Greene, Allison & Tucker. "I was grateful that it didn't fit into my future plans," he recalled. Nor did a stint as a Broadway lawyer, for reasons neatly explained by a cushion on the office couch of a Los Angeles lawyer friend of his. "Be an entertainment lawyer," it urges. "Touch paper that's been touched by stars."

While in Cambridge, Mr. Zippel collaborated on several student shows. He also met Wally Harper, the musical director for Barbara Cook. But perhaps the most important contact was a classmate named Russell DaSilva. Mr. DaSilva's father, Albert, a New York entertainment lawyer, represents Mr. Coleman and Mr. Gelbart. It was through him that Mr. Zippel landed "City of Angels."

To quote some lyrics from the show, Mr. Zippel's new life is "lots of fun and pots of dough." With the show sold out for months, his horizons have broadened, to include such exotica as accountants and taxicabs.

And with recordings, tours and other residuals still in store, the receipts should only increase. Mr. Zippel has, in short, reached the blessed state so many of his classmates covet: he is not a Wall Street lawyer—but he can live it up like one. ❑

VI

ETHICS

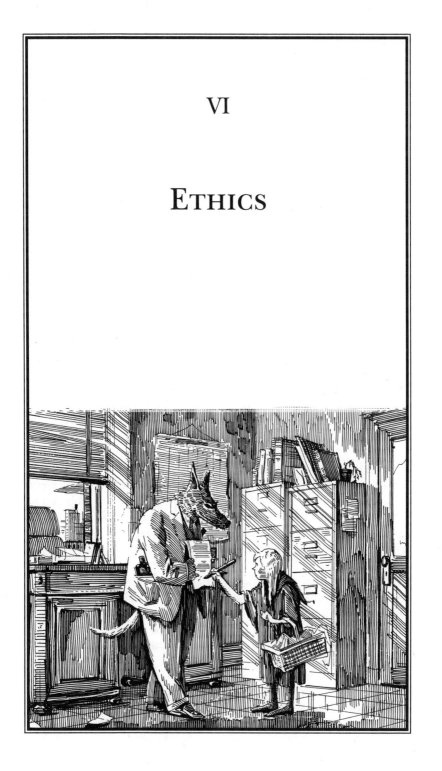

TO ATTACK A LAWYER IN 'TO KILL A MOCKINGBIRD': AN ICONOCLAST TAKES AIM AT A HERO.

2/28/92

IN HER PROGNOSTICATIONS FOR 1992, THE PSYCHIC JEANE DIXON PREDICTED that "anti-lawyer riots will shake the profession." But could even the canniest clairvoyant have foreseen an attack on Atticus Finch?

Atticus Finch, the sagacious and avuncular lawyer-hero of Harper Lee's 1960 novel, "To Kill a Mockingbird," who earned the scorn of his segregated Southern town by defending a black man wrongly accused of rape? Atticus Finch, who stood down a lynch mob that had come to collect his client one night at the Maycomb jail? Atticus Finch, who taught a community and his two young children about justice, decency and tolerance, and who drove a generation of real-life Jems and Scouts to become lawyers themselves?

Monroe Freedman of Hofstra Law School has never been one to duck controversy. His heterodox views on what constitutes vigorous representation of a client once led Chief Justice Warren E. Burger to call for his disbarment. Now, in his column on professional ethics, which appears monthly in Legal Times, Mr. Freedman has taken on Atticus.

Legal scholars concede that Finch has his ethical lapses. In telling his children to pity their grumpy, bigoted neighbor, Mrs. Henry Lafayette Dubose, because she was addicted to morphine, he was arguably betraying a client's confidence. Later, to spare the reclusive Boo Radley from a murder prosecution, he countenances Sheriff Heck Tate's fiction that the nefarious Bob Ewell actually fell upon his own knife.

But in legal literature as much as in the popular imagination, Finch, particularly Gregory Peck's film version of the man, has heretofore remained unsullied. In his trailblazing 1981 law review article, "The Moral Theology of Atticus Finch," Thomas Shaffer of Notre Dame Law School described Finch as someone "who risks everything in order to tell the truth." Two years ago, Timothy Hall of the University of Mississippi Law School wrote of Finch, "Truthfulness was stamped upon his character like an Indian head on an old nickel."

All this is too much for the iconoclastic Mr. Freedman. "Atticus Finch has become the ethical exemplar in articles on topics ranging from military justice to moral theology," he writes. "If we don't do something fast, lawyers are going to take him seriously as someone to emulate. And that would be a bad mistake."

Sure, Mr. Freedman writes, Finch represented Tom Robinson zealously, and for nothing in return. But he took the case involuntarily—failure to accept the court-ordered appointment could have landed him in what Miss Lee called Maycomb's "miniature Gothic joke" of a jail for contempt—and only "from an elitist sense of noblesse oblige." Besides, Mr. Freedman asked, what had Finch done up to that point to combat the forces that brought Robinson down?

Far from attacking racism at its root, Mr. Freedman charges, Finch was complicit in it. For all his gentlemanliness, he does not complain that blacks attending court are relegated to the balcony. He eats in segregated restaurants; he walks in parks where signs say "No Dogs or Colored Allowed." And he is too willing to excuse racism in others, dismissing the local chapter of the Ku Klux Klan as "a political organization more than anything else," and the leader of the lynch mob as "basically a good man" with "blind spots."

More than a racist, Finch is a sexist. Mr. Freedman notes that in his closing argument to the jury Finch dismisses Eleanor Roosevelt as "the distaff side of the executive branch in Washington." Worse, while encouraging Jem to follow in his footsteps and become a lawyer he does not similarly encourage his daughter. "Scout understands that she will be some gentleman's lady," Mr. Freedman writes.

Professors Shaffer and Hall, both of whom regularly assign "To Kill a Mockingbird" in their legal ethics classes, good-naturedly accuse Mr. Freedman of compulsive contrariness. "There isn't a sacred cow in the world Monroe Freedman doesn't enjoy taking on," Mr. Shaffer said. In addition, they accused Mr. Freedman of what Mr. Hall called "chronological snobbery": that is, unfairly subjecting a New Deal-era Alabama lawyer to contemporary standards of behavior.

Mr. Freedman, they added, also has a mistaken notion of perfection, one that would require lawyers not only to stand vigilantly by their oppressed clients, but also to separate themselves entirely from all agents of oppression.

"What Monroe really wants is for Atticus to be working on the front lines for the N.A.A.C.P. in the 1930's, and if he's not, he's disqualified from being any kind of hero," Mr. Hall said. "Monroe has this vision of lawyer as prophet. Atticus has a vision of lawyer not only as prophet, but as parish priest." ❑

A CRUSADER'S ISSUE: WHAT SHOULD BE DONE WHEN A WHISTLE-BLOWER IN A LEGAL FIRM IS DISMISSED?

3/15/91

HOWARD WIEDER'S CRUSADE TO MAKE LAWYERS MORE HONEST SNUCK INTO Albany last week, two years and at least $100,000 in out-of-pocket expenses after it began. Soon, New York's highest court, the Court of Appeals, will decide whether to take on Mr. Wieder's case, and thereby enter the legal and moral thickets it represents.

Authorities on legal ethics are closely watching. So too, perhaps, are the photocopying and paper pulp industries, A.T.&.T., the United States Postal Service and other enterprises Mr. Wieder has been subsidizing.

Whistle-blowers, to paraphrase F. Scott Fitzgerald, are very different from you and me. And in his obsession for his cause, the 37-year-old Mr. Wieder is extreme even by whistle-blower standards.

In September 1987, Mr. Wieder, a lawyer at the Manhattan firm of Feder, Kaszovitz, Isaacson, Weber & Skala, told his superiors that the lawyer they had supplied for his house-closing had acted unethically, and should be reported to disciplinary officials. Under the Code of Professional Responsibility, lawyers must disclose misconduct by peers; they can lose their licenses if they don't. But instead of following his recommendation, Mr. Wieder said, the firm dismissed him. He has filed suit, charging wrongful discharge.

The firm has called the charges "the product of an unstable and depraved personality," even though the lawyer at issue later conceded that Mr. Wieder's accusations were accurate. But whom you believe hasn't mattered, at least not yet.

In August 1989, Acting Justice Edward H. Lehner of State Supreme Court in Manhattan ruled that laws authorizing employers to dismiss employees at will apply to lawyers, too. Last November the Appellate Division unanimously upheld that ruling. Now Mr. Wieder has gone to the Court of Appeals.

He argues that lawyers, unlike other workers, must blow the whistle when they see wrongdoings in their profession. Further, he argues, because lawyers are officers of the court, the courts and not the Legislature can regulate the terms of their employment and exempt them from dismissal for whistle-blowing.

Mr. Wieder has become a familiar figure at Tower Copy, an Upper West Side store whose machines have duplicated the legal materials and letters—elaborate, handwritten affairs up to 35 pages long, filled with references to Emile Zola, Dietrich Bonhoeffer, Winston Churchill and Benjamin Cardozo—with which he deluges those whose support he seeks.

He has become a fixture at the philatelic window of the Vanderbilt Station post office, where he has cleaned out the supply of Chief Justice John Marshall commemorative stamps and done his part to keep the first-class rate from rising beyond 29 cents.

Recipients of the Wieder file include Senators Daniel Patrick Moynihan and Alfonse M. D'Amato; Justices William J. Brennan Jr. and Lewis F. Powell Jr. of the United States Supreme Court; and President Bush.

Mr. Wieder said he now owes his trial lawyer, Jeremiah Gutman of New York, some $30,000. To defray those costs, Mr. Wieder plans to nominate himself for the first annual Rolaids Relief Hero Award, a $25,000 jackpot earmarked for "an unsung individual or group who improves the quality of life in a community."

His financial picture grew more bleak last month when, a day after an article on his case appeared in the magazine Manhattan Lawyer, he was dismissed from his post as vice president and counsel at the Manufacturers Hanover Trust Company—though whether out of dissatisfaction with him or distaste for his conspicuous crusading is not clear.

But Mr. Wieder has enlisted allies to file friends-of-the-court briefs for him, including the New York City Bar Association's Committee on Professional Responsibility and 11 experts in ethics and labor law, including Leonard Gross of Southern Illinois University, Charles W. Wolfram of Cornell and Clyde W. Summers of the University of Pennsylvania.

"If the decision of the Appellate Division is not reviewed, what shall I tell my students who plan to practice in New York?" Mr. Summers, an authority on labor law, asked in an affidavit submitted to the Court of Appeals. "Shall I warn them not to report misconduct lest they lose their jobs? Shall I tell them that the Court of Appeals does not care?"

To Mr. Gross, an ethics specialist, as to many of those he deals with, Howard Wieder is exasperating, endearing and, ultimately, convincing. "I enjoy talking with Howard, even though I can't always get him off the phone," he said. "He is monomaniacal on seeing that justice is done. That's not necessarily a bad thing, because it requires a Don Quixote to be willing to buck the establishment." ❑

In December 1992, the New York Court of Appeals unanimously ruled in Mr. Wieder's favor, and reinstated his lawsuit. The requirement that lawyers re-

port misconduct, Judge Stewart F. Hancock Jr. wrote, was "nothing less than essential to the survival of the profession," and nothing should be done to undermine it. But Mr. Wieder must prove his case in court—a formidable and expensive task, particularly since he owes Mr. Gutman $75,000. Mr. Wieder, who now works as a court attorney for the Unified Court System of the State of New York in Brooklyn, said his ordeal has convinced him of one thing: he will blow no more whistles.

State Bar Funds Are Acting
as a Practical Conscience for
Lawyers Who Bilk Their Clients.

1/1/88

THERE'S NO WAY OF KNOWING WHETHER MORE CLIENTS WILL BE FLEECED BY unscrupulous lawyers in 1988 than in previous years. One thing, however, seems clear: A growing percentage of them will be reimbursed for at least some of what they lost.

Pressured by legislatures, prodded by judiciaries, or in some cases acting on its own, the legal profession has taken steps to atone for its most disreputable members. Since Vermont set up the first such system of reimbursement in 1958, all states but Alabama and Maine have created funds, paid for primarily from lawyers' dues, to compensate victims of venal attorneys.

Most of these deviant lawyers are graduates of marginal law schools, eking out livings from vulnerable clients. Many of them are alcoholics, gamblers or, in recent years, cocaine addicts. Invariably they cannot make restitution themselves, because they have died, been disbarred or imprisoned, are broke or have disappeared.

No program in the nation has been more active in helping the victims of such lawyers than the Clients' Security Fund of New York, a reflection, no doubt, of the size, integrity and variety of the state's bar. Since it was set up in 1981, the fund's seven trustees, appointed by the state Court of Appeals, have awarded a total of $5,805,000 to 1,153 victims. The fund awarded $2 million of that in 1987 alone.

Fund officials expect even more to go out this year, an increase due not so much to a nose dive in legal ethics as to growing public awareness that will prompt more victims to file claims with the fund. The fund recently began running television advertisements, and next month will unveil slick new messages featuring one of the state's most famous lawyers, Gov. Mario M. Cuomo. "Even in a barrel of New York's finest, there's bound to be a bad apple or two," he declares, standing behind a bushel of McIntoshes.

If Eleanor Breitel Alter of Rosenman & Colin in New York, the fund's chairman, has her way, the publicity would not always be so benign. She hopes newspapers will one day list the panel's dispositions as routinely as they do unsanitary restaurants.

A review of the New York fund's cases resembles nothing so much as a few pages from Miss Lonelyhearts. Consider these cases:

⁋ The Nassau County lawyer who stole $167,000 in pension money from a widow recovering from a nervous breakdown suffered after her husband died the previous Christmas. The fund awarded the widow $100,000, its maximum.

♬ An attorney near Rochester who not only lifted $71,000 from an elderly client but also stole her piano.

♬ A Rockland County father-and-son legal team who appropriated $75,000 from a boy orphaned after his sister had arranged to murder his parents, and $150,000 from another estate earmarked for an organization training Seeing Eye dogs.

♬ The Manhattan lawyer who stole $44,000 from 11 clients, then raised a novel defense: that he had licked his alcohol problem, only to realize once he had sobered up that he hated the practice of law and let his ethical standards deteriorate.

♬ The Otsego County lawyer who, seeking to steal the savings of an illiterate client, invented an heiress in the client's will and provided that she receive half the $66,000 estate. To document the bogus heiress's existence, he dressed up as a woman and checked into the Best Western motel in Little Falls, N.Y., under her name.

♬ The Manhattan lawyer who took $250 from 92 clients, principally on divorce and name changes, then did nothing for them. One victim sought compensation not only for his lost fee but also for his lost fiancée, who had grown fed up over his lingering engagement and left him.

Some attorneys have committed crimes of almost olympian proportions. The gold medalist is Barry J. Grandeau of Poughkeepsie, with 496 claims against him. Among those he robbed was an 81-year-old widow who for many years had invested $5 a week in I.B.M. stock. As a result of the theft, she was forced to work at a local market that Mr. Grandeau patronized.

The largest payouts, meanwhile, have come in the cases of a former Brooklyn lawyer, Jerome Spiegelman: $697,000. He settled cases surreptitiously, then pocketed the proceeds. Both Mr. Spiegelman and Mr. Grandeau were later imprisoned.

With over $4 million in its kitty, the fund appears to be prospering. Always, however, there is the prospect of some truly colossal crime, like the Danbury, Conn., probate judge recently accused of stealing as much as $3 million from his clients. "We have to be cautious," said Mrs. Alter. "We're terrified that there's someone out there who's ripped off $5 million from 500 people." ❏

Mrs. Alter's worst fears were very nearly realized with the appearance of one Jack Solerwitz, a Long Island lawyer who stole $3 million from 99 clients.

(Among Mr. Solerwitz's victims was Sarah Kiss; see next column.) In 1993, the fund—now called the Lawyers' Fund for Client Protection—paid out $7.5 million to 318 unlucky clients, and 1994 promises to set another record.

TWICE STUNG BY CROOKED LAWYERS, AND TWICE SAVED BY THE CLIENT PROTECTION FUND.

3/19/93

BEFORE LONG, A CHECK FOR $74,917 WILL ARRIVE AT SARAH KISS'S APARTment in Far Rockaway, Queens. Then, at long last, the 32-year-old Ms. Kiss, a mortgage broker's representative and part-time makeup artist, will be able to buy some furniture and send her three children to summer camp.

She may also reflect on her horrific experiences with lawyers, which recently led The New York Law Journal to call her "New York's Unluckiest Client."

The New York Lawyers' Fund for Client Security, created to reimburse the victims of crooked lawyers, has done a brisk business in its 11-year history, paying out $29 million to 2,200 defrauded clients. But only one of them, Ms. Kiss, has had to come before the panel a second time, when her stolen money was stolen again by a second thief with a law license.

To some degree her story is a nightmarish aberration, like one of those tales of tornadoes hitting the same trailer twice. At the same time, it reflects a far more common, perpetual problem: the terra incognita ordinary people tread upon whenever they look for a lawyer.

In 1989, the lawyer who handled Ms. Kiss's divorce, Jack B. Solerwitz of Mineola, L.I., absconded with the $70,834 she received from the sale of her house required by the settlement. Ms. Kiss then hired a second lawyer, Bertram Zweibon of Manhattan. In 1990, with Mr. Zweibon's help, the fund compensated Ms. Kiss for most of her losses. But Mr. Zweibon promptly stole everything she had just recouped. "Aside from the fact that my ex was driving me nuts, all these guys were taking my money," she recalled.

It is in her religious tradition, said Ms. Kiss, an Orthodox Jew, to take people at their word. It is also, she thinks, in her stars. Asked how she could have judged legal talent so badly, she replied: "Maybe it's because I'm an Aries and I trust people. Don't you think it's a better way to be?"

But bitter experience, she concedes, has made her a bit warier—a feeling, she said, that has spilled over to her children. "The latest line of the oldest one," she said, "is, 'Lawyers are liars.'"

Fiorello La Guardia liked to say that when he made a mistake, it was "a beaut," and for Ms. Kiss this is doubly true. In New York legal lore, Mr. Solerwitz is the Babe Ruth of rip-offs, having been convicted of stealing more than $5 million in the 1980's. He is serving 5 to 15 years in prison for grand larceny.

"I didn't know any lawyers, and he was a very nice man," said Ms. Kiss, whose children were 3, 4 and 6 when she left her husband in 1987. "Someone finally wants to help you; you jump at it. What did I know? When you're dealing with a woman with three small babies, it takes a lot of chutzpah to do something like that."

Compared with Mr. Solerwitz, Mr. Zweibon, now serving one to three years, was a piker: he was convicted of stealing only $2 million, including $45,000 from the estate of his mother-in-law and $30,000 from Ms. Kiss's father, a rabbi. For Ms. Kiss, however, his betrayal was even greater, for Mr. Zweibon came highly recommended from friends in an insular, closely knit Orthodox Jewish community center along Central Avenue in Far Rockaway.

"He convinced me to leave the money with him, so I did," she said. "He said it was safe there, it would be secure for my kids. 'You have a job, you're managing, you'll get your interest, leave it where it is! When you need it, you'll tell me.' So when I did I called him, and he never returned my calls.

"I felt raped. I live with a conscience every day. Just because he has a license to practice law, doesn't he have a conscience?"

Her money out of her reach for four years, receiving no child support, Ms. Kiss scraped by. "I'm always behind on bills," she said, adding, "I can't describe to you how degrading it is to go before the parents' tuition committee at the Hebrew school, literally breaking down, pleading to get your kids in when you don't have a dime, knowing that the money was stolen."

But with the help of her parents, along with Frederick Miller and Tim O'Sullivan of the client protection fund in Albany and her first honest lawyer, Charles Liechtung of Manhattan, she is ready to start anew. She even has a bit of pity for Mr. Zweibon, who earlier this month sent her a contrite letter from prison. Forgiveness, too, she said, is part of her tradition.

Mr. Miller, whose panel approved the payment to Ms. Kiss last Friday in Albany, is looking out for the fund's most faithful patron.

"Fred said to me: 'Sarah, what are you going to do with the check? You're not going to give it to another lawyer, are you?' " Ms. Kiss recalled. "I told him, 'It's not going to go to another lawyer's escrow account in my lifetime.' "

About her old friends at the fund, she said: "I think they were pretty wonderful. They have a tough job up there. Every day, you hear about another lawyer doing this." ❏

Ms. Kiss finally got her money, and had only good things to say about her third lawyer, Mr. Liechtung, both because she fell in love with him and he did not charge her a dime in fees. "He's a sweetheart," she said. "He served me well, in more ways than one."

THE FLEECING OF THE CLIENT,
A CAUTIONARY REPORT ABOUT
THE LAWYER'S CONFLICT OF INTEREST.

5/4/90

"TELL ME A MAN IS DISHONEST, AND I WILL ANSWER HE IS NO LAWYER," Daniel Webster told the Charleston, S.C., bar in 1847. "He cannot be, because he is careless and reckless of justice; the law is not in his heart, is not the standard and rule of his conduct."

It is a lofty ideal. But Lisa Lerman, a law professor at Catholic University in Washington, reports that it is also a self-serving myth. That, at least, is what is suggested by her interviews with 20 lawyers. Once promised anonymity, they spoke with her with a candor and contrition more appropriate to a confessional than a scholarly journal.

All lawyers face a fundamental conflict of interest, between clients and careers, Professor Lerman writes in the current issue of the University of Pennsylvania Law Review. The latter usually prevails, particularly in times of cutthroat competition and straitened economics. But never, never is the client to know.

What results is a House of Games; a panoply of deceits: padding bills, puffing expertise, ducking responsibility, meter-running, posterior-covering. Lying to clients, she writes, is "a serious and pervasive problem" in law firms, whose subculture "does not put much emphasis on truthfulness." Or, as she paraphrases Nietzsche, for some lawyers, "lies are necessary in order to live."

Professor Lerman concedes her survey is not scientific. What she did, essentially, was turn over 20 rocks at random, and with great delicacy.

The lawyers who spoke with her—most of them youngish and in private practice—were given comic strip pseudonyms like "Miles Marcus," "Beth Forrester," "Martin Richards" and "Alison Price," with a "Deborah Greenberg" and "Arthur Katz" thrown in for ethnic flavor. No locales are mentioned; presumably they work in Metropolis and Gotham City. Once she got her quotations, all interview tapes were promptly destroyed.

Some of these lawyers practice in the personal injury bar, which tony lawyers have always loved to hate. One, "David Larsen," tells of a defense lawyer who settled a $100,000 case for $4,700 because he was short of cash. But the professor's examples suggest that cheating may be even more rife in the ostensibly impeccable large firms, whose clients have deeper pockets and, often, less of a ringside seat.

The lawyers describe a world in which clients can be charged just about anything. There is the tale of a client who farmed out similar assignments to two firms, and got bills of $100,000 from one and $5,000 from the other.

"Winston Hall," described as "an associate at a large firm," tells of how his employer updated Robin Hood to the Boesky era, regularly bilking the mega-rich, often foreigners. He put the prevailing attitude this way: "They've got so much money in these countries where there is nothing to buy, they might as well give it to me."

Then there is "Mary Helen Murphy," an associate at a "middle-sized firm" who recalls her futile efforts to blow the whistle on a senior associate who, under pressure to get his billable hours up, routinely charged a couple of clients for 12 to 16 hours of labor a day when he averaged only two. When the lawyer discovered her snitching, he came into her office.

" 'You're not going to get away with this,' he said," she recalled. "And he closed the door and he started gesturing. His face was splotchy. I said 'Get out!' and I started to scream. One of the senior partners came down and said, 'We'll have to up his dose of lithium again' and then the partner said to me, 'Don't leave your scissors on that side of the desk.' That was their response to what this man had done." She later quit the firm in disgust.

The only clients smart enough to see through the make-work, double-billing and other assorted rip-offs, "Winston Hall" said, are people who presumably used to do it themselves. "The worst clients from the point of view of a lawyer are the ex-partners, who know damn well that lawyers do work to run up the meter," he explained. He tells of a time when a client paid an inspection call on his firm, and saw how little the eight lawyers he was bankrolling were producing. "It was like a customer going into the kitchen of a restaurant," he said. "They were utterly horrified."

What clients also don't know, the interviewees said, is that lawyers routinely blame secretaries for their own foul-ups, take credit for the work of underlings, exaggerate their expertise, say work they still haven't started is off "in word processing" and forever duck phone calls.

The article has already provoked its share of curmudgeonly criticism. "One gathers that Professor Lerman does not like lawyers," Edmund B. Spaeth Jr. wrote in a comment in the same issue of the publication.

Professor Lerman, a graduate of New York University Law School, denies the charge. "I work with lawyers all day," she said. "And I'm also married to one." ❑

COURT ASKS A LAWYER,
IF A COMPUTER IS DOING MOST OF THE WORK,
WHY THE BIG FEE?

11/12/93

"SOME WILL ROB YOU WITH A SIX-GUN, AND SOME WITH A FOUNTAIN PEN," Woody Guthrie warbled in "Pretty Boy Floyd." And, according to a California judge, were Guthrie around today, he might have added that some lawyers use CD-ROM.

Craig Collins, a lawyer in San Mateo, Calif., specializes in family law. Recently he was representing a woman who hoped to move across the country with her 7-year-old son to White Plains. Her former husband, who was also the boy's stepfather, wanted to keep the boy in California.

What rights does a stepparent have under the circumstances? Once, the Collinses of the world would have cracked open their law books. But Mr. Collins, who once taught legal research and writing at San Mateo Law School, had recently purchased the West CD-ROM Library, a system that has reduced every court opinion published in California in the last 33 years to three compact disks of computer memory.

Punch in the magic words and backslashes and quotation marks—in this case, "stepparent /5 custody," and up pops all the relevant cases and statues. Push "DEFINE BLOCK" and "MOVE," and one can turn huge chunks of other people's words into one's own work product without even retyping.

Mr. Collins swore under penalty of perjury that he had devoted 22 hours, 10 of them over the Fourth of July weekend, to retrieving the information and turning it into memorandums. At his normal rate of $225 an hour, that worked out to $4,950, part of his total tab of $9,591.50. The money was to come from the stepfather, who lost the case, provided it was approved by Judge Roderic Duncan of the Alameda County Superior Court.

That was not quite what happened. Indeed, after deconstructing the mechanics of modern computer research, Judge Duncan not only balked, but handed over Mr. Collins to the disciplinary enforcement section of the State Bar of California.

The first person to detect something amiss in Mr. Collins's memorandums was the stepfather's lawyer, Sarah Leverett of Berkeley. Initially she was impressed. "As I was reading, I thought, 'Boy, this is written better than anything else Collins has done,' " she recalled. There then followed, however, a sense that what she was reading was not a case of first impression. "I thought, 'Not only is this well written, but I've read it before.' "

In fact, large portions of Mr. Collins's memorandums had been copied verbatim, without attribution, from various printed court decisions. In one seven-page stretch, all but three paragraphs had been lifted; in another nine-page memorandum, only six lines were original. Ms. Leverett called the matter to Judge Duncan's attention at a hearing held to discuss Mr. Collins's fee request.

The judge reacted with incredulity, particularly since Mr. Collins had depicted himself as an experienced practitioner, someone who in his two decades of practice had represented more than 1,000 clients in family law cases and tried numerous cases—either 50 or 100, depending on how one read his fee request—to a verdict.

"It is difficult to believe that even a first-year law student could have spent 22 hours cutting and pasting the draft of these pleadings," Judge Duncan wrote. He awarded Mr. Collins $3,000, a third of what he sought.

Mr. Collins asked Judge Duncan to reconsider his ruling, and the court held a hearing on Sept. 7. As a kind of computer-character witness, Mr. Collins produced the man who sold him his computer library, William P. Eppes 3d of the West Publishing Company. Mr. Eppes testified that by typing "cd Westpub/prs" after the "C prompt," he determined that Mr. Collins had used the system for 9 hours and 33 minutes since he had purchased it. (Apart from his sales job, Mr. Eppes said, he had been a licensed lawyer in Tennessee since 1978, and it seemed entirely plausible to him that Mr. Collins had put in the time he claimed.)

All of the computer time, Mr. Collins explained in a memorandum to the court, was spent on the custody case. As for the lifted language, he explained that he had quoted the courts at length because their language "was better written than I would have composed it myself," but that he had made minor alterations to it.

After the hearing, Judge Duncan gave Mr. Collins a split decision. He declined to give the lawyer any more money. But apparently impressed with Mr. Eppes's research, he withdrew his claim that Mr. Collins had not worked as long as he had said. All those hours at the computer, the judge seemed to say, reflected inefficiency rather than dishonesty. As a result, Mr. Collins said, disciplinary officials have told him that his case will proceed no further.

But he is still miffed at Judge Duncan. In an interview, he described the jurist as a "cavalier" judicial "maverick" whose ill-considered opinions had periodically been criticized by the California courts of appeal. How did he know? He consulted his trusty CD-ROM, and plugged in the words "Duncan" and "reversal." ❏

LIFTING A BRIEFCASE CAN BE A TERRIFIC STRAIN.
BUT A LITTLE CASH CAN EASE THE PAIN.

4/30/93

JAMES BENFER, ESQ., WHO INJURED HIS SHOULDER WHILE LIFTING AND IN-
specting the underbelly of his leather office chair, will collect
$107,913.75. Robert Anderson, Esq., received $30,000 after throwing
out his back stretching for a statute book on a top shelf of the law library at the Kansas Supreme Court.

Michael Harris, Esq., wrenched his shoulder reaching into the
backseat of his car for his briefcase. He will receive nearly $35,000. A
briefcase also proved the undoing of Fletcher Bell, Esq. He hurt himself trying to lift his out of his car trunk. The injury did not cause him
to miss any work, or even to miss his golf game. Still, a workers' compensation judge awarded him $95,000 for it.

Practicing law has its perils. But nowhere, it seems, is it more dangerous than in Kansas, where a dozen lawyers stand to receive more
than $670,000 in workers' compensation for work-related injuries. It
is a subject they know something about, for in one capacity or another
all are veterans of the workers' compensation system.

Mr. Harris, now a Republican State Senator, specialized in workers'
compensation cases as a lawyer. Mr. Bell was the Insurance Commissioner of Kansas, supervising companies that offer workers' compensation insurance. Mr. Anderson was once director of the division of
state workers' compensation. Indeed, he approved the award to Mr.
Bell, who, according to The Topeka Capital-Journal, beat his own
handicap at the Alvamar Country Club in Lawrence four months after
his crippling confrontation with his briefcase.

Collectively, the lawyers' claims reveal previously hidden dangers
lurking in the law, like slipping on ice to and from courtrooms; getting out of a chair, carrying files and bending over while preparing
for court; falling down during business trips; or aggravating an old
back injury by sitting too long at an office desk. "Somebody needs to
look into the dangers of being an attorney in the workers' comp
field," Bob Getz, a columnist for The Wichita Eagle, wrote last month.
"You'd think these guys were quarterbacks in the National Football
League, the way they've been racked up."

But in Kansas, where workers' compensation is a charged issue, not
everyone is so good-humored. "The general reaction is that while peo-

ple are struggling to be compensated at all, those inside the system have been busily taking care of themselves very, very well," said Pat Lehman, an official with the state A.F.L.-C.I.O. "The whole stinking mess just wants to make you lean over and throw up."

The damage awards, first reported by The Associated Press and The Capital-Journal, have become an important part of the debate over the future of workers' compensation now raging in the Kansas Legislature. It has not been overlooked, for instance, that Mr. Harris is leading the campaign to cut back on compensation awards.

They have also unleashed an orgy of lawyer-bashing and briefcase jokes in the letters-to-the-editor pages of the state's newspapers. Most of the letters focus on what the writers see as the silliness of the lawyers' injuries and the generosity of the damage awards, which, because they are based on annual income, are higher for lawyers than for most people. The money generally comes from insurance companies, though as onetime state employees, Mr. Bell and Mr. Anderson received state funds.

In one of many letters on the subject in The Wichita Eagle, Norman Smith of Wichita told of receiving only $6,000 a year after the murder of his wife in a local bridal shop. "When I go to the cemetery," he wrote, "I'm going to tell her that I miss her, I still love her, and I wish to God she had just sprained her back lifting a dress instead."

Daryl Glamann Sr. of Augusta was one of the many letter writers to focus his fire on Mr. Bell. "That tender, white-collar sissypoo would not have lasted one day as a railroad switchman, or an assembler, or a welder, or a tool and die maker," he wrote. Or as M. Elaine Skelton of Wichita put it: "We housewives should be collecting workers' compensation for our tired and strained backs! Those sacks of groceries are heavy!"

Writing to The Eagle in defense of the awards, David Jackson, the senior workers' compensation judge in the state, said the lawyers were not "thieves or cheats or exploiters" but merely "aware of workers' compensation laws." That reasoning did not satisfy Debra Smalley of Newton, Kan.

"By his judging standards, 20 kids who learn how to manipulate a candy machine into giving free candy would not be guilty of stealing," she wrote. "They were just 'aware' of how it worked."

Mr. Benfer, Mr. Anderson and Senator Harris did not return phone calls. Nor would Mr. Bell, according to his lawyer, Derek Shafer of Topeka. But amid calls for reform, Mr. Shafer disclosed that at least one thing had already changed. No longer, he said, was Mr. Bell playing golf. ❏

THE ACTION OF A LAWYER IN OCCUPIED FRANCE
RAISES THE QUESTION: IS NIT-PICKING COLLABORATION?

5/17/91

FROM THE LITTLE WE KNOW ABOUT HIM, JOSEPH HAENNIG WAS A RESPECTED lawyer in his day. Besides his practice, he wrote for one of France's most prestigious legal publications. Contemporary American legal periodicals are filled with the words of lawyers like him.

But Mr. Haennig's day was during World War II, his venue Paris under the Nazis. And what he wrote has reverberated beyond the era of Marshal Pétain and Pierre Laval, the leaders of unoccupied Vichy France.

In the current issue of the Cardozo Law Review, Richard Weisberg assesses the complicity of French law and lawyers in the slaughter of 90,000 French Jews. In that drama, he contends, Mr. Haennig was a kind of Everylawyer—an exemplar not just of the banality of evil but of its hyperlegality as well.

Mr. Haennig was not one of those Frenchman who, in effect, pushed Jews on Auschwitz-bound transports with a zeal even the Gestapo found impressive. He played no role in drafting Vichy's version of the anti-Jewish Nuremberg Laws. Nor was he among those judges who scrutinized baptismal records or circumcisions or the frequency of synagogue attendance of those desperately disclaiming their Jewishness.

All Mr. Haennig did was write a learned article for the Gazette de Palais, the official French compilation of cases, statutes and analyses. In form and flavor, that article resembled something out of the Harvard Law Review or New York Law Journal. It parses legal language, advises practitioners, analyzes precedents and original intent. There is the usual ever so reasonable editorializing ("We believe that neither good sense nor the law could lead to the view that . . ."), the usual garlands of citations.

Then there is the title: "What Means of Proof Can the Jew of Mixed Blood Offer to Establish His Nonaffiliation with the Jewish Race?"

The role played by the German judiciary in the Nazi era has been explored recently in Ingo Müller's "Hitler's Justice" (Harvard University Press). But Mr. Weisberg, who teaches at Cardozo, argues that with its constitutional tradition of liberty, equality and fraternity, the French experience is really of far greater relevance to American lawyers.

He came across the Haennig article nearly 20 years ago at Columbia Law School. Since then he has traveled many times to France, interviewed often reluctant functionaries from the Vichy era and reviewed thousands of documents, including the vast jurisprudence spawned by the 1941 French law defining "Jewishness" by the ethnicity of one's grandparents.

The statute, Mr. Weisberg writes, was rife with the ambiguities and caveats lawyers love. Did the individual or the state bear the burden of proof on the question of "belonging to the Jewish race"? What if one's grandparents had been atheists? Of what legal effect was baptism? What if the spouses were first cousins and thereby shared grandparents?

Mr. Haennig urged the courts to construe non-Jewishness generously. He cited a 1938 case from Leipzig involving a girl who, though baptized, had two Jewish grandparents. Despite her having attended religious school and Rosh Hashanah services for a time, the court had held her "Aryan." Mr. Haennig commended the ruling to French jurists, noting its "largeness and objectivity of spirit."

Lawyers pride themselves on being reasonable people. But there are times, Mr. Weisberg argues, when reasonability itself is unreasonable. To him, it is precisely its "benign aura of liberal, legalistic eloquence" that makes the Haennig article so pernicious; he nit-picked and hair-split rather than address the underlying barbarity of the racial laws. To Mr. Weisberg, such hyperlegalistic thinking was an element of the Holocaust as surely as Zyklon B.

After Mr. Weisberg first criticized Mr. Haennig in 1984, Richard Posner, a Federal appeals court judge in Chicago, took issue. What Mr. Haennig reflected, he argued, was not complicity but humanity: what had spared a half-Jewish German could presumably spare a half-Jewish Frenchman. "Maybe he thought the racial laws grotesque but knew it would not help to let his feelings show," Judge Posner wrote. "What would Weisberg have Haennig do?"

Plenty—or nothing—Mr. Weisberg responds in his new article. Some lawyers, he writes, did challenge the Vichy legal system, and without retribution. Or Mr. Haennig could have chosen another course, however counterintuitive for an ambitious lawyer. He could have remained silent.

Whether Mr. Haennig is still alive is a mystery to Mr. Weisberg. So, too, is how many other Haennigs there may be. ❑

FOR TEXAS FIRM, THE PRICE OF CIRCULATING
A VIDEOTAPE PROVES QUITE STEEP.

6/1/90

HOUSTON—THE LETTERHEAD SAYS HIRSCH, GLOVER, ROBINSON & SHEI-ness. But a local legal newspaper referred to the firm as "Hirsch, Glover & Shameless" for its role in the Houston bar's version of "Sex, Lies and Videotape," and many people here agree.

Hirsch, Glover was counsel for a 17-year-old in Houston who, aided by three confederates, filmed a sexual encounter between him and his unknowing girlfriend. Last July, a local jury awarded the woman, Susan Kerr, $1 million for invasion of privacy. But the case, and the collecting, has not ended there.

Within days Hirsch, Glover found itself in the dock for violating a court order to keep the tape out of circulation. And last month, under threat of a lawsuit, the firm quietly pledged Ms. Kerr an additional $600,000. But to her counsel, Ronald Krist, even that isn't enough. As offensive as the conduct of the four teenagers was, he maintains, the conduct of the firm was more reprehensible still.

In August 1985, as a primitive video camera hidden in a nearby closet recorded the scene, Dan Boyles Jr. made love with Ms. Kerr, who was 19 at the time. He brought the tape with him to the University of Texas and showed it to 10 people, primarily his fraternity brothers in Alpha Tau Omega. One of them even forgave a $25 gambling debt for the privilege.

Only that December did Ms. Kerr learn of the tape. She confronted Mr. Boyles, retrieved the cassette, then filed a $60 million suit against him and the friends who had assisted in his scheme. Mr. Boyles retained Jaime Drabek of Hirsch, Glover; representing Ms. Kerr was Mr. Krist, a flamboyant trial lawyer here who previously represented the families of several Challenger astronauts.

Anxious to keep the tape out of circulation, Mr. Krist resisted Hirsch, Glover's requests for a copy. But Judge David West overruled him. "You've got to trust the lawyers," he said. Still, he ordered that the copy given to defense counsel be viewed only by the lawyers and their experts, and that no additional copies be made.

When the case finally reached court last June, a Houston jury rejected the defense—that, as Mr. Drabek put it, the taping was simply "an impromptu, stupid, adolescent mistake." After the verdict came down, the Hirsch, Glover team returned to its office. Relieved over the outcome, since the $1 million award could have been much higher, Mr. Drabek ordered champagne for his troops. With most of the firm's top cats away at a retreat at nearby Lake Conroe, the mice began to play, according to Susan Hardy, a temporary secretary who was there.

One lawyer, Barbara Hackenberg, asked to view the tape once more, ostensibly to prepare for an appeal. But as many as 16 other employees—secretaries, paralegals, clerks—filtered into the room, with another goal. "Let's get to the good part," a secretary said.

"It made me sick to my stomach when I learned what they were doing in there," recalled Ms. Hardy. "They were watching it like a stag film." She stormed out of the office, vowing that "every attorney in town" would soon learn what had happened. The first she called was Mr. Krist.

Mr. Krist asked Jay Hirsch, a partner at the firm, for an explanation. Mr. Hirsch assured Mr. Krist and Judge West that he had investigated the matter "thoroughly" and that only employees "directly involved" in the case had seen the tape. But that same day, Mr. Drabek informed Mr. Hirsch by memo, at least five staff members, not all involved in the case, had been watching. Mr. Drabek also conceded in the memo that a copy of the tape had been sent to Mr. Boyles's insurance company, where at least four more people got to see it.

A copy of that memo was sent anonymously to Mr. Krist. (The alleged culprit at Hirsch, Glover was given a lie detector test and, upon failing, was dismissed.) Mr. Krist promptly and publicly charged that Hirsch, Glover had not only violated the court order but had also misrepresented its conduct. "Lawyers in Houston's notorious sex-tape trial apparently could not resist the urge to watch the lurid video one more time," The Texas Lawyer reported.

Judge West fined Hirsch, Glover $2,000. But that did not placate Mr. Krist, who threatened to sue Hirsch, Glover for invading Ms. Kerr's privacy anew. A settlement quickly followed.

Mr. Hirsch conceded that the firm had done a poor job of limiting viewing of the tape. But he insisted that the costly settlement was a reflection not so much of any additional injury Ms. Kerr had suffered as of the firm's desire to leave the whole painful experience behind—an impossibility, he said, given Mr. Krist's penchant for generating publicity.

But the case won't go away. It will soon be a made-for-television movie. There is no word yet on who will portray Ms. Kerr, Mr. Boyles, Mr. Krist or any of the Hirsch, Glover lawyers. ❏

The miniseries was never made, and the Supreme Court of Texas reversed the $1 million verdict against the main perpetrator. But Ms. Kerr settled with him for $500,000, which brought her total winnings in the case from the lascivious teenagers and the voyeuristic Hirsch, Glover lawyers to $1,600,000. Mr. Krist reports that Ms. Kerr married a wealthy rancher in the Texas panhandle and is now the mother of two children.

ACCUSED OF PUTTING THE VICTIM ON TRIAL, A TOP DEFENSE LAWYER IS ON TRIAL HIMSELF.

1/22/88

MOST PEOPLE, ACCEPTING THE MAXIM THAT EVERYONE IS ENTITLED TO HIS day in court, are willing to forgive a lawyer for his clients. Attorneys spend legal lifetimes representing drug dealers or Mafia kingpins or murderers, and remain invulnerable. Not so Jack T. Litman, the man representing Robert Chambers in the death of Jennifer Levin in Central Park.

The Guardian Angels are picketing his office. One television commentator called him "a vulture preying on the dead." The American Lawyer named him the "hands down" winner of its annual "Now You Know Why People Hate Lawyers Award." And, according to his friends, he's been the target of dirty tricks of the sort normally directed at child molesters rather than lawyers.

Why Mr. Litman? The reason seems to be simple. First, his case simultaneously involves the most unpopular of defendants and defenses: a man who admits to killing a young woman, but offers the explanation that he was provoked by her sexual conduct. And second, at least in the public mind, Mr. Litman pulled the same sort of thing in another celebrated case 10 years ago.

That time, his client was Richard Herrin, accused of hammering to death his ex-girlfriend, a fellow Yale student named Bonnie Garland. There, Mr. Litman argued that Mr. Herrin, distraught after learning that Miss Garland was involved with another man, could not be held fully accountable. The defense worked, to a point—Mr. Herrin was ultimately convicted of manslaughter.

Afterward, Mr. Litman (who has refused all interview requests) was asked by a psychiatrist, Willard Gaylin, whether legal attacks on crime victims were inevitable, and Mr. Litman said they probably were. There were those, he said, who held that defense lawyers must resuscitate the deceased so that the jury can kill them one more time. He'd stopped far short of that in the Garland case, he insisted, but confessed it was necessary "to taint her a little bit" so that the jury would understand the nature of her relationship with her killer.

The remark has come back to haunt Mr. Litman, particularly after he sought Jennifer Levin's diary, which Mr. Litman called "a chronicle" of the 18-year-old girl's "kinky and aggressive" sex life. As a result, his very presence has come to inflame an already explosive case.

As a general rule, the more notorious a case, the more a lawyer covets it. Mr. Litman is already among the city's top defense lawyers. He is particularly expert with medical testimony of the sort that could prove crucial in the Levin case. But should he overcome the implausibility inherent in Mr. Chambers's story—that he was just defending himself during rough sex—Mr. Litman could end up the homicide lawyer of choice in New York.

This may account in part for his accepting a case that, at least in the short run, is economic suicide. With lawyers like Mr. Litman charging around $300 an hour, the Chambers defense could be worth over a million dollars. No one thinks the family could pay even a fraction of that, nor is anyone else offering to.

But in the process, Mr. Litman has become what no good lawyer wants to be: a lightning rod. With clients, juries and judges alike it is crushing to become known as a Peck's bad boy of the bar, synonymous with an unpopular cause. Similarly, even in an age of specialization it's no better to be a Johnny One-Note. "If someone shot a man in the subway tomorrow, I wouldn't take his case," said Barry Slotnick, who represented Bernhard Goetz.

Thus, Mr. Litman faces two challenges in the Chambers case. He must not only vindicate his client but also, at least to some extent, himself.

That he finds himself the target of such contempt is paradoxical. For one thing, he handles relatively few homicide cases—only a dozen or so in 14 years of practice. His clients, including Rabbi Bernard Bergman, the nursing home owner convicted of fraud, may not always be savory, but they have been varied.

And, as a morning in court reveals, Mr. Litman is the unlikeliest of ogres. His demeanor is subdued and his style stolid, perhaps as a matter of habit, perhaps because, after the raft of bad publicity, he's on his best behavior. In the promiscuous puppy love world of the Levin case, a world populated with characters like "Larissa" and "Alexandra" and "Brock," where you half expect to hear advertisements for Ivory Liquid during recesses, the lawyer seems incongruous, almost ill-at-ease.

Furthermore, the kinds of aggressive tactics Mr. Litman is accused of inventing are as old as the adversary system itself—a system, defense lawyers and ethics experts agree, that not only condones what he does but requires it. Seventy years ago, the legendary Max Steuer won acquittals for the Triangle Shirtwaist Company owners, in part by badgering the surviving workers, mostly immigrant women, who testified against his clients.

"There are no synagogues named for him, but Steuer did what a good defense lawyer should do," said Leon Stein, who has written about the trial. "He won his case." ❑

After the jury voted, 7 to 5, to acquit Mr. Chambers of murder, Mr. Litman accepted the deal he had demanded before trial: manslaughter, with a sentence of 5 to 15 years. His client remains in jail; Mr. Litman has since become president of the New York State Association of Criminal Defense Lawyers.

ON LAWYERLY LASCIVIOUSNESS
AND NEW EFFORTS TO DEAL WITH
A 'DIRTY LITTLE SECRET.'

5/22/92

THE STATE OF INDIANA BARS PLUMBERS FROM ENGAGING "IN LEWD OR IM-moral conduct" while on house calls. But the lawyer-legislators who drafted that statute have not applied the same standard to themselves. Indeed, what is sauce for doctors, psychotherapists and at least some pipe fitters is not necessarily sauce for lawyers—in Indianapolis or anywhere else.

Perhaps, one state bar disciplinary official speculated, this is because lawyers are asexual. More likely it is because until very recently lawyers have been reluctant to acknowledge, much less discuss, what one judge has called the bar's "dirty little secret": that however sex between lawyers and clients complicates and compromises zealous representation, it is hardly extraordinary.

But bar associations in several states have finally begun dealing with the issue. Two of the profession's reigning superegos, Monroe Freedman of Hofstra and Geoffrey Hazard of Yale, have assailed lawyerly lasciviousness. So has the American Academy of Matrimonial Lawyers, perhaps because divorce clients—often overwrought, fearful or impoverished—prove the likeliest prey.

Never has the academy, the American Bar Association or any other lawyers' group sought to chart the dimensions of the problem. The task fell, instead, to two Boston lawyers, Linda Jorgenson and Pamela Sutherland. Their findings, based on reports from cooperative bar officials in every state except Michigan, Nevada and Rhode Island, will appear next month in the Arkansas Law Review.

In one sense the statistical pickings are slim: only 90 cases over the last two years. Alabama, Pennsylvania and Oregon topped the list, but all remained in single figures. The vast majority were brought by female clients against male lawyers, although one, in North Carolina, concerned a male inmate and his male counsel, while an Oregon case involved a female lawyer and a male prisoner (the two were married after charges in the case were dropped).

But according to J. Warren Bettis, disciplinary counsel for the Ohio Supreme Court, what is visible is only the "tip of the iceberg."

"This is a sensitive topic and many women choose not to report it," he wrote last year to the general counsel of the Ohio State Bar Association.

Two years ago, in a case known as "Suppressed v. Suppressed," an Illinois appellate court agreed. "This is a case of first impression despite the fact that the activity involved has been considered a wrong since biblical times," the court said. "Certainly, this court is not so naive that it believes that lack of case law is due to an absence of such activity within the legal community."

But the cases are as illuminating as they are skimpy. For example:

❡ In Wisconsin, a woman already receiving counseling and medication because of spousal abuse and the sudden death of her infant child consulted a lawyer about a divorce. While on a house call, the lawyer pushed her onto a bed and tried to remove her clothes, she said. The woman subsequently contemplated suicide—her note mentioned the lawyer by name—and post-traumatic stress disorder was diagnosed.

❡ A West Virginia lawyer peppered his client in a divorce case, she said, with inquiries about the number of orgasms she usually experienced during intercourse and regaled her with tales of his own resilience, boasting that he was in good enough shape to have sex seven times a day.

❡ After maneuvering a client into having sex, an Illinois lawyer billed the woman for the time, she said. The same lawyer—Mr. "Suppressed" in the aforementioned case—made a second divorce client inhale a liquid solution out of a brown bottle that made her feel "light-headed" and "tingling" before inveigling her into bed. The woman, claiming that the lawyer had harassed other women, tried suing him and his law firm under the Federal racketeering law.

❡ Another Wisconsin lawyer told his distraught divorce client that an amorous relationship was necessary "to relieve sexual tensions," she said. The woman spurned him, but over the next few days she suffered from repeated nightmares, from which she would awaken screaming and crying uncontrollably.

Some of these lawyers were penalized under criminal statutes or existing provisions in the Code of Professional Responsibility. But Ms. Jorgenson and Ms. Sutherland urge that sexual liaisons, like business transactions between lawyers and clients, be made presumptively unethical—a presumption rebuttable only by clear proof that the lawyer did not take advantage of the client's vulnerability and that the client offered informed, possibly even written, consent.

"It is hardly likely that a lawyer about to begin a sexual relationship with a client would meet that rigorous standard," Justice Alan J.

Greiman wrote in the Suppressed case. He called such a requirement "the legal equivalent of a cold shower." ❑

Three states—California, Oregon and Minnesota—now regulate the circumstances under which lawyers may have sex with the clients. New York does, too, but only for matrimonial lawyers. Similar regulations are under discussion in several other states.

VII

IN THE TRENCHES — AND BEYOND

COURT STREET BIDS GOODBYE TO IZZY HALPERN, A LEGENDARY FIGURE OF THE BROOKLYN TRIAL BAR.

2/9/90

ALONG COURT STREET IN BROOKLYN, IN THE HIGH-RISE ROOKERIES WHERE trial lawyers congregate, there are 65 years' worth of Izzy Halpern stories.

There is the one about how, during one of his typically impassioned summations, a woman on the jury pleaded with him to stop. "It's not worth it!" she shrieked in Yiddish. "You're going to have a heart attack!"

There is another about how he once asked an overconfident doctor on the witness stand whether he had examined the plaintiff for some obscure disease. "Of course," the doctor said huffily, only to learn that the "ailment" was actually some atoll in the South Pacific.

Still another has him looking on in horror as his co-counsel, oblivious to the jury's reaction, harassed an elderly woman who had fallen in an elevator and was suing his client. When Mr. Halpern's turn to cross-examine her came, he got up, gently kissed her hand, purred, "Feel better, Mother," then sat down. His client, incidentally, was acquitted.

From the era of Al Smith and Jimmy Walker on, Isidore (Izzy) Halpern was a fixture in the courtrooms, corridors and cafeterias of Court Street. He was also a familiar figure on Court Street itself, sitting in the front seat of his Rolls-Royce, alongside his chauffeur. Like many who'd grown up poor, he was proud of his success; unlike many, he never wanted to seem too uppity about it.

But when Izzy Halpern died last week at the age of 88, he did so in a most uncharacteristic way: quietly. Only a few were around to mourn him—an occupational hazard of outliving all of your contemporaries. In fact, the world Izzy Halpern represented died long before Izzy did himself.

It was a world in which Court Street was the hub of a vital community rather than some seedy adjunct of Manhattan, a separate world rather than merely a separate area code. It was a world in which courts were less crowded, crime less menacing, juries less jaded and sophisticated. It was a world in which oratory, forensics, even histrionics mattered more than erudition.

A few years ago, after he had gone into hemidemisemiretirement, he lamented that his younger colleagues on Court Street tried cases "like ulcerated accountants."

"We're in an era of settle, settle, settle, and advocacy is going down the drain," he complained. "The swashbuckling, gallant guys are gone."

When old-time trial lawyers speak of Izzy Halpern or his bar contemporaries like Harry Gair or Emile Zola (Zuke) Berman, they sound much like old baseball buffs talking about Josh Gibson and other stars of the Negro Leagues. They talk of how much better they were than those who played in arenas barred to them, how they beat the pants off their so-called superiors whenever they squared off.

When he got out of New York University Law School in 1923, Mr. Halpern didn't go to Wall Street; Jews or Italians or Irish couldn't. But he prided himself on being more resourceful, more shrewd, faster on his feet than the "paper men" across the East River, and others agreed. When William Randolph Hearst needed a trial lawyer, it was Izzy Halpern he hired. (Hearst was dropped as a client after Mr. Halpern's wife, Lillian, objected to the publisher's right-wing politics.)

Still, if Mr. Halpern was not a Wall Street lawyer, nor was he a Court Street lawyer, at least as that term is usually used—a synonym for ambulance chaser, fast talker, exploiter of the miserable. He was one of the few lawyers versatile enough to represent either side in the "eye-out" and "leg-off" cases in which Court Street abounded. He was a man of great learning and breadth, who read Freud and Jung and Ibsen.

And yet he knew Jean Harlow, drank with Dutch Schultz, represented Gypsy Rose Lee. What Reginald Marsh painted, Izzy Halpern appreciated: the surreal performers, carnival barkers, prostitutes.

As he aged, his style changed. "You'd see this tiny thin guy shuffling into court," one lawyer recalled. "Then he'd stand up in summation and it was magic: he was transformed. When he spoke, he was 10 feet tall. He just took over a courtroom."

But in his twilight years, spent sequestered in his apartment on Willow Street in Brooklyn Heights, he despaired of the real value of a lawyer's work. It was all a game, he feared. Perhaps, he'd say, he'd have been better as a rabbi, like his two brothers, or a teacher. In fact, that's what he always was, even at the end.

For years, he taught classes in trial tactics. Then, in his final days, as a childless widower, he tutored young lawyers by telephone, speaking to them for hours, offering pointers, asking questions, reviewing transcripts, even as his eyesight failed. As one of them, Richard Harrow, put it at the funeral, Mr. Halpern was more than just his dear friend. Always, he said, "Izzy was my co-counsel." ❑

OF LIFE, LIMB AND THE PURSUIT OF UNHAPPINESS: AN INJURY LAWYER'S EXCHANGE.

1/26/90

EVER REPRESENT ANYONE WHO'S BEEN THROWN OUT OF A HOVERCRAFT OR who's slipped on some terrazzo stairs? Has any client been forced at gunpoint to withdraw money from a cash machine? Or has a client been bitten by a hog and lost a leg? If so, your fellow lawyers are looking for you.

You can find them through Lawyers Alert, a biweekly publication for the profession. Each issue offers a "readers' exchange" in which personal injury practitioners from around the country try to learn whether their clients' latest and most perplexing calamities have arisen anywhere else.

The exchange is a kind of professional flea market or swap meet in which lawyers, primarily small practitioners without the resources of larger firms, share intelligence. It is also an atlas of the dangers posed by everyday objects and an inventory of emerging areas of tort liability.

Since the service began two years ago, there have been inquiries into deaths or injuries from tire inflators, measles vaccines, straitjackets, rupturing swimming pools, nasal sprays, abusive door-to-door vacuum-cleaner salesmen, wart-remover kits, falling cartons of beer, bowling alleys with sticky floors, hot tubs, steering axles in semitractors, improperly labeled gas pumps, improperly released prisoners, protruding shelves at Montgomery Ward, desk chairs, diving boards and venetian blinds.

Many of the notices are intriguing, especially for those with a bizarre sense of humor or a vivid imagination. "Attorney seeks information on the use of Alcon or other aluminum-based antacids with dialysis patients," one read. It was from Gerald D. McBeth, Esq., of Nevada, Mo.

Lawyers have inquired into Ford seat belts, Oldsmobile throttle-control springs, Renault hoses and Volkswagen brakes. Apart from life and limb, there have been queries about defective mobile homes, falling mirrors and crop damage from phone cables.

Some lawyers offer information in ads, which are free, like all the notices in the exchange. Whitney L. Schmidt of Tampa, Fla., has data on "depression or psychosis allegedly resulting from physician-supervised diet programs such as HMR 500 and Optifast." Christian Stegeman of Cincinnati knows all about fires caused by electric heat tape.

Thomas F. Harrison, the editor of Lawyers Alert, turns the lawyers' often loquacious requests into succinct and printable prose. "The only ones I haven't run are where people wanted dirt on particular experts who are appearing against them," he said. "There we drew the line."

Lawyers Alert, read by 20,000 lawyers, costs subscribers $130 a year, an investment that its publisher, Laurence Bodine, promises is not just tax-deductible but pays for itself. "Win lawsuits and prosper," Mr. Bodine states in his promotions. "No gossip. No propaganda. No puff profiles. Just concise up-to-date information you need to win lawsuits and make your practice thrive."

Those who have advertised in the reader's exchange seem satisfied with the response and, in some instances, elated by it. Take Edward K. Madruga of Indio, Calif. A client of his was maimed when a bottle of lye blew up in her face. Mr. Madruga advertised for comparable cases and received "just a plethora of information" from his bar brethren— information that he said could turn a real loser of a case into "a six-figure win." "It was absolutely phenomenal," he said. "People called and wrote; busy lawyers took time to write me memos. It was a wonderful, heartwarming experience, and I loved it."

Other results, if less dramatic, are nonetheless satisfying. Stephen J. Fallon of North Attleborough, Mass., had a client whose eyelids swelled after a salesman in Filene's basement gave her a sample application of some Lancôme mascara. Mr. Fallon advertised last fall and heard from four or five other lawyers with similar stories. While he is no longer contemplating a lawsuit, Lancôme has agreed to pay his client's dermatological bills.

Not everyone has had such happy results. Some, like Michael Havrilesko of Rockford, Ill., whose farmer client lost a leg and developed leukemia after one of his boars bit him, got responses from a computer research concern but no one else. Daniel Pritchett of Dallas found no one else whose olfactory nerves or tastebuds had been dulled by nasal spray, and anyway, his client's condition disappeared.

The experience of Mr. McBeth, who placed the advertisement about Alcon, proves the lesson of his namesake: "If it were done when 'tis done, then 'twere well it were done quickly." One lawyer did respond, but by the time Mr. McBeth got around to calling him back, he had died. It was not clear whether the poor lawyer was on antacids or dialysis at the time. ❑

WHEN A LAWYER ASKING CLIENTS TO DIAL INJURY 1 TAKES ON THE ONE WITH INJURY 9, WHO IS INJURED?

7/3/92

ABOUT EIGHT YEARS AGO, HARRIS J. SKLAR OF PHILADELPHIA SPOTTED A FELlow personal injury lawyer named Paul Perlstein approaching him at a wine and cheese party. "Well, here comes Mr. 'INJURY 1!' " Mr. Sklar said cheerily.

Mr. Perlstein had mixed motions about the greeting. On the one hand, it was yet another indication that his new phone number—the one he was advertising in broadcasts, on benches and buses, at bus stops, on magnets and ballpoint pens and in newspapers—was catching on. INJURY 1 might be clunkier to dial than "465-8791," but it was so much catchier. And it was far more memorable than "Dranoff-Perlstein Associates," the name embossed on his stationery.

Mr. Perlstein was not the first Philadelphia lawyer to use a mnemonic device. That distinction goes to Marvin Goldberg, a.k.a. LEGAL 10. But all that time he spent at the telephone, typing out different combinations on the number pad, were bearing fruit. Thousands of Philadelphians knew the drill: "Automobile accident? Dial INJURY 1. Medical malpractice? Dial INJURY 1. Death claims? Dial INJURY 1. Slip and falls? Dial INJURY 1."

On the other hand, Mr. Perlstein thought he detected a bit of gentle ribbing in Mr. Sklar's greeting. Lawyer advertising was still in its awkward adolescence, and even among personal injury practitioners, who had pushed for it most aggressively, it still had a vaguely schlocky air. As for mnemonic devices, they were still the preserve of loan sharks and hemorrhoid specialists.

The two lawyers went their separate ways. So happy was he with his first mnemonic that Mr. Perlstein acquired another, for cases beyond the city limits: 1-800-732-HURT. But in February 1990 he heard something disconcerting on a local radio station: anyone who had been injured by a product that had either been poorly designed, manufactured or labeled was being told to call INJURY 9. On the other end of the line was none other than Harris J. Sklar.

"It was a rip-off," Mr. Perlstein recalled. After some threatening letters to Mr. Sklar proved unavailing, Mr. Perlstein took his erstwhile litigating and drinking companion to Federal District Court, claiming copyright infringement and unfair competition.

Of all the areas of law, perhaps none is as superficially simple and technically impenetrable as the law of patents and trademarks. In it, otherwise intelligible words like "arbitrary," "suggestive," "descriptive" and "generic" take on new and baffling meanings and blend inextricably. From this morass the competing lawyers' competing lawyers—Stuart Beck for Mr. Perlstein, Manny Pokotilow for Mr. Sklar—fashioned arguments that telephone numbers can or cannot be protected.

Mr. Pokotilow maintained that injury is "generic" rather than distinctive, citing the plethora of practitioners who use various forms of the word in their advertisements or phone numbers. An Illinois lawyer, he noted, used INJURY 5. Others, of unspecified venue, use 1-800-INJURED or 1-800-4-INJURY or "Personal Injury Hotline."

But Mr. Beck countered by resting on the landmark case of Dial-a-Mattress v. Page. There, a Federal appeals court barred a company from using 1-800-MATTRES, noting that it infringed on the rights of another company that had built its business around the slogan "Dial MATTRES and leave off the last 's' for savings."

Judge John P. Fullam, a senior judge who heard the case, sided with Mr. Pokotilow and Mr. Sklar, throwing out the case. If the two sets of lawyers were selling injuries rather than legal services, he ruled, Mr. Perlstein could have leaned on the Dial-a-Mattress doctrine. Besides, the numbers were different and distinguishable.

Last month the United States Court of Appeals for the Third Circuit agreed, but only in part. The INJURY portion of the Dranoff-Perlstein number, it held, was indeed generic and unprotectable. To deny Mr. Sklar or others in his field the right to use INJURY in his advertising, the court held, "would be to deny competitors the right to call the practice of personal injury law by its name."

But whether the numbers in their entirety—that is, INJURY 1 and INJURY 9—can be confused as Mr. Perlstein asserts, the panel continued, is a question that the lower court cannot shirk.

Mr. Perlstein has at least one ally: Teresa Rydzewski, a Philadelphia housewife who can be reached at 465-8792—that is, INJURY 2. His advertisements, which she has seen on local buses, have made a believer out of her. "If I had ever needed a lawyer, that's who I would have called," she said. ❏

After a bout in the courts, INJURY 1 won.

In Which a Personal Injury Lawyer Trips Over His Porsche and Thereby Dents His Own Case.

4/5/91

PORSCHES. MERCEDES. JAGUARS. BMW'S. THEY ARE THE PULITZER PRIZES of the legal profession. But as a Dallas personal injury lawyer named John Cracken was recently reminded, fancy cars are sometimes best left at home.

Only four years out of the University of Texas Law School, the 30-year-old Mr. Cracken has become one of the hottest plaintiffs' lawyers in Dallas. He has done so partly by picking up the secrets of his craft—among them, that conspicuous consumption has no place in a courtroom. Jurors must never think a lawyer is rich, lest they fear making him richer. As much as 40 cents of every big buck awarded to clients ends in the pockets of their lawyers.

This is particularly true in a conservative community like Dallas, whose jury boxes are filled with insurance adjusters, bank employees and other constituencies wary of windfalls. "Dallas County is a tough place to be a plaintiffs' lawyer," Mr. Cracken said.

Thus, on days when he is due in court, Mr. Cracken leaves his Rolex at home. He doffs fancy clothes and dons a somber, somewhat ill-fitting suit. And he usually trades off his $40,000 red Porsche 911 to a colleague with less ostentatious wheels, or rents the kind of generic late-model American-made vehicle, respectable but dull, that congregates like a herd of hippopotamuses in the watering holes of Hertz or Avis.

It is a changeover he can make convincingly. Mr. Cracken is a slight man with a vaguely Ivy League look; someone who recently saw him in court likened him to Pee-wee Herman, better suited to a red Columbia two-wheeler than a red Porsche.

In personal injury practice, a family's calamity is a lawyer's bonanza, and in Martinez v. Rock-Tenn Company that appeared truer than ever. Representing the widow of a Salvadoran mangled by a baling machine, and facing a defense hobbled by court sanctions, Mr. Cracken was understandably eager to get to court when the case got under way in January. He left his house early enough to make it by 7:30 A.M.—early enough to beat the jurors and so, he figured, early enough to take his Porsche.

But when he drove into the courthouse parking garage, he found himself in a flock of jurors. "They flanked me on the right and left and behind me," he recalled. "It was amazing." With a trial lawyer's instincts, Mr. Cracken ducked down toward the glove compartment and began fumbling among its contents until the jurors had passed.

But he'd been spotted, and nothing—not even the 1988 Buick Regal he used afterward—could undo the indelible. Waiting for the elevator, three jurors discussed what they'd just seen. One of them, Narween (Narky) Blackwell, recalled what one of her colleagues vowed: "There was no way I'm going to buy that lawyer another fancy car."

Anyone who has ever served on a jury can tell how jurors, having little else to do and little else in common, focus minutely on the lawyers appearing before them. Thus, though they apparently overlooked the kind of car Mr. Cracken's opposing counsel, Mike Schmidt, drove to court each morning ("a little Mercedes," Mr. Schmidt said), they noticed that he kept wearing the same dark suit, its jacket lining held in by a safety pin.

It was not surprising, then, that Mr. Cracken's Porsche became part of the banter over coffee and doughnuts in the jury room each morning. "It was just something to talk about," said another juror, Frances Hensley of Seagoville. "Everyone knows that lawyers make money."

And with the jury deadlocked over how much to award—the numbers ranged from $60 million to nothing at all—the Porsche became part of the deliberations. That much became apparent early on, when the jury sent Judge Anne Ashby Packer a note: Just how much, it asked, did the lawyers in the case stand to make?

After a day of deliberations, the jurors awarded the plaintiff $5 million. Mr. Cracken says ruefully that but for that confounded car, it could have been far more—two or three million dollars more, according to Melissa McMath, the jury expert he imported from Little Rock, Ark., for the case. "It's the most expensive Porsche in the United States," Ms. McMath said.

Several weeks have passed, and some jurors are irate at the turn of events. "It seemed to me that a form of justice was decided on the fact that Mr. Cracken was driving a Porsche," grumbled Beti Hauser of Dallas, who favored a higher award. "That wasn't what we were there to do."

But a chastened Mr. Cracken has moved, or driven, on. The following week, after motoring to court in a borrowed Sterling—"a nice car but not particularly flashy," he said—he collected another million-dollar verdict. ❑

BIRMINGHAM'S TOUGHEST LAWYER
IS FACED DOWN BY HIS OUTRAGED
COLLEAGUES OVER A FUNERAL WREATH.

6/7/91

BIRMINGHAM, ALA.—ANYONE HERE WATCHING RERUNS OF "PERRY MASON" or "Mayberry R.F.D." has heard of Robert M. Norris.

In televised advertisements—which he had to sue the Birmingham Bar Association to be allowed to run—Mr. Norris promotes himself as "the toughest lawyer in town." His name can also be seen on wristwatches, baseball caps, church chairs, plastic business cards and bumper stickers that warn: "BACK OFF! MY LAWYER IS ROBERT NORRIS."

But Mr. Norris may soon be silenced, hanged by a $25 wreath of yellow flowers.

Four years ago, shortly after 19-month-old Randy Carter died after spending five sweltering hours in a van, where workers for a day care center left him, Mr. Norris sent the wreath to the funeral home where the baby had been taken. Accompanying it was a brochure about his firm and a note to Randy's family.

"Please accept our deepest sympathy in the loss of Randy," it stated. "We know you are presently being faced with many difficult decisions and will soon be faced with others. If we may be of assistance to you in any regard, do not hesitate to contact us at 870-8000."

The funeral directors dumped the flowers, but not before the boy's anguished mother had spotted them. She was outraged, particularly since a spiritualist named "Sister Carol," to whom Mr. Norris denies having any connection, already called her with word that God, too, wanted her to call 870-8000. Randy's mother called the wreath "real tacky," and the lawyers who sent it "vultures."

Mr. Norris's bar colleagues were outraged. "With lawyers trying to rehabilitate a negative image, some clown like you comes along and destroys everything," one wrote Mr. Norris. "Robert, that was a real class act. The person who invented the word 'shyster' obviously had you in mind."

An investigation was begun, and last year the State Bar Association's disciplinary panel handed Mr. Norris a two-year suspension, for improper solicitation.

Mr. Norris has clearly displaced the Houston lawyer who sprinkled business cards along with pepperoni on the pizzas he sent to emergency room orderlies as the most vilified marketer of legal services.

Robert M. Hill Jr., the chairman of the disciplinary panel, said Mr. Norris's conduct was "just not acceptable."

Mr. Norris admits he made a mistake. But however tasteless his gesture may have been, he insists it was constitutional, and that in throwing the book at him the bar association had acted vindictively, sanctimoniously, hypocritically and illegally.

The tale of the wreath began on July 7, 1987. A woman calling herself a friend of Carter family members told one of Mr. Norris's assistants that they needed legal help but were too poor even to buy flowers for the boy's funeral. Mr. Norris said he sent the flowers, but only after checking the rules, which state that while in-person or telephone solicitation are improper, direct mailings are not.

"To say we wouldn't have liked to have the case is ridiculous, but I'd have sent the flowers anyway," said Mr. Norris, a soft-spoken man who hardly seems like the toughest lawyer in any town, except perhaps Mayberry R.F.D.

But over the past decade, Mr. Norris's shtick antagonized just about every segment of the bar. To compound matters, he is a Mormon, a Virginian and a non-joiner, who says he would rather play golf with one of his eight children than with any fellow lawyer. "Norris is not a good old boy," said his partner, D. Michael Barrett. "He doesn't smoke, drink, curse or chase women, and that's against the norm down here. He sued the bar, and he's not a Deep-in-the-Heart-of-Dixie Southerner. Down here Virginia's practically a border state."

This antipathy, Mr. Norris says, helps explain why his accusers broadened their definition of "solicitation" after the fact and eviscerated his free speech rights. He said it also explains why his sanction was so severe while lawyers committing more serious sins—botching cases, dipping into escrow accounts, showing up in court drunk, punching the opposing party during a recess—have received only private reprimands.

Already, Mr. Norris has lost an appeal to the Alabama Supreme Court. Should that panel decline to rehear the case, as he has requested, he will appeal to the United States Supreme Court. But expecting the worst, he is preparing to hand the practice to his younger brother, David.

In the meantime, some decisions can't wait. "We're out of baseball hats and we're afraid to reorder," he said. "We don't know what name to put on them." ❑

Mr. Norris sold his practice to his brother, and served a two-year suspension. The hiatus scarcely dented either his income (he had been running a law office more than actually practicing law) or his ego. "I never really had any buddies in the law anyway," he said. But he remains bitter, noting how a drunken lawyer who'd run over a young girl was suspended for only six months. "I sent flowers and got two years," he complained. "I'd have been better off killing someone."

Disciplinary authorities have now gone after the Norris firm for its latest television advertisement. "Attention, injury victims: let's face facts," it stated. "Norris & Associates are greedy lawyers. Greedy to get you as much money as we can as fast as we can because the more you get, the more we get."

"I can imagine why the bar didn't like that, but the public loved it," Robert Norris said. "It's the best ad of all time. It's so overwhelmingly honest. Lawyers are finally telling the truth."

FOR PERSONAL INJURY MAVEN, A CHRISTMAS CARD TRADITION FUELS A SUIT WITH BITTER FEELING.

12/14/90

"CITY SIDEWALKS, BUSY SIDEWALKS," THE CLASSIC GOES. "IT'S CHRISTMAS time in the city." For thousands who have tripped and fallen on those sidewalks or might know someone who has, Christmas time in New York City has always included a holiday card from Harry Lipsig.

For 60 years Mr. Lipsig, personal injury lawyer nonpareil, has sent Christmas cards to virtually everyone he has ever buttonholed. He records their names on color-coded index cards—pink for lawyers, orange for firefighters, and so on—and stores them in a vast card catalogue.

With Mr. Lipsig, it is always Christmas in July. That is when his secretaries have begun addressing the 60,000 or so cards he mails out annually. For personal injury lawyers, for whom personal contacts are crucial, holiday cards are not sent for the reasons Bing Crosby crooned of in "White Christmas." In fact, Mr. Lipsig's season's greetings have become the crux of a most unmerry lawsuit. As bells jingle and children laugh these days, the discordant sounds of Lipsig v. Sullivan & Liapakis emanate from State Supreme Court in Manhattan.

Mr. Lipsig, who will turn 89 on Dec. 26, built his career on outrageousness. He is someone who not only chased ambulances but did so flamboyantly. For thousands of accident victims, the first words out of their mouths after "Ouch!" have been "Harry Lipsig."

Even by Mr. Lipsig's boisterous standards, however, the twilight of his career is noisy indeed. In the last two years he has legally adopted his former office manager, a woman in her 30's; left his law firm in a huff; formed a new firm with a woman who has since sued him; formed yet another firm, where he currently practices; and most recently, took his original partners from two firms ago, Robert Sullivan and Pamela Liapakis, to court. That's where the Christmas cards come in.

Mr. Lipsig maintains he has been unable to send out his full complement of cards this year because Mr. Sullivan and Ms. Liapakis won't disgorge the card file. Worse than that, he says, they have traded on his good name and deprived him of millions of dollars in referral fees, all in violation of the pact they signed upon separating.

Sullivan & Liapakis counter that not only does he have the file but
also that he stole it from them. In a letter included in court papers, a
former secretary to Mr. Lipsig wrote that she knew he had the file because "I could not count how many envelopes I typed last year from
cards, some of which seemed to be eons old."

Mailing the cards, the former partners say, violates both the pledge
and a court order not to solicit clients from the firm where he worked
for decades. Taking the matter to court, they add, is simply Mr. Lipsig's—or his adopted daughter's—way of keeping his name in print,
propping up his practice and persuading the public that he can still
practice law.

Mr. Lipsig has in fact been homebound for weeks, recuperating
from pneumonia and adjusting to a new pacemaker, and has been declining interviews for the first time since Hoover was President and
Babe Ruth roamed the Bronx. But in a brief conversation this week,
he said: "I'm in constant contact with my office and enjoying every
blasted minute of it. My law firm is doing fabulously—doing fabulously in the millions."

In recent years Mr. Lipsig has been as much a broker as a lawyer.
Relying on a name than is to torts what Sacher is to tortes, he has sat
back as clients brought him cases that he promptly farmed out to
other lawyers, claiming one-third of whatever the lawyers eventually
collect.

His lawyers, Susan Dwyer and Mara Levin of Herrick & Feinstein,
say he had 2,000 to 3,000 such referrals pending when he left Lipsig,
Sullivan & Liapakis in March 1989, and that he has been denied some
of those fees. His former partners maintain they effectively bought
those cases, along with the card file, for $2 million at the time of the
split.

Further, Mr. Lipsig has contended that anyone calling Sullivan & Liapakis looking for him has been told he was dead, incapacitated or retired. He also charges that Sullivan & Liapakis has exploited his name,
most notably by referring to itself as "Formerly Lipsig, Sullivan & Liapakis" in the Manhattan Yellow Pages.

One thing everyone can agree on is that for Mr. Lipsig, Christmas
cards have always been something of a religion and that his mailing
list would be the envy of Publishers Clearing House. What they differ
on is whether or not sending them out constitutes improper overtures
to another firm's clients.

"This is not a case where he knows our clients personally and is
sending a Christmas card because of Christmas cheer," said Edward
Brodsky, who represents Sullivan & Liapakis. "It's the first step in so-

licitation. The next step would be a call: 'Did you get my Christmas card? How's everything going? Are you satisfied with the lawyers representing you?' He's not supposed to be doing that." ❑

In the courtroom of Justice Martin Schoenfeld, it was Christmas in July in 1992. That was when Justice Schoenfeld ruled Mr. Lipsig should get the disputed addresses (but that his rivals be allowed to copy them first) and that both sides could send out Christmas cards to as many addressees as they wished. Mr. Lipsig's usual card, he noted, featured a reindeer and stated "Season's Greetings, Mildred and Harry Lipsig." "Whatever Lipsig's personal or professional magnetism may be, this hardly seems like a powerful device to lure away clients," the justice wrote. Ms. Liapakis has since added names of her own, and now mails 100,000 cards every Christmas. Actually, she sends them out the week before Thanksgiving, to make sure they are actually read.

A PIONEER IN PERSONAL INJURY
ADVERTISING STILL FINDS HIMSELF
ON THE CUTTING EDGE.

5/26/89

IN THE FIRST, HEADY DAYS OF LEGALIZED ADVERTISING BY LAWYERS, PHILIP Damashek was the king of the New York classifieds—and the crown prince and regent, too. While others hesitated to hawk themselves a decade ago, whether out of taste or timidity or frugality, Mr. Damashek went unabashedly ahead.

Like most trailblazers, he took his share of collegial heat. Another personal injury lawyer, Bert Subin, called Mr. Damashek's advertising "low-class," while still another, Perry Pazer, said it was unprofessional. It burned up Mr. Damashek, head of the 14-member Philip M. Damashek firm and now president-elect of the New York State Trial Lawyers Association, but only temporarily. "One day I woke up, checked the newspapers, and found that Bert had joined the low-class brigade," he recalled. "And here's Perry Pazer in the Yellow Pages— with his picture."

Ten years into the Madison Avenue era, only a few law firms, and only certain kinds, use the newspapers. One will never see Sullivan & Cromwell alongside the bartending schools or high-school equivalency courses. Most are personal injury firms, whose names, like Longhi & Loscalzo or Gersowitz & Libo could have been lifted from the log at Ellis Island as easily as from the pages of Martindale-Hubbell.

No longer, though, is it enough to run an ad; now that ad must stand out. Even New York has only a finite supply of "slip-and-fall" or "leg-off" cases. And this is where Mr. Damashek excels. His ads in The Daily News and Newsday are the biggest, the costliest and the catchiest of the lawyer blurbs.

While doctors may no longer make house calls, Mr. Damashek and his associates will, and the first one is an "on-the-house-call." Mr. Damashek is listed in "Who's Who in American Law." While Weisen, Gurfein & Jenkins can boast of being mentioned on "60 Minutes" and "20/20," he does better: he's in "The Guinness Book of World Records," under "greatest personal injury damages."

And recently Mr. Damashek tried something new, with his own toll-free number: 1-800-FACT-LAW. That is the leitmotif of his ads, a follow-up to his "This Week's Legal Tip" theme of 1984-85. Each ad includes a bite-size tale of woe—collapsing scaffolds, negligent landlords, drunk drivers—along with the applicable law. "INJURED?" he asks. "Give us THE FACTS—We'll give you THE LAW."

Even Mr. Damashek concedes that as a brand name, "FACT-LAW" is no Kodak or Coca-Cola. Theoretically he had 10 million different combinations to choose from in selecting his hot line number, but several of the choicest were already gone, like 1-800-LAWYERS. Others, like 1-800-GET-EVEN or 1-800-GET-CASH, were considered but rejected as undignified.

The calls start around 8:30 in the morning and average 75 to 100 a week. Mondays and Tuesdays are the busiest, weekends apparently being prime time for torts. The calls are routed to lawyers like Fern Finkel or Jeffrey Marder rather than secretaries or paralegals. "People who respond to newspaper ads are impulse shoppers," Mr. Damashek explained. "Either you respond to them immediately or they'll call someone else."

Only 5 percent of the calls lead to cases. The rest either fall outside Mr. Damashek's practice, are from cranks or aren't actionable, like one from a G.I. seeking to sue the Army for D-Day injuries. There are the Miss Lonelyhearts, for whom 1-800-FACT-LAW is a toll-free sympathetic shoulder. And there are the weirdos, who complain of being bombarded by alpha rays or tailed by the C.I.A. One lawyer in the office, Richard Ancowitz, spoke to a woman who said she'd just been killed in a car accident. "I asked her 'When did you first realize you were dead?' " he said. "Then I told her it was outside the scope of our expertise."

Mr. Damashek said he might branch out to radio and television, but nothing else. He considered buses and subways and even developed one of those posters with tear-off pads, of the sort favored by the Wilfred Beauty Academy. But they're expensive—about $5,000 a month—and didn't work, at least for a Brooklyn lawyer who tried them, Paul Mirman. Nor is he about to go the way of stamp companies and driving schools and use matchbook covers. "Maybe it's just a hangup of mine, but I just don't think you get a serious case from a matchbook ad," he observed.

"People are constantly asking me whether it works," he went on. "I say: 'Of course it doesn't work! That's why we've been doing it since 1978.' " He estimates that every advertising dollar brings in five more.

Up to now, at least, the ads have brought in no Guinness-like verdicts, which is not to say that 1-800-FACT-LAW doesn't produce an occasional dream client, say, a sympathetic soul claiming to have been horribly maimed by some heartless ogre with plenty of insurance. Mr. Damashek knows all about such "victims."

"It's one of my colleagues," he said, "yanking my chain. ❑"

VIII

OF JUDGES, REAL
AND WOULD-BE

AFTER TWO DECADES' LABOR,
A CHRONICLE ON THE LIFE OF PERHAPS
THE FINEST JUDGE EVER.

2/22/94

PALO ALTO, CALIF.—HANGING ON PROF. GERALD GUNTHER'S OFFICE WALL here at Stanford Law School is Philippe Halsman's 1957 portrait of Learned Hand, maybe the most famous photograph ever of a judge. It shows Hand, four years before his death at the age of 89, with his chiseled features, bushy eyebrows, close-cropped hair and intense eyes, staring off contemplatively.

"That was the human being I was trying to capture: a human being who knows sadness and tragedy and self-doubts and flaws, the kind of person whom I remember," Mr. Gunther said the other day. "All of his reflectiveness, his shaky self-esteem, his melancholy come through for me in that picture."

Forty-one years have passed since Mr. Gunther, who had fled Nazi Germany as a boy, served as a law clerk for Judge Hand, then nearing the end of a legendary career on the United States Court of Appeals in New York. For more than half that time, Mr. Gunther, author of the nation's most widely used constitutional law casebook, has also labored on a biography of his mentor. His efforts have now culminated with Alfred A. Knopf's publication of "Learned Hand: The Man and the Judge," the definitive work on the compulsively conscientious, insecure figure who served longer (a total of 52 years)—and perhaps with more distinction—than just about any other Federal judge in history.

Mr. Gunther, as painstaking as his idol, began working on the Hand biography back in 1972, when he acceded to repeated requests from the judge's son-in-law, a New York lawyer named Norris Darrell Sr. He has lived with Hand's papers even longer, since his days at the United States Courthouse on Foley Square, where he first spotted the innumerable neat file boxes that lined the judge's shelves. In them were decades of correspondence with Felix Frankfurter, Walter Lippmann, Bernard Berenson and other exemplars of an epistolary era now vanished.

No hand was more practiced than Hand's; Mr. Gunther read perhaps 40,000 of the judge's letters in researching the book. Nor was anyone more archivally inclined. Hand saved everything, beginning with the pocket diary he had kept as a 6-year-old boy in Albany. He did so less with an eye toward history—monumentally insecure, he would not have thought his writings lastingly significant—than out of what Mr. Gunther calls "a nice upstate New York Calvinist-Presbyterian" aversion to throwing anything away.

Mr. Gunther quite unwittingly helped save the Hand archive in the late 1950's when the judge, aroused by Frankfurter's warnings against allowing personal papers to fall into the hands of bad biographers, resolved to burn them. Only when Frankfurter promised Hand that Mr. Gunther, then teaching at Columbia Law School, would chronicle his life did Hand relent. Frankfurter made the pledge, incidentally, without consulting Mr. Gunther himself. "To him," Mr. Gunther said, "it was a white lie in a good cause."

Through correspondence and interviews, Mr. Gunther documented the Learned Hand he had known: the man who wrote all of his 4,000 opinions, without committees of law clerks; who wanted those clerks to be sounding boards rather than sycophants; who agonized, sometimes to a fault, over the most obscure patent case no less than over the most wrenching tests of the First Amendment. "Damn it, I have to get off the pot sometime!" he once shouted after Mr. Gunther the law clerk objected to some parts of a 13th handwritten draft of an opinion. "I get paid to decide cases, not just to argue them!"

In the course of his research, the author also encountered some surprises. Perhaps the greatest was that for all his protestations of indifference, Hand had been deeply disappointed at being passed over for the United States Supreme Court, where Oliver Wendell Holmes Jr., Benjamin Cardozo and countless others said he belonged. Twice he came close, in 1930 and 1942, but he never got the nod.

"I can say it now without the shame that I suppose I should feel—I longed as the thing beyond all else that I craved to get a place on it," he wrote of the High Court in a letter to Frankfurter in 1950. "It was the importance, the power, the trappings of the God damn thing that really drew me on, and I have no excuse beyond my belief that I am not by a jugful alone in being subject to such cheap and nasty aspirations."

Mr. Gunther, himself touted frequently for the Court—in 1987, when The National Law Journal asked a group of lawyers who, ideology aside, was most qualified to serve there, he was the runaway winner—says his discovery of Hand's longing was "startling."

"I never asked him about it, and he never volunteered," said Mr. Gunther, who had remained close to Hand after clerking for him.

"But I had taken at face value the notion that not being on the Court was not a big deal to him."

In recounting Hand's life, Mr. Gunther's greatest worry was that biography could become hagiography. "I began despite the fear that my admiration might preclude an absolutely unprejudiced portrayal," he writes in his preface. "I end hoping I have pictured him fully, warts and all. He remains my idol still."

At times, Mr. Gunther said in an interview, he even felt like offering Hand a posthumous pat on the back: "I just wanted to reach out and shake him by the shoulders and say, 'For heaven's sake, Judge, live a little, enjoy the applause. You do deserve some.' " Along with Mr. Gunther's admiration and love was also gratitude—not just for enriching his life four decades ago but, in a sense, for legitimizing it now.

"Hand gives substance to the alleged myth I believe in, one trashed repeatedly in recent years: that judges can be independent, restrained, detached," Mr. Gunther said. "I spent my life criticizing what judges do, sometimes with a fair amount of fervor. It would be a pointless exercise if I thought the judging business were predetermined by who your parents were, or your political affiliations, or what you had for breakfast." ❑

THE LONELY VIEW FROM THE BENCH
FOR THE NEW JUDGE WHO MUST
UNDERGO A RITE OF PASSAGE.

1/6/89

THE NEW JUDGE, CLAD IN A T-SHIRT AND SHORTS, WALKED PAST A COUPLE OF lawyers at a local health club. Only a few years ago, he knew both of his onetime bar brethren would have ignored him. "Good evening, your Honor," said one, thinking he was leaving. In fact, the judge was only going to the Nautilus machine, and when he emerged a few minutes later he passed them again. "Good evening, your Honor," the lawyer unctuously repeated.

Even as private practice has grown logarithmically more lucrative, many lawyers still aspire to the bench, or at least say they do. They consider judging the capstone of a career, a way of forsaking mercenary, partisan concerns for the loftier pursuit of truth and justice.

But there is another side of life on the bench, one even potential judges rarely recognize in advance. Judges feel a sense of instant isolation, almost quarantine. Activities that were once routine become awkward; old relationships are distorted, new ones inhibited or stillborn. And, suddenly, they're placed on a kind of lifelong probation, where even the slightest peccadilloes are magnified.

There are monkish men like Benjamin Cardozo, for whom taking the bench actually represented a coming-out. But most judges are instinctively affable, social sorts; that, after all, is how they became known, an essential part of becoming a judge. For new judges like the one in the health club, the first months on the bench are a time of profound adjustments.

No one has yet invented a protractor fine enough to measure the angle to which even the most respectable lawyers bow and scrape before judges. No matter what their personality, when approaching the bench they tend to sound like Eddie Haskell of "Leave It to Beaver" talking to June Cleaver. They compliment the judge's appearance, lavish him with honorifics, pore over his decisions, praise his erudition, double over with laughter at even his lamest jokes.

Not every new judge is sufficiently self-aware to realize that what these lawyers are groveling before is the robes rather than the intellect inside them.

"Someone who would not have given me the time of day a year ago

now says 'How are you, your Honor?,' " the new judge observed.
" 'You look like an altar boy in your robes, your Honor.' 'I read your
opinion last week, your Honor.' 'It's about time someone said that,
your Honor.' Before I was on the bench, this same character would
take every opportunity to misrepresent what I said, and pepper me
with ridiculous, harassing motions."

Since taking the bench he has mastered the arcane language in
which lawyers address judges. "I know you know the law better in this
area than anyone else, but . . . ," for instance, means "You're all wet."
He's learned how lawyers, knowing that to most mortals there is nothing sweeter than the sound of their name, repeat his incessantly. One
lawyer did so so excessively that the judge actually told him to cease
and desist.

And he has come to realize how rulings from the bench are not the
only ones he must formulate. For partisan advantage lawyers will seek
to exploit a judge's humanity and, like an overly aggressive suitor with
a date, they will go as far as he lets them. Thus, he has devised a rule
for every occasion: which dinner invitations to accept, who should pay
for them, whether to attend Christmas parties, when to leave, how
much he can say when on what subjects and to whom.

In the past couple of years old and trusted friends have become
more precious, new friends much harder to make. There have been
other changes. Although his political instincts are keen, he can no
longer dash off letters to the editor or pontificate on current events.
And the distractions are not only more sparse, they are more spartan.
Broadway shows, new cars, fancy dinners, all once routine, are now
extravagances for someone whose salary fell by at least half.

All of this makes him cleave to his work still more devotedly.
Evenings, he is far more likely to be found home catching up on summary judgment motions than anywhere else. Which may be just as
well, given the fishbowl in which judges swim. "I can no longer jay-
walk," he said. "I can't go five miles over the speed limit or drink too
much or use four-letter words or borrow my neighbor's newspaper. In
court, judges have to hurdle mountains, but outside they get in trouble if they stumble over a pebble.

"Is it worth it?" the new judge went on. "Unqualifiedly, yes. In private practice, lawyers measure success by beating the other side, persuading a jury to acquit someone who is probably guilty, getting a
million dollars in a case worth half that much. In this position, I can
always do what I believe is right. There's nothing to compare with the
satisfaction of doing justice, even in the smallest case. That's why this
is the best job in the world." ❑

CONSPICUOUS COMPASSION DOES NOT EQUAL BIAS. THAT IS TO SAY, EVEN A JUDGE IS ALLOWED TO CRY.

5/21/93

WHEN PRESIDENT CLINTON LISTED HIS PREREQUISITES FOR THE SUPREME Court, he included what some see as a contradiction in terms: a lawyer with a big heart. But as Judge Paula Lopossa of Indianapolis recently learned, big hearts can sometimes prove problematic, at least when worn on one's sleeve.

One day in April 1992, a lawyer named Portia Douglas appeared before Judge Lopossa, not as advocate but as victim. A year earlier a young man had entered Ms. Douglas's apartment, shot her in the chest, struck her with his revolver and raped her. He then placed a pillow over her head and pulled the trigger. Ms. Douglas survived only because her forearm blocked the bullet.

Now the man, Rodney Cook, was about to be sentenced, and the 33-year-old Ms. Douglas shared her thoughts on the subject. She said she did not seek vengeance, because nothing the court could do could change the past. If the mildly retarded Mr. Cook could somehow be rehabilitated, she said, she was all for it. If not, he should be kept out of circulation for as long as he could harm anyone. To her mind, the 25 years in prison that prosecutors were seeking for the 22-year-old man was not enough.

"I wasn't in there pounding the table saying, 'This S.O.B. should go to prison,' " she said. "I was saying, 'This guy has problems, and if we can help him, let's help him. Otherwise, let's make sure he doesn't do this to someone else.' "

Judge Lopossa initially listened impassively in Marion Superior Court. But when the victim said she sought no vengeance, the judge began to sob. "I thought she was blowing her nose or something, then I realized she was quietly crying," Mr. Cook's lawyer, Steven J. Glazier of Indianapolis, recalled. "Then she broke down and was crying openly."

The judge tried to explain. "All of you know that I am crying, and I want you to know the reason is because of her forgiving nature," she said, referring to Ms. Douglas. "It is unusual for a victim of such a vicious crime to have such a forgiving attitude. And I think that that reflects the best that there is in human nature."

Having praised Ms. Douglas, she tried placating the defense. "I want Mr. Glazier and Mr. Cook to realize, that even though I'm emotional and I'm crying, that you will have nothing to fear," she told them. But Mr. Glazier was not reassured, and after a short recess he asked Judge Lopossa to remove herself from the case on the ground of bias. His motion was denied. The judge then sentenced the defendant to 80 years in prison.

Mr. Cook, with a new lawyer, appealed on the same ground.

In his opinion for the three-member panel that rejected Mr. Cook's argument, Judge Ezra Friedlander of the Indiana Court of Appeals said that conspicuous compassion did not necessarily equal bias. He cited a 1954 New Jersey case for the proposition, not always apparent to lawyers or litigants, that a judge is actually human, entitled to human feelings.

The matter may rest there; Mr. Cook's appellate lawyer, Howard Howe of Indianapolis, would not comment on whether the sentence would be appealed further. But while she has mostly recovered from her injuries—her right arm, she said, is now "very ugly" and does not function very well—Ms. Douglas said she remained "appalled" over Mr. Glazier's recusal motion, which she deemed sexist.

"I've seen male judges yell and scream and pound the table at defendants, and that's acceptable," said Ms. Douglas, who handles personal bankruptcies for members of the United Automobile Workers. "What's the difference between anger toward the defendant or compassion toward the victim? Judge Lopossa did nothing different from what I've seen male judges do; she just did it in a different way."

Mr. Glazier maintained that good lawyering, and not sexual politics, accounted for his maneuver. "I didn't want to anger her," he said of the judge, "but I had to protect the record."

To him, Ms. Douglas's oration and its aftermath reflected what defense lawyers elsewhere have maintained about victims' rights: that defendants whose victims are white, middle class and articulate are dealt with far more harshly. Mr. Cook was doubly unfortunate for having chosen a lawyer as his target. Mr. Glazier said that while the human being in him listened to Ms. Douglas's remarks with admiration, the defense lawyer in him listened with horror.

"Unfortunately, there's a two-tiered system of justice, depending on the type of victim," he said. "If Rodney Cook had grabbed some hooker or homeless person off Skid Row, then our legal system may have dealt with him more leniently."

In an interview, Judge Lopossa said she was surprised neither when Mr. Glazier filed his recusal motion—"He would have committed malpractice if he had not," she said—nor when the appeals court upheld her handling of the case. "I believe the citizens of Marion County and the United States want to have judges who have feelings and who are human beings," Judge Lopossa said. ❑

A CALIFORNIA APPEALS COURT
COMES TO GRIPS WITH A QUESTION:
JUST HOW STUPID CAN SOME JUDGES BE?

3/4/94

CAN A JUDICIAL EDICT BE SO OUTRAGEOUS, SO IRRATIONAL, SO MEGALOMA-niacal that it simply cannot be real? Or, given the errant behavior of some judges, can even the most bizarre mandate appear genuine? That question was recently before an appellate court in California.

In recent years, Judge Ricardo Torres of Los Angeles County Superior Court and Roger Grace, editor and co-publisher of The Metropolitan News-Enterprise, a newspaper serving the Los Angeles legal community, have been locked in combat. Mr. Grace says it stems from his paper's gutsy, unflattering coverage of Judge Torres's performance as presiding judge in 1991-92. In one editorial, the publication called him "a despotic twit."

Judge Torres counters that the newspaper set out to ruin him, and insists that the feud really runs only one way. But in late 1991 he persuaded the court's executive committee to cancel 350 of 384 subscriptions to the News-Enterprise, ostensibly for budgetary reasons. The cancellations were a serious matter to a daily whose entire paid circulation is around 2,400.

In July 1992, the dispute moved from outraged commentary to outrageous satire. That was when Mr. Grace picked up his laptop computer and banged out a bogus memorandum from Judge Torres to "all judicial officers," pasted it onto Judge Torres's official letterhead and ran off about a hundred copies.

"It has been determined that The Metropolitan News-Enterprise contains material of a questionable nature," the bogus memo began. "For example, use of such epithets as 'despotic twit,' when applied to a judicial officer with august status, cannot be countenanced. Accordingly, it has been determined that henceforth, the possession of that publication within the confines of a Los Angeles Superior Court facility shall not be permitted."

"Judge Torres" went on to say that all offices would be searched after hours for copies of the newspaper. "You are advised that amorous escapades would more appropriately be conducted in off-site locations to avoid embarrassment," he advised. He then declared a court emergency, one allowing him to suspend the election of his successor.

Three News-Enterprise employees distributed copies of the memorandum in the courthouse—until court officers stopped them and took them into Judge Torres's chambers. The judge proceeded to interrogate the leafleteers, first there, later in open court. The employees, with Mr. Grace's backing, soon sued Judge Torres for false arrest.

Judge Torres responded by saying that whatever he had done was proper, part of his supervisory responsibilities over the court. Then he sued the News-Enterprise for libel, declaring that the memo had made him look silly among his peers, many of whom, he said, thought it was genuine.

The false-arrest case still awaits trial. But last month Judge Torres's defamation suit was thrown out by the California Court of Appeal in an opinion plumbing the nature of parody and the range of plausible judicial behavior.

"The formality (and, no doubt on too many occasions, outright pomposity) of judges and legal proceedings provide rich ground for mockery and parody," said the majority opinion, written by Presiding Justice David G. Sills. And the reasonable person, the opinion said, is sophisticated enough to have seen the phony memorandum as a spoof rather than the false statement of fact that a defamation case requires. "It is unreasonable to believe that any judge appointed by any of California's governors in this century would be so stupid as to seriously author such a memo," the majority stated.

But Justice Thomas F. Crosby Jr. was not so sure, recalling one local judge who had kept her dog with her on the bench and another who had prodded a lawyer with a dildo. "Los Angeles legal history does not lack for examples of the occasional judge gone off the beam," Justice Crosby wrote in his dissent. "The majority has its rose-colored glasses on when it thinks people familiar with the local legal scene could not be taken in by the phony memo. Stranger, much stranger, things have come from Los Angeles judges."

Indeed, one of Judge Torres's colleagues, Judge Ernest G. Williams, had found the memo so believable that he called Judge Torres about it immediately. "I had three or four Met Newses in my drawer," he said in a deposition, "and I wanted to know whether or not he wanted me to take them home."

The lawsuits have afforded Mr. Grace, who is a lawyer as well as a newspaper publisher, a chance to interrogate his nemesis, asking him whether he passed his law school course in constitutional law or smoked marijuana on the day he questioned Mr. Grace's employees. (The answers were yes and no, respectively.)

Judge Torres declined a reporter's request for comment. But his attorney in the false-arrest case, Frederick Bennett, a lawyer for Los Angeles County, said the judge was only the latest of many people Mr. Grace had vilified through his newspaper. And simply for saying so, Mr. Bennett said, so, too, will he be vilified. "I will no doubt be the subject of an editorial or two," he predicted. "That's the normal pattern."

Mr. Bennett said he expected the donnybrook to continue. "These are cases that involve great emotions and egos," he said. "They're the hardest cases to settle." ❏

A GUIDE (IN LAWYERS' WORDS) TO THE PALOOKAS AND THE CARDOZOS ON THE FEDERAL BENCH.

2/1/91

ONE FEDERAL JUDGE IN MANHATTAN IS "UNSTABLE." ANOTHER IS "UNDULY concerned with publicity." A third is "a kind of stumbler on the bench" and a fourth "talks as if he just come off the Bowery." As for a fifth, "You get the feeling that he's getting a little old, it's boring and he'd rather be out on the golf course."

A sixth is "not a rocket scientist" while a seventh is "not what I'd call an intellectual powerhouse." An eighth is "no Cardozo, but he's not a Palooka by any means." Of a ninth, one lawyer advises, "You're either going to get a raging maniac or a sweet pussycat." A tenth draws the harshest reviews: "He's rude, nasty, intemperate and not very smart. Other than that he's a fine judge."

These are among the findings in the latest edition of the "Almanac of the Federal Judiciary," a compilation of facts about and lawyers' opinions of every Federal trial and appellate judge, published twice each year by Prentice-Hall Law and Business. The facts about the judges, all of whom are referred to by name, are mundane. But the evaluations, gleaned from interviews with 12 to 20 lawyers who have appeared before them, can be pungent, irreverent or downright nasty. Promised anonymity by the editors who selected them, the lawyers interviewed enjoy a rare chance to take potshots at the judges with impunity.

The Almanac has been around since 1984. But only with its purchase by Prentice-Hall in 1989 have the appraisals become so biting. "We're trying to approximate what you'd get from another lawyer rather than something that's been sanitized," said Steve Nelson, the Almanac's executive editor.

Some comments offer fraternal tactical advice. "You can't change his mind about anything until the Second Circuit tells him to, and even then he thinks he's right." Others try psychoanalysis. "He seems to react on the basis of a fear of his own fears and insecurities," a lawyer said of another Manhattan judge.

One judge in Detroit "needs to remember that he was appointed, not anointed," while another is "a rotten person to everybody." A Philadelphia judge is described as "one of our hacks." "You can buffalo him by making arguments that sound plausible because he doesn't understand," the lawyer said. Anyone appearing before a certain judge in Atlanta is advised to "read a Kafka novel before you go into his courtroom—you'll feel right at home."

For the most part, those panned in the two-volume Almanac, for which lawyers and law libraries pay $250, have taken their lumps stoically. Not so two judges who sit in the Southern District of Texas, which has the largest backlog and largest per-judge caseload in the country.

Judge David Hittner of Houston is variously described as "very erratic," "a tyrant," "arrogant," "rude," "the consummate politician," "real cranky," "obnoxious," "very volatile," "very impatient," "pompous," "an egomaniac," "stuffy," "overrated" and "tremendously overrated." "He treats you like his brother off the bench, but he puts on that robe, and it's like the phantom mask," one critic observed.

And while one lawyer described Judge Ricardo Hinojosa as "brilliant," another accused him of contracting "Federal judge-itis" while a third called him "a pompous dictator."

According to The Texas Lawyer magazine, both men, who had scored well in previous surveys, notified Prentice-Hall after their reviews appeared and asked to be re-evaluated by a different group of lawyers ahead of schedule (they are normally done every three years).

Judge Hinojosa would not comment on the matter. But Judge Hittner said in an interview that what bothered him was not so much the anonymity of his critics—"I understand that, because judges have the opportunity to retaliate," he said—but the limited range of the lawyers sampled.

His re-evaluation is not yet complete. But Judge Hinojosa's is, and if the Almanac were the Michelin Guide, his rating would have jumped from one star to three. "He's a sharp man, and down here, that's something," one lawyer observed. Most of those re-evaluated stay the same or score higher—proving, Mr. Nelson said, either that different lawyers have different opinions or that the judges took their poor report cards to heart.

Some negative comments are omitted for reasons of taste. Thus, a Midwestern judge will be spared this epitaph: "Her contribution to jurisprudence has been in getting coffee barred from the courtroom area."

Mr. Nelson explained, "It's one thing to be angry at a judge and it's another to make fun of them." And a Southern judge will not be known as having "a good legal mind—for someone who went to Georgia Tech."

"We're evaluating judges, not colleges," Mr. Nelson said. ❑

FALSELY ACCUSED: IN A HUMILIATING ARREST, A BLACK JUDGE FINDS LESSONS OF LAW AND RACE RELATIONS.

1/7/94

NEWARK—ALMOST A MONTH HAS NOW PASSED SINCE JUDGE CLAUDE Coleman's fateful visit to the Bloomingdale's at the Mall in Short Hills, N.J., when an innocent Christmas shopping trip turned into a nightmare of false accusations, public humiliation and eventual vindication. He is back behind the bench in Newark Municipal Court and back, at least superficially, to his old good-natured self.

But despite apologies from Bloomingdale's and the Millburn, N.J., Police Department, Judge Coleman, who served as director of Newark's fire and police departments before joining the judiciary, is still smarting—and thinking. He is pondering just how fragile things like a reputation and the presumption of innocence can be. He is also wondering what, if anything, a black man must achieve to be beyond suspicion.

On Dec. 11, the 53-year-old judge entered Bloomingdale's and bought two pairs of women's gloves, presents for friends. He charged them to his Bloomingdale's credit card, then left for the Georgetown Leather store a few doors away. There, he suddenly found himself surrounded by walkie-talkie-toting security guards from Bloomingdale's, who accused him of using a stolen credit card. They made him put his hands in the air, then spread them on the counter, as they summoned the Millburn police.

When the officers arrived, Judge Coleman protested his innocence, asked to see his accusers and showed identification. He was nonetheless handcuffed—tightly and behind his back—and was dragged through crowds of shoppers to a police car. At the station house, he was chained to a wall and was prevented from calling a lawyer or even from urinating. There, he said, the officer guarding him seemed to delight in his predicament and seemed flabbergasted to meet a black man who had actually gone through life without ever having been handcuffed.

It took the Millburn police three-and-a-half hours to book Judge Coleman on charges of theft and fraud. It did not take Bloomingdale's much longer to realize it had erred; a black man had tried to use a stolen credit card that day, but the clerks who waited on him later said his skin tone, facial hair and clothing did not match Judge Coleman's.

By the time Bloomingdale's recognized its mistake, however, the case had taken on a life of its own. The Essex County prosecutor's office launched an investigation, and Judge Coleman was suspended. Moreover, the arrest was reported by WCBS News Radio 88, prompting calls—some comforting, others disconcertingly accusatory—from friends and relatives.

"They thought that perhaps I was unraveling, that I was going through some mid-life crisis," said the judge, who is separated from his wife.

On Dec. 17, the charges against Judge Coleman were officially dropped. Four days later, Bloomingdale's called a press conference and apologized. It has since fired two of the security guards involved in the episode and has suspended the third.

The store's lawyer, Peter Harvey of Morristown, who is black, conceded that in stores, as in life, blacks endure indignities. "I've been in stores where people have followed me," he said. "Hell, I've walked into court with white colleagues and had people assume I was the defendant." But, he continued, "Sometimes people make an honest mistake. This could have happened to someone whether he was white or black or Asian or Hispanic."

The Millburn Police Department has 55 officers, three of them members of minorities but none of whom were at the mall that day. The department is every bit as embarrassed as Bloomingdale's. "I don't want this ever to happen to anyone, much less to Judge Coleman or anyone in his position," said Warren Ebert, the town's police chief. "I feel miserable about it." But he, too, said race was irrelevant. "It was a severe case of stupidity," he said.

Judge Coleman said that initially, he had been inclined to agree. But he said he had changed his mind as the facts had come into focus and as black friends had shared similar unhappy experiences in the Bloomingdale's at Short Hills Mall. "I'm not one to cry 'racism!' all the time, but I don't see any other explanation," he said, adding that he was considering suing Bloomingdale's or the Millburn Police Department.

Once, as a police-officer-turned-judge, he said, he had felt compelled to convince defense lawyers that he did not favor prosecutors; now, as a judge-turned-victim, he would have to show prosecutors he did not favor defense lawyers. "I'll have to prove myself all over again," he said.

And he must now weigh the larger meaning of his ordeal.

"This experience," he said, "has brought home to me what Arthur Ashe said shortly before he died: that no matter how many achievements you have, you can't shuck the burden of being black in a white society.

"So long as any black person is thought of as a nigger, until all persons of color are looked upon with respect, none of us are going to be. And it doesn't matter whether you're a lawyer or a judge or a prosecutor." ❑

The store may have fired the offenders and the Millburn Police Department is now getting racial sensitivity training, but that hasn't stopped Judge Coleman from suing them both, along with the town of Millburn. He has yet to return to Bloomingdale's.

The Marshall Islands Has Blue Lagoons, Warm Pacific Breezes and an Opening on a Court.

4/3/92

Some enchanted evening, you may see a plaintiff.

The Marshall Islands, a collection of 1,136 bits of land sprinkled like confetti over the South Pacific, has an opening on its High Court. None of the country's 12 resident practicing lawyers among the 50,000 islanders is in the running. So the newly independent republic is advertising the opening in The National Law Journal.

Even with what the advertisement calls "favorable tax rates," the salary—$49,000 per year—would be, for most American lawyers, a mere bag of betel nuts. Still, some 60 cockeyed optimists, either enticed by images of Ezio Pinza or Paul Gauguin or intrigued by the chance to play John Marshall in a young democracy, have already applied for the post.

Not surprisingly, they tend to come from the Rust Belt. "The job may spark their imagination, especially at the end of a long, cold winter," said the High Court's current Chief Justice, Neil Rutledge.

The only South Pacific most Americans know is the one written about by James A. Michener and set to song by Rodgers & Hammerstein. Cognoscenti of the Marshall Islands tend to be either G.I.'s once stationed there or students of atomic weaponry who know that two of its atolls, Bikini and Enewetak, were partially vaporized during the heyday of fallout shelters.

In fact, after tortured relations with Germany, Japan and the United States, the Marshall Islands became an independent country in 1986. Its legal system combines British, American and local customary law; its bill of rights was drafted by Laurence H. Tribe of Harvard Law School, locking into place some Warren Court-era standards that have since been eroded by the Rehnquist Court.

The three-member High Court hears appeals from community and district courts, conducts trials in felony and civil cases and handles wills and divorces as well. The Marshall Islands has a Supreme Court, but it meets rarely; its Chief Justice actually practices law in Honolulu.

The new Justice will be a stranger to Marshallese law; he or she will, as the song says, have "got to be taught." But according to Justice Rutledge, erudition is not enough. "What's equally important are adaptability, availability and cultural sensitivity," he said. "If you come in here thinking you're a hotshot American judge or lawyer, that's a recipe for disaster."

Not surprisingly, all of the applicants are presenting themselves as profiles in sensitivity, offering all manner of happy talk about their world travels, open-mindedness and sense of adventure.

A corporate lawyer from Dayton, Ohio, noted how, at one time or another, he had lived and worked in Brazil, Argentina, Norway, Egypt, Tunisia, Yemen, Somalia, Scotland, Saudi Arabia, Ethiopia, Kuwait, Colombia, Chile, Bolivia and Mexico. A litigator from North Dakota said, "I have a strong personal belief that we are all brothers and sisters."

And this from a sole practitioner in Alabama: "My wife and I both have a deep concern for the welfare of the earth and its peoples."

The 42-year-old Mr. Rutledge—no relation to the late United States Supreme Court Justice Wiley Rutledge—hails from Detroit. He taught at Wayne State University Law School and was counsel to the Michigan State Senate before he followed the sun, first as legal adviser to the Solomon Islands, later as the Marshall Islands Assistant Attorney General.

There are, Justice Rutledge confesses, some drawbacks to the job. Atop the usual isolation of the expatriate is the isolation of a judge. He is a thousand miles from good restaurants, junk food, movie theaters and television. He not only researches his own landmark decisions, but, at times, types them, too. He may be the only Chief Justice anywhere without a home telephone. "When people need me, they know where to get me," he said. "It's a small island."

There are also Americanisms he does not miss. "I don't miss the rampant commercialism, the bombardment with material things, traffic, pollution," he said. "Here it's just a beautiful lagoon. It's so stimulating and seductive that I've lingered much longer than I ever thought I would." Should those idyllic conditions ever change, he need only complain to his wife, Elizabeth Harding, who is legal counsel to the Marshall Islands Environmental Protection Authority.

The Islands' Judicial Service Commission will screen the applicants, then recommend a candidate to the Cabinet. The winner must eventually be ratified by the Nitijela, or parliament. The also-rans? They can sing "This Nearly Was Mine." ❏

The High Court received several hundred applications, from lawyers, professors, law students and—after Judge Rutledge promised in one radio interview to provide "on-the-job training"—from assorted plumbers and carpenters. "A lot of people were wildly underqualified," said Judge Rutledge. "Quite a number were just fed up with their careers." The job ended up going to a retired judge from Sacramento, but he quickly O.D.'d on paradise. As of the fall of 1994, the position was open again.

A JUDGE-MAKER LEARNS WHAT IT IS
TO WIN SUPPORT, TO BE NOMINATED
AND THEN TO LOSE.

12/9/88

FEW LAWYERS KNEW MORE ABOUT HOW JUDGES ARE MADE THAN STUART Summit. For 12 years, he helped two Mayors of New York select judicial appointees, and then he spent 9 more combing through candidates for the state's highest court.

Nothing, however, prepared him for the fate of his own nomination to the prestigious United States Court of Appeals for the Second Circuit. It is, he admits, an experience from which he will never fully recover.

After President Reagan selected him, Mr. Summit fended off ethics charges. Then he survived the departure of the man responsible for his nomination, former Deputy Attorney General Arnold I. Burns. Then he won over wary Democrats on the Senate Judiciary Committee. All was for naught. The nomination was killed by Senator Alfonse D'Amato, who had previously said he'd been "honored" to submit Mr. Summit's name to the Senate.

While Senators in effect pick Federal trial judges, the Justice Department selects Federal appellate judges. Thus, when Judge Irving Kaufman assumed senior status in May 1987, Attorney General Edwin Meese 3d asked Mr. Burns to suggest a replacement. Mr. Burns recommended Mr. Summit, his former law partner, and persuaded the initially reluctant Mr. Summit to accept.

The choice was ratified by the Justice Department, the White House and, it seemed, Senator D'Amato himself. Introducing Mr. Summit to the Senate Judiciary Committee last April, the Republican Senator called him "outstanding," "prestigious," "important," "major" and "steeped in the law." And he said, "I am certain that as a judge he will continue to distinguish himself."

Quickly, problems arose. Mr. Summit's ethics were challenged by Lee Kreindler, a prominent New York personal injury lawyer who had faced Mr. Summit in court. Then, after Mr. Burns resigned and quarreled publicly with Mr. Meese, Mr. Summit was caught in the crossfire.

But he prepared for the bench. He read a three-volume history of Anglo-American law and every decision by Judge Learned Hand. He picked his law clerks and pondered writing decisions. He bought an apartment near Foley Square. He would cut back on clothes and cabs and calories to get by on a quarter of what he made at Summit, Rovins & Feldesman.

Anticipating a more monastic life, he pulled back from his practice and sought contentment in his own company. He stopped swearing, at least publicly. He began detecting the fawning that lawyers always lavish on judges and girded against it—just as the man for whom he'd once clerked, former Chief Judge Charles Breitel of the New York Court of Appeals, always did.

In late August the Senate Judiciary Committee approved Mr. Summit unanimously, and champagne flowed at his office. But within weeks it became clear that some Senator had put a "hold" on the nomination. The procedure, a courtesy Senators extend to one another, is normally used to stall in the hope of exerting political pressure. Coming late in the Congressional session as the hold did, and apparently from Mr. Summit's own state's Senator, it was permanently crippling.

Suspicion first focused on the opposition: Senator Daniel Patrick Moynihan. But the source turned out to be Mr. D'Amato. Initially, the Senator and his aides denied placing the hold, then offered a number of explanations: it was only temporary; it was somehow beyond the Senator's control; it reflected opposition from some unidentified Federal judges; it stemmed from the Senator's pique over two nominations that had failed.

Others speculate that Mr. D'Amato saw a chance for the appointment of someone closer to him, or to send a message to the Bush Justice Department: "talk to me before submitting another name." Mr. D'Amato's real motive remains unclear, however. He did not return phone calls, including three from Mr. Summit. Nor did he consider entreaties from other Senators, the White House, officials in the Justice Department, including Attorney General Richard L. Thornburgh himself, bar officials or prominent New York Republicans. When the Senate adjourned, the Summit nomination died.

Mr. Summit, 52 years old, remains in his law office, though once again he must adjust, and without any glittering incentive. He still doesn't know what hit him. Sobbing quietly as he discussed his fate, he was clearly a man in mourning.

"That a single Senator, never mind one who introduced me to the committee, could simply stop the entire process only a few days before my confirmation without having to explain himself to anyone and without the courtesy of explaining himself to me, is simply beyond my understanding," he said. "It's not in my makeup to be bitter. But no matter how exciting or thrilling my life now is, I will carry a sense of sadness with me. I had visualized myself dying in that job. I'll be grieving, probably all of my life." ❑

JEWS ON THE SUPREME COURT:
WERE THEY DIFFERENT AND
WHY ARE THERE NONE NOW?

12/22/89

NO JEW HAS SAT ON THE UNITED STATES SUPREME COURT SINCE 1969, when Abe Fortas resigned. It is an odd phenomenon, given the prominence of Jewish lawyers in the United States. In that period, Jews have led the American Bar Association, dozens of major law firms and virtually every major American law school.

But for many Jews, even touching the topic is taboo. Perhaps because of fear of seeming either chauvinistic or parochial, there is no longer much talk about a "Jewish seat" on the High Court, even during Judge Douglas Ginsberg's short flirtation with the post. Jewish law professors have shied away from the subject or, for that matter, anything concerning the distinctiveness of Jewish judges.

This is what makes a recent scholarly exchange between Robert Burt of Yale Law School and Judge Stephen Reinhardt of the United States Court of Appeals in Los Angeles so unusual. In it, the two men broached subjects that remain touchy even in an ethnocentric age, like the dearth of Jews on the nation's highest court and whether Jewish judges differ from their Christian counterparts.

Last year, the University of California Press published Mr. Burt's book "Two Jewish Justices: Outcasts in the Promised Land." It examines how the ethnicity of Louis D. Brandeis and Felix Frankfurter, the Supreme Court's first and third Jewish members, affected their jurisprudence. The question is important, even obvious. But until Mr. Burt's book, it was not only unanswered but also unasked.

True, legal academia has many Jews, including at one point the law school deans at Harvard, Yale, Columbia, the University of Pennsylvania and Berkeley simultaneously. But older professors, perhaps fearful of generating the anti-Semitism many had encountered in their youth, avoided such questions; middle-aged professors, thinking themselves enlightened secularists, were not interested in them; and younger ones, many imbued with economics, thought them too squishy.

Enter Mr. Burt. His answer to the question was that the Jewishness of the two Justices left them both "outsiders," never at home in the American mainstream.

Brandeis, according to Mr. Burt, remained in, and even relished, the role of outsider, or, to use the political philosopher Hannah Arendt's term, "pariah." He resolutely stood apart, disdained social acceptance, sympathized with the unpopular. Frankfurter, on the other hand, was the "parvenu," in Miss Arendt's term, a judicial Sammy Glick, so desperate for acceptance that he became, Mr. Burt wrote, "an over-eager apologist for the existing order."

Judge Reinhardt's reaction to the Burt book is striking, and would undoubtedly have caused a great stir had it not appeared in the Bermuda Triangle of contemporary legal debate: an academic law review, specifically the Cardozo Law Review.

The judge argues in a review of "Two Jewish Justices" that Brandeis and Frankfurter had more in common than Mr. Burt suggests. "I doubt that either would have felt at home in a Bush—let alone a Reagan—Administration," he wrote.

But he agrees that most Jewish judges are different, that they have an "instinctive sympathy for the underdog." He also divides them into two categories, better described perhaps as "mensches" and "curmudgeons" than "pariahs" and "parvenus."

The former group includes judges like Brandeis and, presumably, himself. In the latter he places the Jewish judges appointed by President Reagan. On issues like affirmative action, abortion and capital punishment, he writes, their attitudes "are remarkably similar to those held by the majority of white Protestant males." And, like Frankfurter, "they are sticklers for procedure; view the judiciary as having a limited role; and tend to be intellectuals."

Judge Reinhardt then confronts the absence of Jews, of whatever political stripe, from the Supreme Court. "Given the prominence of Jews in the legal profession, both in numbers and talent, the appropriate question is not whether there should be a Jewish seat, but why are there not several Jews on the Court today," he writes.

The blame, he says, lies partly with Richard Nixon, the man who filled the Fortas seat and a President, he wrote, "who did not speak or think kindly of Jews." But it also lies, Judge Reinhardt added in an interview, with Jews who did not complain when the tradition was broken and who have remained silent since. "Avoiding the issue," he said, "is part of the reason that we've just been frozen out."

A Jewish colleague of Judge Reinhardt's, Alex Kozinski, said the absence of Jews on the Supreme Court "has been an issue among Jews for 20 years, but most aren't willing to speak out on it."

"Reinhardt," Judge Kozinski said, "has more courage than most of us." ❑

With President Clinton having appointed Ruth Bader Ginsburg and Stephen G. Breyer, the Supreme Court now has two Jews for the first time since the days of Brandeis and Cardozo. That few have even noticed is perhaps the best sign of how much things have changed.

A FORMER VIKING WILL ADMINISTER JUSTICE IN MINNESOTA AFTER DEALING HAVOC ON THE GRIDIRON.

1/1/93

THE MINNESOTA VIKINGS AND THE MINNESOTA SUPREME COURT play their respective games in different parts of the Twin Cities. But the gap will close next week when Alan Page completes a remarkable migration from the gridiron to the bench.

Last November, the 47-year-old Mr. Page—10 times an All-Pro defensive tackle and a member of professional football's Hall of Fame— was overwhelmingly elected to the state's highest court. On Monday, after three of his four children help him don his robe and the fourth reads from the speeches of Robert F. Kennedy, Mr. Page will become the court's first black justice.

Mr. Page won fame as an athlete for getting around obstacles: the guards and tackles and centers protecting an opponent with the football. But whatever he faced on the field was less formidable than what blocked his route to the court: turf-protecting politicians, blacks who deemed him too aloof and insufficiently ardent about their cause, a wary bar and what Mr. Page calls "the dumb jock syndrome," or the claim, raised by his opponent in the race, that Mr. Page was a legal lightweight capitalizing on his name.

The assertion, Mr. Page maintained, was unfair. In two more years, after all, he will have practiced law as long as he practiced mayhem professionally, and with at least as much dedication. Besides, he said, his two lives share some values.

"People who watched me play saw someone who worked hard, was focused, was an independent thinker, believed in fair play, was disciplined, sought excellence and achieved it," he said. "Those are qualities I think we would like to have in government."

Fair or unfair, in a state where he is still revered as a member of Bud Grant's famed defensive line, the "Purple People Eaters," any reference to Mr. Page's athletic past proved to be political suicide for his opponent. Mr. Page, who spent little time on the bench during his playing days, is about to become a fixture there.

Mr. Page is not John Updike's Rabbit Angstrom, forever bathing in bathos over past athletic triumphs. Apart from a crooked pinkie on his left hand, he carries few tokens from his former life.

His playing days, he said, are "sort of all a blur" to him now. While millions of couch potatoes and armchair quarterbacks watch bowl games today, Mr. Page won't be among them. "A fine, mindless activity," he called such pursuits. Though two teammates, Jim Marshall and Carl Eller, campaigned for him, he rarely fraternizes with old Vikings. This week, when Mr. Page's wife, Diane, tried finding friends tickets to tomorrow's Vikings-Redskins game, she got the same busy signals as everyone else.

Soft-spoken and reticent, contemplative and modest, the very personality of the 6-4, 220-pound man seems to repudiate his macho, manhandling past. The University of Minnesota, where he has served as a regent for the past several years, looms larger to him than Notre Dame, where he was an All-American.

The Minnesota Democratic-Farmer-Labor Party, the D.F.L., matters more than the N.F.L. And the Page Education Foundation, which he founded in 1989 to grant scholarships to minority students, clearly matters more to him than either.

Watching "Perry Mason" as a boy, Mr. Page said, inspired him to pursue law. It offered a far more palatable option than the steel mills of Canton, Ohio. Over time, particularly while active in the National Football League's Players' Association, his appreciation became more substantive. For him, football was a lucrative, enabling detour to the profession of his choice. "With football, you leave an image on film and that's about it," he said. "The law is far more interesting and challenging, and when you're done, maybe you'll leave something behind."

Mr. Page enrolled briefly in law school in 1968 after his rookie season with the Vikings. He enrolled again, at the University of Minnesota, in 1975, and graduated three years later. Over three off-seasons—and full time after hanging up his cleats in 1981—he practiced at the corporate law firm of Lindquist & Vennum in Minneapolis. In 1985 he moved to the office of the Minnesota Attorney General, where he specialized in employment litigation, and he dreamed of the State Supreme Court.

Slots there are ostensibly elective, but since most justices are appointed between elections, then run as unopposed incumbents, no seat had been contested for decades. Twice, Mr. Page prepared to run, only to be thwarted by 11th-hour appointments by Governors Rudy Perpich and Arne Carlson.

Mr. Page took Mr. Carlson to court—the Minnesota Supreme Court—over the last maneuver. The entire court recused itself, naming seven retired judges to serve in their stead. This judicial taxi squad invalidated Governor Carlson's appointment, clearing the way for the nasty race for the court seat.

"I don't believe anyone would be taking Alan Page seriously if it were not for his fame as a football player," his opponent, Kevin Johnson, a Hennepin County prosecutor, asserted in the campaign. The state's lawyers apparently agreed, giving Mr. Johnson an eight-point edge in a straw poll.

But for Mr. Johnson, the support of the bar proved about as deadly as harping on Mr. Page's athletic exploits. "I believe the lawyers' recommendation should be given consideration by the voters," wrote Nick Coleman, a columnist for The Saint Paul Pioneer Press. "When lawyers endorse someone, the public is wise to vote for the other guy."

That they did in the November race. Mr. Page overwhelmed his rival by nearly two to one. In doing so, he became the first black ever elected to statewide office in Minnesota.

Now Mr. Page is poised to join a new squad, one in which, unlike any other state supreme court in the country, a majority of his six teammates are women. As his wife arranges for the Page Scholar, the Minneapolis Gospel Sound and groups of fourth-graders from Minneapolis and St. Paul to participate in his swearing-in, Mr. Page has been meeting his future colleagues and reading briefs. Half an hour after he is sworn in, he will begin hearing cases.

There is little he can do, Mr. Page conceded, to placate his critics. But on the field or behind the bench, being underestimated has its advantages. "If you lower expectations," he said with a laugh, "they're easier to meet." ❑

WITH A CHANCE ENCOUNTER HER ONLY WEAPON, A JUDGE'S WIFE MAY HAVE K.O.'D A FORMER CHAMP.

10/22/93

HIRING A LAWYER LIKE ALAN DERSHOWITZ HAS ITS ADVANTAGES. THE ME-diagenic Harvard law professor is one of the few lawyers as effective on cathode-ray tube as in court. But one Dershowitz client, the former heavyweight champion Mike Tyson, has learned that sometimes a lawyer can be just too recognizable.

In fact, Mr. Tyson languishes in jail, Mr. Dershowitz contends, because an Indiana judge could not control his talkative and starstruck spouse.

Flash back to lunchtime on Oct. 3, 1992. Mr. Tyson was in the Indiana Youth Center in Plainfield, serving a six-year term for raping a contestant in the Miss Black America pageant, while his appeal proceeded. Mr. Dershowitz was at Yale Law School for his 30th reunion. As the ubiquitous camera crew—this one was Australian—filmed him in the University Commons, Mr. Dershowitz reminisced with Stephen Joel Trachtenberg, a fellow '62-er who is now president of George Washington University.

Suddenly a woman recognized Mr. Dershowitz—is any lawyer *more* recognizable?—and began shrieking "Alan Dershowitz! Alan Dershowitz!" Mr. Dershowitz says she declared excitedly, "I've got to talk to you!" and with that, she broke the nostalgic spell. "She was very pushy and enthusiastic and had all the qualities of a gossip," Mr. Dershowitz recalled. "In the neighborhood I grew up in, they would have called her a yenta."

The woman, who had not introduced herself, proceeded to sec-ond-guess Mr. Dershowitz's performance at Mr. Tyson's bail hearing a few months earlier. "Indiana is different from New York," she counseled. Mr. Dershowitz asked her what she meant. "The kinds of arguments that work in New York don't always work in Indiana," she continued. As an example, she cited the professor's pledge to drop the case if his client fled the state.

Mr. Dershowitz then asked the woman, whose name was Amy W. MacDonell, Are you an Indiana lawyer? She was not, she said, but her husband, Yale Law School '72, was the Chief Justice of Indiana. That was Randall T. Shepard, before whom Mr. Dershowitz would soon be arguing the Tyson appeal. Sensing he was entering an ethical mine-field, Mr. Dershowitz abruptly broke off the conversation.

But that hardly ended the matter. In November, before the appeal reached his court, Chief Justice Shepard suddenly disqualified him-self from the case. He cited Canon 3 of the State Code of Judicial Conduct, which bars judges from sitting where their impartiality may be reasonably questioned. Beyond that, he gave no explanation. Ob-servers were mystified; rumors ran rampant.

The Chief Justice, then, was not present when his four colleagues considered arguments over whether Mr. Tyson, three of whose wit-nesses had been barred from testifying in his defense, should receive a new trial. Nor did the Chief Justice vote last month, when the rump court split on the question 2 to 2. That left the boxer's conviction in-tact and the boxer in prison.

Alone among his legal team, Mr. Dershowitz believed that the chance conversation accounted for the Chief Justice's decision. That recusal smarted even more when, according to Mr. Dershowitz, a source in the court informed him that the Chief Justice would proba-bly have voted Mr. Tyson's way.

A month ago Mr. Dershowitz asked Chief Justice Shepard to recon-sider and cast a vote in the case. "Your Honor's attempt to avoid even the appearance of injustice has now resulted in an actual injustice," Mr. Dershowitz pleaded.

In a little-noted decision issued last Friday, the Chief Justice de-clined to reverse himself. But for the first time, he acknowledged what had led to his withdrawal.

"My wife is not a lawyer, and she did not fully appreciate the princi-ples underlying these rules," he wrote, after offering a version of events in New Haven akin to Mr. Dershowitz's. "She regrets very much having initiated this colloquy and feels a deep sense of embarrass-ment about it." But were he to have remained in the case and voted in Mr. Tyson's favor, people would have wondered why: Had Mr. Der-showitz won by taking Ms. MacDonell's advice? Had the Chief Justice voted with Mr. Tyson precisely to keep the story quiet? Given these possibilities, he wrote, he thought—and continued to think—with-drawal was appropriate.

Mr. Tyson is convinced the entire episode was a setup; he wants to sue Ms. MacDonell for negligence. Mr. Dershowitz does not go quite so far, but he is furious over the turn of events.

"It's frustrating as hell to have worked so hard on a case and lose by something that was so totally beyond my control," he said. He fumes because the judge failed to instruct his wife in the rudiments of lawyerly conduct, and dismisses as "arrant nonsense" any suggestion that he followed Ms. MacDonell's strategic advice.

Mr. Dershowitz will soon ask the entire Indiana Supreme Court to consider the propriety of the Chief Justice's decision and, failing there, will tell the story to the United States Supreme Court. In the meantime, he weighs the moral of the tale. "I love attending reunions," he recently wrote Yale Law School's dean, Guido Calabresi. "But I didn't realize until last week how dangerous that wonderful activity can be to the liberty of my clients." ❏

The Indiana Supreme Court never reviewed Chief Justice Shepard's recusal, and Mr. Dershowitz concluded it was pointless to ask the United States Supreme Court to do so. Nor did Mr. Tyson ever sue Ms. MacDonell. "It would be an uphill fight, and he has other fish to fry," Mr. Dershowitz explained.

SIXTY-THREE YEARS AFTER HIS DISAPPEARANCE, THE SEARCH FOR JUDGE CRATER CONTINUES.

8/6/93

MENTION "A DATE WHICH WILL LIVE IN INFAMY," AND MOST AMERICANS think of Dec. 7, 1941. But to Mrs. R. D. Amelar, that date is Aug. 6, 1930, when Judge Joseph Force Crater was last seen alive. It is a mystery Mrs. Amelar has pondered most of her life, and labored over—as she puts it, "obsessively and incessantly"—for the last 13 years.

Today, the 63rd anniversary of Judge Crater's disappearance, will be a day like any other for Mrs. Amelar. Working out of her apartment on Washington Square, within walking distance of numerous landmarks in Crater lore, she will compile and organize the 3-by-5 file cards that will one day become "Crater Knew Too Much," her treatise on the case.

That book, she believes, will finally crack the case of the 41-year-old New York State Supreme Court Justice who vanished inexplicably less than four months after Gov. Franklin D. Roosevelt named him to the bench. It will rehabilitate Crater. And it will turn what has become a bit of American kitsch, like the exploits of Billy Carter or the "memoirs" of Howard Hughes, into real history: a cautionary tale of murder, betrayal and corruption in the highest political places.

When Judge Crater first vaporized, it was a serious story. But as the investigation languished, in came the clowns. "Think I'll step out and look for Judge Crater!" Groucho Marx declared in the stage version of "Animal Crackers" in 1931. Increasingly, explanations for the mystery centered on Crater himself. This absolutely outrages Mrs. Amelar.

"People say he got mixed up with gangsters, that he had unsavory innards, that he chased chorus girls or ran off with a beautiful blonde, that he made shady deals," she said disgustedly. "All of these are absolutely unfair. Crater's good name has been traduced by people who know nothing about him. I want it restored."

Though Mrs. Amelar never actually met Crater—she was born shortly after what she calls his "assassination"—she usually calls him "Joe." She describes his features with exactitude—"exceptionally tall, a comparatively small head for a man his height, prominent eyes and broad shoulders that made his neck look long"—and speaks of him reverentially: "intensely brilliant," "extraordinarily articulate," "extremely personable," "always very kindly."

Her relationship to him is not only familiar but also familial. Her father, Samuel Zinman, considered Crater his mentor and was with him the day he disappeared. Mr. Zinman, now 90, once aspired to the bench and would have made it to the United States Supreme Court, his daughter believes, if Crater had stuck around.

Shattered by Crater's disappearance—"If politics is this dirty, it's not for me," he declared—Mr. Zinman vowed to write about the case someday. Thirteen years ago, he passed the torch to his daughter. She has carried it, ferociously, ever since.

She carried it to the New York Public Library, where she pored over contemporary newspaper accounts of the case. She carried it to Easton, Pa., where Crater grew up, and Hershey, Pa., where his elderly sister lived. She carried it to Pine Bush, N.Y., where Crater's wife was born. She carried it to Hallandale, Fla., and Cincinnati, where the sister and niece of Crater's mistress could be found. She carried it to Belgrade, Me., where Crater had a summer home. "It was not only still there but was for rent, by the week," she said.

And she carried it to the home in Bronxville where, she contends, Crater was murdered—and where she marched to the front door and rang the bell. "I wanted to see whether anyone was home before I went running around to the backyard," she explained. Actually, Mrs. Amelar believes Crater was later reburied somewhere near the newly constructed Hutchinson River Parkway.

At one point she asked the Yonkers police to investigate. "Of course, they weren't in the least bit interested," she said.

Mrs. Amelar believes that Crater was killed to keep him from testifying before a grand jury investigating the sale of judgeships. That investigation, she says, would have ruined Roosevelt politically, and it is primarily at his doorstep that she places the blame for Crater's demise.

"If I had finished the book before the centennial of Roosevelt's birth, there wouldn't have been a celebration, and Clinton would not have marched up to Hyde Park," she said.

There will be those who disagree, and heatedly, when Mrs. Amelar's book appears. "I think she should get in touch with Oliver Stone," said Arthur M. Schlesinger Jr., the historian and Roosevelt biographer.

Mrs. Amelar does not have a publisher. But passion she has aplenty.

"I lie in bed every morning planning what I'm going to write," she said. "I revise it 17 million times. I have become allergic to TV, radio, concerts, anything that interferes with my thought processes, my vibes. I never stop thinking about it." ❑

WHEN HERSCHEL FRIDAY DIED,
FEW PEOPLE OUTSIDE ARKANSAS NOTICED.
IT MIGHT HAVE BEEN DIFFERENT.

4/1/94

MAYFLOWER, Ark.—IN 1971, WHEN PRESIDENT RICHARD M. NIXON SEEMED poised to place Herschel Friday on the Supreme Court, a local civil rights lawyer, Philip Kaplan, called Mr. Friday "the wrong man for the wrong job at the wrong time." As a prominent Arkansas lawyer, Mr. Friday, in the late 1950's, had represented the school districts of Little Rock and several other towns that resisted the pace of desegregation, and Mr. Kaplan had not forgotten.

Last month, after Mr. Friday was killed in the crash of his private plane near his home here, Mr. Kaplan was among the 1,400 mourners at his funeral. The ceremony was but one part of a community's extraordinary farewell to a man who practiced law in Little Rock for almost 50 years. Over the last 23 of them—a period when Mr. Friday saw Mr. Kaplan regularly around town but never mentioned his criticism—Mr. Kaplan came to reassess Herschel Friday.

"I grew to know him better," Mr. Kaplan said. "I learned he was a very gracious, wonderful man, a person who was very giving of his time and his resources, a leader of a profession I love, a man who set an example for kindness and gentility in an age where they're not always at a premium."

Mr. Friday's death, at 72, brought condolences from President Clinton and was front-page news in The Arkansas Democrat-Gazette. The newspaper was filled for days afterward with large—in some cases, full-page—paid tributes that noted not only that he had built Arkansas's largest law firm and headed the state bar association but also that he was perhaps the state's leading citizen, active in innumerable charities.

But outside Arkansas, Mr. Friday will always be just an "almost" in American judicial history. Like Webster L. Hubbell and Vincent W. Foster Jr. a generation later, he thrived in a little pond called Little Rock, only to drown out of town.

In October 1971, with Hugo L. Black dead and John Marshall Harlan dying, the Nixon Administration went looking for two conservative and uncontroversial Supreme Court nominees, one from the South. Attorney General John N. Mitchell suggested Mr. Friday, a Democrat. Years earlier the two had become friends through their bond practices, and they had resumed their friendship that summer during a long cab ride at the American Bar Association convention in London. Mr. Friday had another ally in Martha Mitchell, the Attorney General's famously outspoken wife, a proud native of Pine Bluff, Ark.

Forty-nine years old, rearing three children, busy building Friday, Eldredge & Clark—a firm even now far more politically connected than the Rose Law Firm—Mr. Friday was flabbergasted by Mr. Mitchell's interest. But when history and country call, who can say no, or will want to ask too many questions? Into the valley of death rode Mr. Friday.

The F.B.I. came to Little Rock to check him out. So did the White House counsel, John Dean. And Mr. Friday—who along with Mildred Lillie, a California appeals judge, topped the list of six candidates for the two seats—went to Washington, where he was interviewed by an Assistant Attorney General named William H. Rehnquist.

Mr. Nixon's list came in for plenty of ridicule—The Chicago Sun-Times called the candidates "Lilliputians"—and Mr. Friday took more than his share. James Youngdahl of the Arkansas A.F.L.-C.I.O. called him "the smiling face of the old Faubus crowd." Then as now, Mr. Friday's friends decried that characterization as an injustice, saying that as counsel for the school district he had done all he could in his quietly persuasive way to foster desegregation, not thwart it.

Mr. Mitchell assured Mr. Friday that his way was clear. The Attorney General was apparently unaware that his White House rival, the Presidential adviser John D. Ehrlichman, was pushing his own candidate, Lewis F. Powell Jr. Mr. Ehrlichman's case was advanced by Mr. Dean's review of Mr. Friday: a fine man and a lawyer, but so unlettered in constitutional law that "we would take a beating trying to get him confirmed."

Then the A.B.A. screening committee split badly over Mr. Friday's qualifications. Some of those involved still feel he was not up to the job; others, like James Manire of Memphis, blame Eastern Establishment bias.

"They couldn't believe that someone like Herschel Friday—a name right out of Dickens—from Little Rock, Ark., would be nominated for the Supreme Court of the United States," said Mr. Manire. "They were trying to get a more uptown lawyer."

Mr. Nixon was to announce his nominations on the evening of Oct. 21, and Mr. Friday was told to expect a phone call from the White House shortly beforehand. Friends gathered in the Friday home for what everyone thought would be a celebration. Reporters milled on the front lawn.

The phone rang, and it was Mr. Mitchell. "This is the hardest telephone call I will ever have to make, I guess," he told Mr. Friday. When Mr. Friday hung up, his guests shouted: "What happened? What happened?"

"And he said, 'It didn't turn out the way we thought,' " his widow, Beth Friday, recalled in an interview. "He had on his face his little smile that I knew meant he was very hurt."

Moments later, Mr. Nixon named Mr. Powell and Mr. Rehnquist to the two seats.

According to Mrs. Friday, her husband ultimately had few regrets. Most people forgot about the episode, and that was fine with him. But last fall, when the law school at the University of Arkansas at Little Rock proposed to name its moot courtroom for him, some of the old questions about his school-district representation surfaced again. The law school went ahead with the honor after some digging by the dean, Howard Eisenberg.

"The more I investigated Herschel's background, the more I was certain that naming the courtroom in his honor was absolutely the appropriate thing to do," he wrote Mrs. Friday after the funeral. "I honestly do not know if I would have agreed with the opinions Justice Herschel Friday would have written, but I do know that there is no person who would have had greater integrity, honesty and kindness on that Court." ❑

A JUSTICE FINDS THE FUNNY BONE
CAN BE AN APPEALING WAY
TO CONNECT WITH LAW CLERKS.

7/5/91

JUSTICE RICHARD NEELY OF THE WEST VIRGINIA SUPREME COURT OF AP-
peals describes himself as a judicial pragmatist. No one who reads his
annual pitch to prospective law clerks could quarrel with that characterization.

These days, some state court justices find themselves scratching for
qualified applicants for these jobs. With more Federal judges hiring
more clerks more aggressively than ever for their more prestigious
clerkships, the competition is tough. The George Steinbrenner of the
process, Judge Alex Kozinski of the United States Court of Appeals for
the Ninth Circuit, in Pasadena, Calif., even felt compelled to defend
himself in the current issue of the Yale Law Journal.

And so, given West Virginia's perpetual identity crisis, few feel the
keenness of the competition as much as Justice Neely.

"Not only am I on a state court," he said, "but I come from a state
that half the world doesn't even understand is a state."

Rather than lament his state, or his state's state, Justice Neely has
taken a lesson from Madison Avenue. Each spring for three years,
he has placed large display ads in the University of Virginia Law
School's weekly newsletter. The product, and the results, are worthy
of Ogilvy & Mather.

"Would you like to be a Supreme Court Justice your first year out of
law school?" asks the most recent ad, for the 1992-93 clerkship. "America's laziest and dumbest judge seeks a bright person to keep him
from looking stupid. Preference given to students who studied interesting but useless subjects at snobby schools. For instance, a classics
major at Wellesley will have an advantage over an engineering major
from M.I.T."

The ad instructed applicants to get in touch with one of two Virginia law professors, Pamela Karlan or Dan Ortiz, to arrange on-
campus interviews with Justice Neely. But it further specified that
should they be "dead drunk" and miss their appointments, they could
always write him at his chambers in Charleston.

As things turned out, there were enough applicants for two days of interviews. "They've doubled in numbers and quality," Justice Neely crowed.

He may adopt an air of insouciance in his ads, but in truth, he is not easily satisfied. He fishes for clerks in Virginia, not in his own state, because he believes students from Charlottesville are more likely to have been "exposed to the greatest minds of this century." And he much prefers to hire someone well versed in Latin.

Like any good (Juris) doctor, Justice Neely has refined his approach in light of empirical evidence. Last year, for instance, he specified that all applicants "must be capable of applying feminist criticism, Critical Legal Studies techniques, and structuralist and deconstructionist textual theory to workers' compensation statutes and Article 9 of the U.C.C. [Uniform Commercial Code]."

Suggesting that every arcane fad in legal academia can be relevant to the bread-and-butter, real-world statutory questions that come before his court was his attempt at humor. But his joke was lost on many students in Charlottesville, who went on to cite their trendiest credentials.

"They could actually believe a judge could be interested in that stuff," Justice Neely said with wonderment. "It was a little too subtle."

In that sense, the ad was less effective than the 1989 campaign for what he touted as "America's most exotic clerkship." "Are you an Ivy League (or Potted Ivy) graduate with enormous depth of background in fields other than law?" it asked. "Did you really want a Ph.D. in English, history or physics, but sold out? Are you in the bottom half of your class? Do you smoke like a fiend? Well, then, have we got a job for you!"

"The object of the ad is to get people to ask the simple question, 'Who is this turkey?' " explained Justice Neely, a Yale Law School graduate. "The reason lawyers are pompous and pretentious is that they've never had any role models for being unpompous and unpretentious," he said.

To understand why Justice Neely's notices work so well, one must consider the usual appeal of judicial clerkships. Sure, they can be interesting and edifying. And, like law school itself, they can be prestigious ways to put off yet again the harsh realities of the workaday world. But few of those seeking such positions actually expect their judges to be bundles of laughs, or the jobs themselves to be fun.

"One of the reasons I picked him is because of his sense of humor," explained the winner of the 1992-93 lottery, Douglas Kornreich of Reston, Va., who spurned a Federal trial court clerkship. "It's going to be a lot of work, but he's definitely a character, and hopefully I'll get some laughs in between." ❏

Justice Neely continued advertising for clerks in the same vein; his pitch for 1994 listed the following as prerequisites: "ability to drive standard automobile or flatbed truck; bachelor's degree in useless subject e.g. Greek or Sanskrit or Byzantine history; bottom half of law school class coupled with a chronic, groaning disinterest in law school and intermittent bouts of disillusionment and embitterment with the legal profession as a whole." It added, "Low classroom attendance is a must" and urged applicants to send "letters and gum wrappers" to him in Charleston.

Alas, there will be no more such solicitations, for in what he called a "self-imposed term limit," Justice Neely will soon leave the bench to open up his own law office in Charleston. He said it will be "a specialized practice, for people who are in deep shit."

IX

ACADEMIA

CONCLAVE IN HERRINGBONE PONDERS
LOFTY AND MUNDANE IN LEGAL
EDUCATION'S MUDDLED MISSION.

1/13/89

NEW ORLEANS—SPEAKING TO A PACKED HOUSE OF HIS PEERS, JAMES BOYD White of the University of Michigan talked of Shakespearean sonnets, Burmese art and the evolution of the Gothic arch. And Dante, Gertrude Stein and Jaroslav Pelikan. And Picasso's "Guernica," Mont St. Michel and the cathedral of Chartres.

Anyone stumbling into Grand Ballroom B of the New Orleans Hilton during the talk might have assumed he was amid art historians or architects. Then he'd notice the legend on the lectern: "Association of American Law Schools."

Once a year Mr. White and the rest of the nation's law professors meet to discuss the congenitally muddled mission of American legal education. Judging from this year's gathering, things are more confused than ever.

The seminar at which Mr. White spoke (and where Harvard Law School's Martha Minow later recited a poem by Adrienne Rich) was on the fledgling "Law and Humanities" movement. The program notes described the subject as "that of personal and community wholeness, characterized by dialogue, the translation of disciplinary languages, and the grasping together of scattered realities."

One couldn't help but feel that if they had their druthers, many of the professors, like many law students and many lawyers, would rather be immersed in something besides law, like history, sociology or literature.

As the law practitioners have proliferated, so have the pedagogues. A record 2,800 of them attended this year's convention here last weekend.

The teachers represent the greatest concentration of herringbone this side of the North Sea. And the genotype seems as uniform as the uniform. To avoid the kind of confusion that results when mail for Robert Rabin of Syracuse ends up with Robert Rabin of Stanford, the program featured names like Ronald Harlan Rosenberg, Alan David Freeman, Stephen Bruce Cohen and Ira Mark Bloom.

This year's conclave was comparatively placid. By now it is old news that legal education is schizophrenic and that law faculties are factionalized. The situation sounds like the old Tom Lehrer song "National Brotherhood Week": The radicals hate the economists, the economists hate the clinicians, the clinicians hate the humanists, and everyone hates the traditionalists. One calls this either ferment or chaos depending on one's point of view.

This only intensifies criticism that law schools have little connection to law practice. Detractors charge that far from leaving their ivory towers, legal academics have erected a skyline of them, from which they spin out increasingly sophisticated forms of irrelevancy.

Just about the hottest panel discussion was "Feminist Theory and Gender Bias in Contracts Casebooks," which a group of professors who are women sponsored after the Section on Contracts rejected the idea as not serious enough. It apparently considered "Adjustment of Contract, Limitation of Remedy, and Excuse of Performance for Unexpected Conditions or Events" more meaty.

Even Duncan Kennedy of Harvard, a stalwart of the left-wing Critical Legal Studies movement as well as Peck's bad boy of conventions past, was more distinguishable sartorially—he was wearing a lavender-and-indigo-striped shirt under a green corduroy sports jacket—than substantively. At one point, in fact, the exuberantly ultra-conservative Richard Epstein of the University of Chicago accused him of creeping into middle-aged conventionality: "Put on your tie," he urged him. "Join the crowd."

Ethereal discussions about the Uniform Commercial Code or the Rule Against Perpetuities were not the only or even the principal item on the agenda here. Nor was faculty hiring, since the annual mating ritual, or "meat market," has been moved to December. More importantly, it was a chance to pick up the freshest gossip in what was undoubtedly the cattiest corner of the legal profession.

The topic most talked about this year was the Harvard deanship, and whether that most inbred of institutions might actually approach an outsider—people mentioned were J. Robert Prichard of Toronto, Gerhard Casper of Chicago and Judge Stephen Breyer of the United States Court of Appeals in Boston—or stick with an insider like Lance Liebman or Richard Stewart.

And Alan Dershowitz's tongue is apparently faring better in the classroom and courtroom than on a plate. He reports that his new delicatessen in Cambridge is continuously packed but has yet to turn a profit. ❑

The Harvard deanship ended up going to none of the above; the winner was Robert Clark, a member of the school's faculty. Mr. Casper became president of Stanford, and Stephen Breyer did even better, reaching the United States Supreme Court. As for Mr. Dershowitz's restaurant, it eventually went deli-up.

A PRE-EMPTIVE STRIKE AGAINST
LAURENCE TRIBE, BY THOSE WHO
DO NOT CARE TO CALL HIM 'MR. JUSTICE.'

10/12/90

IT CAN ONLY BE DESCRIBED AS A DIA-TRIBE.

In the vanilla-flavored world of law reviews, Benchmark, the quarterly journal of the conservative Center for Judicial Studies, stands out. And no issue stands out more than Vol. IV, No. 2, which is devoted to one topic: Prof. Laurence H. Tribe of Harvard Law School.

In articles with titles like "The Many Faces of Laurence Tribe," "God Save This Honorable Court—And My Place on It," "Tribe on Legalized Abortion: Where There's a Will There's a Way" and "Pettifogger of the Year," a collection of authors dissect the life, work and psyche of Professor Tribe. The result reads like a roast, but hardly of the affectionate Friars Club variety.

"A lot of people don't like Larry Tribe, and a lot of people take shots at him, but a lot don't really have the intellectual brainpower to really take him apart, which is what these scholars do," said Edward Tiesenga, a Chicago lawyer who is an editorial assistant for Benchmark. He called Professor Tribe a "constitutional cancer."

To these conservative critics, still smarting over the prominent role Mr. Tribe played as an adviser to the Senate Judiciary Committee in the defeat of Robert H. Bork's nomination to the Supreme Court, Laurence Tribe is many things. Or, more accurately, many people.

He is Sammy Glick, relentlessly clawing his way to the top. He is Machiavelli, always ready to cut corners or tailor principles for personal gain. He is Socrates, the corrupter of impressionable law students and professors. He is Gary Kasparov, who manipulates constitutional principles like pawns. He is Iago, a man who having spearheaded what the authors variously describe as the "lynching," "assassination" and "crucifixion" of Mr. Bork, sent the rejected nominee a note afterward. (Perhaps he addressed it to Benchmark, where Mr. Bork is a consulting editor.) He is Professor Harold Hill—in the words of Gary L. McDowell, "as much salesman as scholar, a fellow who, like Meredith Willson's 'Music Man,' is able to sell trombones and band uniforms to every podunk town on his route."

Most of all, he is Captain Ahab, but his white whale is the United

States Supreme Court. "One would think Tribe spends almost every waking moment of his life campaigning for the high bench," Benchmark's editor, James McClellan, writes.

Another contributor, William Bradford Reynolds, puts it differently. "The worst-kept secret around Washington is that Tribe not only wants, he wants desperately, a seat on the Supreme Court," writes Mr. Reynolds, an alumnus of the Meese Justice Department. "Every article, every interview, every speech, even every brief and pleading, seems crafted with an eye on how the written or uttered word will enhance his chances of becoming Mr. Justice Tribe."

Of course, it's been 23 years since a Democratic President named anyone to the Supreme Court, and given political realities, Prince William of England could well accede to the throne before another one gets the chance. But the folks at Benchmark aren't taking any chances. Jefferson, via Mr. McClellan, makes the point. "It is better to keep the wolf out of the fold than to trust to drawing his teeth and talons after he shall have entered."

So the issue amounts to a pre-emptive strike, a legal brief, a blueprint for some future "Stop Tribe" movement. Writer after writer portrays Professor Tribe as a constitutional chameleon, more devoted to his own unprincipled preferences than to the vision of the Founders. "There is something unholy about putting heretics in charge of sacred texts, and something foolhardy about appointing pyromaniacs to be fire chiefs," Mr. McClellan writes.

Mr. McClellan said he had received compliments about the critique from law professors, members of Congress and Federal judges (none of whom he would name). Professor Tribe himself wouldn't comment. "I'd rather let my work as a teacher, scholar and advocate speak for itself," he said.

Nor has he spoken about it with the Benchmark contributor Mr. McDowell, a visiting scholar at Harvard Law School. In fact, the two have yet to cross paths. "I would hope there'd be no hard feelings over this," said Mr. McDowell, who writes that Professor Tribe's constitutional jurisprudence owed more to the personal advertisements in The New York Review of Books than to The Federalist.

When it comes to monomania, the authors are on familiar ground. Every page of Benchmark reflects a consuming obsession with Professor Tribe. One Benchmark reader, Yale Kamisar of the University of Michigan Law School, offered a possible explanation for this fixation.

"He's the most famous professor at the most famous law school, he's produced more books and articles than anyone and he's been on 'Nightline' more than anyone," he said. "Sure, he's cocky, but so were

Babe Ruth and Muhammad Ali." Professor Tribe is so talented, he concludes, "they just can't stand it." ❑

With another Jewish Harvard professor, Stephen Breyer, now on the High Court—and with a liberal unlikely to occupy 1600 Pennsylvania Avenue anytime soon—Mr. Tribe's conservative critics surely worried for nothing.

THE FETISH OF FOOTNOTES,
OR THE FOLLY OF TRYING TO ERADICATE
THE PROFESSION'S ENDURING WEEDS.

6/8/90

IT WAS SUPPOSEDLY NOËL COWARD WHO ONCE COMPLAINED THAT ENCOUNtering a footnote was "like going downstairs to answer the doorbell while making love." Or was it John Barrymore, and was his choice of verbs more pungent? For further information, *see* footnote 23 in "Footnote[1] Skulduggery[2] and other Bad Habits[3]," by Arthur D. Austin of Case Western Reserve Law School.

Professor Austin clearly has a fetish about footnotes, those agglomerations of type that protrude upward like stalagmites from the bottom of most pages of most law reviews. The typical legal scholar, a wit once wrote, "may not assert so much as 'the sun rises in the east' without citing Copernicus" (*see* Coleman, Student Lawyer, Feb. 1989), and Professor Austin tries to explain why.

He has already found two publications, the law reviews at Vanderbilt and the University of Arizona, masochistic enough to print his iconoclastic views. Last year, he addressed the subject at the National Conference of Law Reviews. Now, in his "Skulduggery" article, coming soon to a law library near you in the University of Miami Law Review, he tackles it again.

Ridiculing footnotes is nothing new. Fifty-two years ago, Fred Rodell of Yale called them "the flaunted Phi Beta Kappa keys of legal writing," and little has changed.

Footnotes still help allay the lingering fear that legal scholarship is to scholarship as military justice is to justice as military music is to music (*see* Clemenceau). But Professor Austin maintains the problem has become even worse.

The last decade, he notes, has yielded a record for footnotes in a single article—4,824, in Arnold S. Jacobs's "An Analysis of Section 16 of the Securities Exchange Act of 1934," a piece that also set a record for consecutive *see infras* (16). The 1980's also brought perhaps the longest footnote (No. 317 in Sciarrino, "Free Exercise in the Defamation Forest: Are 'New Religions' Lost?," which consumes five solid pages of agate type) and the highest percentage of *ids* since Freud (444 out of 574 footnotes in Buchanan, "Comparative Analysis of Name and Likeness Rights in the United States and England").

What accounts for this scourge? Professor Austin explains the many functions footnotes serve in addition to elucidating texts. For as maligned as footnotes are, he writes, they have many constituencies. Indeed, the footnote lobby is as entrenched in legal academia as the tobacco lobby is in Congress.

For authors, footnotes offer an easy way to look scholarly or curry collegial favor. For schools, they make faculties appear more productive. For editors, they help fill issues. For legal researchers, they provide a livelihood. And for readers, they afford the thrill of turning the pages of turgid texts with lightning speed.

Some citations are, like Piltdown man, outright hoaxes. In an article on the duty to wear seat belts, in the University of Washington Law Review, two professors said—apparently as a prank—that a certain Earl of Andrews once declared: "Quoth, what fool dareset upon the highways of this realm without properly strapping his ass to his cart?" The man, and the quote, were bogus.

But Professor Austin contends that other footnotes, while less explicitly fraudulent, are no more legitimate. Some are soapboxes for ideologues. Others provide authors with a chance to razzle-dazzle readers or escape the editorial straitjacket of the text or simply prove they're regular guys or Renaissance types.

Law-and-economics types throw in graphs or formulas, law-and-psychiatry types throw in Jung, law-and-literature types throw in Tolstoy, law-and-baseball types throw in Yogi Berra or, in Professor Austin's case, Reggie Jackson (in legal literature, he says, footnotes are "the straw that stirs the drink"). "With the Woodstock generation now retiring to the friendly bosom of academe, rock lyrics have become a popular titillator," he writes, noting how Martha Minow of Harvard recently cited the singer Holly Near.

Footnotes provide an easy way to butter up colleagues. For junior professors, they win friends and influence people—particularly people on tenure committees. Acknowledging Laurence Tribe or Richard Posner, even if their contributions were minimal, is a bit like stamping "Reg. Penna. Dept. Agr." on a box of Lorna Doones: that is, it is a sign of wholesomeness and quality. It is also a poor substitute for the kind of peer review found in other disciplines.

In a mere 16 pages of text, Professor Austin's article had 161 footnotes. Reading it is a bit like playing a Bach toccata and having to look not only at the keys of the organ but also at the pedals below.

Of course, it's his way of making a point. But even in his more scholarly efforts, he says, he can't escape footnotes. "I try to be economic as possible, but I have to play the game," he said. Why? [1] ❏

---

1. See supra.

THE MAN WHO HELPED LIBERATE
LEGAL HISTORY, BRINGING IT OUT
OF THE IVORY TOWER DOWN TO EARTH.

3/23/90

MADISON, Wis.—WHEN J. WILLARD HURST ATTENDED HARVARD LAW School in the 1930's, the study of legal history was nonexistent. Oh, yes, some professors had studied obscure legal doctrines and there was one superannuated scholar studying history, but it was Roman history, and he stalked Langdell Hall like a ghost.

Why this dearth, given the inherent overlap between law and history? The explanation came a century ago from Christopher Columbus Langdell, Harvard Law School's intellectual architect: the law was a self-contained science and the law library its laboratory. One need not study how law actually affected people or how legal institutions evolved; all wisdom could be gleaned from appellate decisions. This approach not only gave law professors a shot at omniscience but also spared them from having to learn other disciplines, set foot in a courtroom or state legislature or even step outside.

From the moment he arrived here at the University of Wisconsin Law School 53 years ago, and was mandated to bridge the gap between law and society by studying how laws were enacted and applied, Professor Hurst changed all that. By his intellect and example, he is universally credited with legitimizing legal history. Even in retirement he remains one of the few legal scholars whose work can be measured in shelf feet—and shelf feet of bona fide research rather than of cut-and-pasted collections of cases and comments. In an era when academia, like sports, has been watered down through expansion, he is an old-fashioned towering figure.

In some ways, he is also an anachronism. He is one of the last disciples of Louis D. Brandeis (whom he once served as law clerk), having inherited Brandeis's interest in grassroots democracy. He is a disciple of the LaFollettes, who charged Wisconsin's academics to view the state as their campus and their laboratory. He is the last of the Legal Realists, the Depression-era scholars who tried to place law in a larger social context.

Mr. Hurst is one of those rare figures in academia who are as well-known for their modesty as for their scholarship. And even as he approaches 80, he still casts his long shadow over the field. "You're either a Hurstian or a reviser of Hurst," said Lawrence M. Friedman of Stanford Law School, one of a generation of legal historians either taught or influenced by Professor Hurst.

Mr. Hurst had the academic pedigree to do whatever he wished. He graduated at the top of his class at Harvard, edited its Law Review, served as research assistant to Felix Frankfurter before clerking for Brandeis in 1936.

It was Brandeis who urged Mr. Hurst to head for Wisconsin and study its democratic institutions. While there Lloyd Garrison, then the school's dean, urged him to create a program in "law and society," investigating how the state's legal system and economy cross-pollinated.

The spectacle of law professors doing social research was rare and at times ridiculous, like the Yale scholar who once charted parking-meter use in New Haven. Mr. Hurst focused on the lumber industry in Wisconsin, all to determine how industry both used and molded the laws of contracts, property and other areas. Mr. Hurst discovered Chippewa Falls long before Woody Allen found Annie Hall there; the work of the courts there was, to him, more interesting, less abstract and certainly less pawed over than that of the United States Supreme Court.

Mr. Hurst's was a largely uncharted route to respectability. Once, when he told a leading law dean he was working on "legal economic history," the dean harrumphed: "You'd never get away with it at my place!" But rather than feel excluded from the mainstream, Mr. Hurst simply created his own.

"For me personally, he was an incredible inspiration," Morton Horwitz of Harvard said. Robert Gordon of Stanford added: "Every scholar needs heroes, and Willard is one of the few authentic heroes of our field."

As his studies continued and broadened, recognition came. Three times he turned down the deanship of Yale Law School, as well as a chair at Harvard. "I guess I was just too pleasure-loving," he recalled. "I was having too good a time in Wisconsin."

Mr. Hurst is one of those people who, beneath a deceptively elderly exterior, retain all the fire, impatience and curiosity of youth.

He still goes into his office, still sifts through piles of manuscripts, still grumbles over all the issues—political action committees, Ralph Nader, antitrust laws—younger legal historians are still neglecting.

He takes great pride in his students—which all younger legal historians necessarily are—even when they criticize him. "Part of your function as a teacher is to send out people who've done more than you," he said.

That may be the only scholarly endeavor in which Willard Hurst has fallen short. ❏

IN WHICH A HALLOWED RITE OF PASSAGE INTO THE JARGON OF THE FRATERNITY IS CHALLENGED.

11/4/88

IT'S OFFICIALLY CALLED "A UNIFORM SYSTEM OF CITATION," THOUGH GENerations of law students know it simply as the "Bluebook." And its function seems as bland as its name: to provide rules for referring to cases, constitutions, statutes and other legal materials. The Bluebook, like almost everything else in legal education, comes from Cambridge, Mass.; it was first published in 1926 by the Harvard Law Review (or "Harv. L. Rev.," in Bluebook-ese).

At schools everywhere it is, as one wag put it, "the Kamasutra of citation." At least one publication folded because the Bluebook contained no abbreviation for it. But in the last 60 years, the Bluebook has become more than a ubiquitous style manual. It is an exasperating part of American legal culture. Wrestling with its arcane rules for footnotes and case citations is the hazing ritual of the legal fraternity. It is also a puberty rite, where fledglings first encounter *supra, infra* and *contra, op cit, id.* and *cert denied.*

The Bluebook has swollen over the years, much like the law itself. What took 26 pages to cover in 1926 takes 255 today, and now includes everything from the proper use of "hereinafter" (when *supra* simply won't do) to the correct shorthand for The Manitoba and Saskatchewan Tax Reporter (Man. & Sask. Tax Rep.).

To its critics, the Bluebook is a Napoleonic code for nitpickers. Even they must concede, however, that its very tortuousness makes it the perfect entrée to a legal career. The illusion of omniscience that mastery of the Bluebook confers comes in handy in a profession where claiming to know something can be as important as really knowing it. Like jargon everywhere, the arcana it teaches is cherished because it gives the fraternity a secret code.

But of late the Bluebook is under fire. The attack comes from the University of Chicago Law Review (U. Chi. L. Rev.), which is now offering a style manual of its own: the "Maroon Book," which takes its name from the school's official color.

To the Maroon Book's authors, the Harvard handbook commits the most heinous of sins: it's inefficient.

At 30 pages, the entire Maroon Book is shorter than the index of the Bluebook alone. The economies come, for the most part, by replacing stupifyingly complex provisions with a simple rule of reason.

The Bluebook spends seven pages distinguishing between the use of *see, see also, see generally, but see, cf.* and *but cf.* Section 2.2(c) states:

" *'But'* should be omitted from *'but see'* and *'but cf.'* whenever the signal follows another negative signal." the Maroon Book dispatches the subject with a single morsel of advice: use any English phrase that makes sense.

The Maroon Book deletes the periods from law review citations (for example, "Harv. L. Rev." becomes "Harv L Rev). "Wasted key strokes," huffs Mark Snyderman, one of the Maroon Book's editors. Gone, too, is the "J." that always followed the surname of Supreme Court Justices, as in Brennan, J. No longer, then, would the uninitiated think every Justice was named John or Jethro.

The Maroon Book has been heartily endorsed by Richard Posner, a past president of the Harv. L. Rev. who is now a Federal appellate judge. Thirty years after a persnickety Harvard editor chewed him out for poor cite-checking, Judge Posner still considers the Bluebook abstruse, pedantic and illogical (e.g. the requirement that a certain Renaissance poet be referred to as D. Alighieri). By exalting form over substance, he writes, it gives lawyers an excuse not to think.

"The Bluebook creates an atmosphere of formality and redundancy in which the drab, Latinate, plethoric, euphemistic style of law reviews and judicial opinions flourishes," he wrote in what the book would describe as Posner, *Goodbye to the Bluebook,* 53 U. Chi. L. Rev. 1343, 1349 (1986). In this suffocating world, he continued, the Maroon Book came as "a breath of fresh air."

The battle is one of big bucks as well as philosophy. Every year, Harvard publishes more than 100,000 Bluebooks, which sell for $6.50 each. Half the profits go to the Harv. L. Rev. (the law reviews at Columbia, Yale and University of Pennsylvania, which play smaller roles in its preparation, split the rest) and those funds help keep the publication afloat.

Around Harv. L. Rev., the reaction to the rivalry ranges from indifference to contempt. "People might buy it as a curiosity but I can't imagine them relying on it," Harry Olivar said of the Maroon Book. By sparing authors from having to devise their own citation system, he says, the Bluebook saves time. The uniformity it ensures is more vital than ever in a computer age.

Undeterred, U. Chi. L. Rev.'s Mr. Snyderman plans to proselytize next spring in Toledo at the annual meeting of law review editors. But in a hidebound profession, he faces an uphill fight. Just a month ago, in fact, the people in Cambridge received an order for another 100 copies of the Bluebook. It came from the University of Chicago bookstore. ❏

With sales of the Maroon Book lagging, the Blue Book still reigns.

THE WATERS ROIL IN VIRGINIA BEACH, HOME OF PAT ROBERTSON'S DISTINCTIVE LAW SCHOOL.

10/1/93

IN THE SEA TO SHINING SEA OF LARGELY INDISTINGUISHABLE AMERICAN LAW schools, Regent University School of Law, established seven years ago in Virginia Beach, Va., by the televangelist Pat Robertson, stands alone.

Its curriculum, according to school officials, "presupposes that God impressed upon His creation an objective order that man is bound to obey." All classes begin with as much as 10 minutes of prayer. Every three years, faculty members must acknowledge by contract that they have a "personal relationship" to Jesus Christ; every year, they must subscribe to a seven-point "statement of faith" and are expected to leave if they cannot comfortably do so.

Concerned primarily about academic freedom and student diversity, accreditors from the American Bar Association initially viewed the school warily, and approved it only provisionally. But with a new $13 million building, Regent seemed on the brink of receiving full accreditation this fall. Then war broke out at the school, precipitated by the dismissal of its founding dean. Now Regent is racked by a most un-Christian imbroglio.

Since July the school, which literally sits in the shadow of Mr. Robertson's Christian Broadcasting Network, has gone through three—by some counts, four—deans. A majority of the faculty has filed a formal complaint against school administrators with the A.B.A., and some of the 350 students may soon follow suit. At least one professor has offered his resignation. Mr. Robertson himself complained at one point that the students were "in open rebellion."

Mr. Robertson, a Yale Law School graduate, now dismisses the goings-on at Regent as "sort of a tempest in a teapot." But given all the turmoil, one A.B.A. official remarked, school officials "would have to be out of their minds" to seek full accreditation this year.

The Regent saga, like Regent School of Law itself, begins with Herbert W. Titus, a Harvard Law School graduate and Marxist-turned-fundamentalist Christian who brought 5 faculty members, 25 students and 190,000 books from Oral Roberts Law School after it went belly-up in the 1980's. Mr. Titus, who gave Mr. Robertson legal advice during the 1988 Robertson Presidential campaign, ran Regent with an iron hand, personally passing on every admission to the school. This may account in part for why the student newsletter recently described him as "beloved."

In July, Mr. Robertson, acting on behalf of Regent's trustees, approached Mr. Titus with an offer that he was apparently not supposed to refuse: to give up the deanship, take a year's sabbatical and return as the first occupant of a John Marshall Chair in Constitutional Law. It was a chair with an exceedingly squishy cushion: a $300,000 annual expense account.

Mr. Robertson calls Mr. Titus "an outstanding dean." But what the televangelist wanted, he explained yesterday, was to make of Mr. Titus a conservative counterpart of the liberal law professors who frequent "Nightline" and "The MacNeil/Lehrer Newshour."

"I wanted a Christian Laurence Tribe," he said.

Others speculate that the school, anxious about accreditation, wanted to cultivate a more moderate image than the one offered by Mr. Titus—a strict constructionist in biblical matters who has said, among other things, that Scripture prohibits affirmative action—and to make Regent look less like his personal fief. There was concern, too, about the difficulties Regent graduates have had passing bar exams.

But Mr. Titus refused, and on July 10, The Virginian-Pilot in Norfolk reported that he had been ousted. Pressed by students to explain the decision, William Cheney, chairman of the trustees, reportedly replied, "This board is only accountable to God."

There followed a parade of successors. The first to be offered the post was Keith Fournier of the American Center for Law and Justice, Mr. Robertson's answer to the A.C.L.U., who turned it down. Paul Morken, a professor at the school, was then appointed on an interim basis while trustees pledged to search for a "world class" dean.

Within a few weeks, that search produced J. Nelson Happy of Newport News, Va., an alumnus of Columbia Law School and the New York firm of Patterson, Belknap, Webb & Tyler. Mr. Happy has little prior academic experience. Indeed, until two weeks ago, he says, he never imagined himself dean of anything.

The situation Mr. Happy has walked into is anything but. Eight of Regent's 14 faculty members have complained to the A.B.A. that Mr. Titus's dismissal violates the bar group's tenure standards. Students complain of having a "dean du jour"; some wear T-shirts beseeching "Reunite Us With Titus" and quoting St. Paul's Second Letter to the Corinthians: "I had no peace of mind because I did not find my brother Titus there."

Despite a conclave yesterday between counsel for Regent and the departed dean, Mr. Titus, who remains on the payroll, could still sue. "Though it's a tempest in a teapot, it's a mighty big teapot," said his lawyer, Donald Lemons of Richmond.

But Mr. Happy, who sounds remarkably like Mr. Robertson—a result, he speculates, of years spent watching the evangelist on "The 700 Club"—maintains that things are settling down. Mr. Robertson, too, predicts that with Mr. Happy on board, his school will once more live up to his ideals. "I think it looks like it's time we got our act together," he said. "And I think we did." ❑

Dean Happy ultimately calmed things down at Regent, but not without firing three Titus loyalists on the faculty. Two of them, claiming they were tenured, have turned around and sued the school. So has Mr. Titus—for conspiracy, libel and slander. "The whole year was a nightmare," Mr. Happy said. "There was a holy war going on." He has tried to diversify the school's faculty, a task made easier now that Regent's trustees no longer insist all applicants be able to speak in tongues.

IN A CONFIRMATION BATTLE FILLED WITH YALIES, THE LAW SCHOOL'S DEAN IS CAUGHT IN THE CROSSFIRE.

10/11/91

JUDGE CLARENCE THOMAS WENT TO YALE LAW SCHOOL. SO DID JOHN C. Danforth, his chief sponsor in the United States Senate. So did Anita F. Hill, the law professor who has accused Judge Thomas of sexual harassment. So did Guido Calabresi, the law school's dean.

If Yale Law School, a place that hasn't always deigned to deal with anything as prosaic as life on earth, is all over the still-unfolding Thomas drama, Mr. Calabresi is at its epicenter. He is perhaps the only person who can attest to the sterling characters of both Judge Thomas and Professor Hill, and has done so.

"I like and respect them both, and I have always trusted them both," he said. "Given the complexity of sexual harassment, I could conceive of a situation in which Clarence Thomas thought he was doing nothing abusive, and Anita Hill thought that what he did was terribly threatening. Which perception is correct is something we all, women and men, will have to decide."

Next to the now famous Roman Catholic Sisters of Savannah, it may be Mr. Calabresi who is most responsible for Judge Thomas's remarkable rise. It was he who, in 1974, recommended Mr. Thomas to another of his former students, Mr. Danforth, then Attorney General of Missouri. After Judge Thomas's nomination to the High Court, and as most law professors remained mute, Mr. Calabresi endorsed Judge Thomas in an op-ed article in this newspaper.

Then, in September, he testified on Judge Thomas's behalf before the Senate Judiciary Committee, thereby counterbalancing for swing voters like Arlen Specter, a Pennsylvania Republican (and yet another Yale Law School graduate), the impassioned testimony of four prominent black law professors, including one from Yale, who opposed the nomination.

"Calabresi's testimony was pivotal because, even though he focused primarily on Thomas's character rather than on his constitutional vision, he was someone from the intellectual community standing behind a candidate whose qualifications are shaky," said Prof. Christopher F. Edley Jr. of Harvard Law School, one of those who testified against Judge Thomas.

Basking in television lights, bantering with Senators, ushering a young protégé into a position from which he can dispense a generation's worth of clerkships, moot court appearances and glory on his alma mater—all this can be heady stuff for someone like Mr. Calabresi, who usually spends his days resolving internecine faculty squabbles, placating professorial prima donnas, buttering up rich alumni and teaching torts. But the Thomas nomination has severely tested this dean of deans, this son of a Finzi-Contini whose family fled Fascist Italy in 1939, this man whose amalgam of brilliance and charm, exuberance and elegance have for 58 years helped him finesse the sternest challenges. Most of that time has been spent at Yale Law School, a place he ferociously—and unabashedly—loves.

Such blind Old Blue boosterism, some professors feel, allowed him to be used by the right wing to help legitimize Judge Thomas. In essence, Mr. Calabresi said little more than that a man of Judge Thomas's background, independence and skin color was likely to be better than any other candidate President Bush—another Yalie, by the way—was likely to select. Still, it was enough to make conservatives chortle. "You're the only head man, the only dean that's come in and testified for Thomas, and I want to congratulate you," Senator Strom Thurmond, Republican of South Carolina, told him at one point.

Off the record, some law professors, including several Yale alumnae, contend that given the past week's breathtaking pace of events, Mr. Calabresi was too slow to defend Ms. Hill and urge a delay in the Senate vote on the Thomas nomination, and that when he finally did speak up, his rhetoric was more wringing than ringing.

Mr. Calabresi said he telephoned Senator Danforth Monday morning, both to vouch for Ms. Hill's integrity and to urge him to cool his harsh criticism of her. "I tried to defend her at the place where it really mattered," he said. But only after another day passed did he go public. He did so in The Los Angeles Times, in which he lamented the mudslinging of the confirmation process, cautioned about how subjective sexual harassment can be, referred to Ms. Hill as "a fine person" and bemoaned how Judge Thomas had been besmirched.

It satisfied some of his critics, though not Professor Edley of Harvard. He called the article "mealymouthed" and added: "Calabresi is backpedaling furiously, without disavowing the character reference he provided. He must feel sorry that he got himself into this, particularly since he had very little meaty to say." ❑

Justice Thomas can now review the opinions of Judge Calabresi; in Feb. 1994 Bill Clinton, yet another Yale Law School alumnus, named his former professor to the United States Court of Appeals in New York.

IN ATTACKING THE WORK OF A MURDERED PROFESSOR, HARVARD'S ELITE THEMSELVES BECOME A TARGET.

4/17/92

ON APRIL 4, 1991, MARY JOE FRUG, A PROMINENT FEMINIST LEGAL SCHOLAR at the New England School of Law in Boston, was hacked to death on the streets of Cambridge. Wielding a military-style knife with a 7-inch-long blade, her assailant, as yet unknown, stabbed her four times.

On April 4, 1992, the Harvard Law Review held its annual gala banquet, when the torch of the nation's most prestigious legal journal is passed to a new generation of editors. Among those invited: the murdered woman's husband, Gerald Frug, a member of the Harvard Law School faculty. Had he attended, he would have found on his plate a parody of his wife's last article. The parody, titled "He-Manifesto of Post-Mortem Legal Feminism," was produced by the Law Review's editors and paid for by the school. It depicted Ms. Frug as a humorless, sex-starved mediocrity and dubbed her the "Rigor-Mortis Professor of Law."

The alleged satire poses a question that is certain to outlast all the finger-pointing, ducking, blaming, petitioning and posturing that has overtaken Cambridge in the nearly two weeks since the "joke" came to light: how can Harvard's best and brightest, the men and women who will soon write the opinions of some of the nation's most powerful judges, also be its cruelest and crudest?

Earlier this year, Ms. Frug's article, "A Postmodern Feminist Legal Manifesto (An Unfinished Draft)," appeared posthumously in the Harvard Law Review. Several conservative editors fought unsuccessfully to block the piece, a bluntly worded examination of how, Ms. Frug maintained, the law perpetuated the subjugation of women.

As the banquet approached, the Law Review's editors, their coveted, career-making judicial clerkships in hand, turned their efforts to the Harvard Law Revue, an annual send-up of the publication. Along with others who had opposed publication of the Frug article, Craig Coben and Kenneth Fenyo set about to lampoon it.

The result was a five-page, footnote-laden parody, saturated with inside jokes and sexual innuendoes. The article was purportedly dictated "from beyond the grave" by one Mary Doe, described as the "Rigor-Mortis Professor of Law, New England School of Law, 1981-1991" and "wife of Gerald Frug, Professor of Law, Harvard Law School." In it, Ms. Doe recounts childhood sexual fantasies about men in tight swim trunks, defended the use of obscenities in her scholarly work and reflected on "the irony that I, a postmodern feminist, am being published because of my husband's tenure here.

"Postmodern feminists represent a diverse group of people," the parody continued. "Some of us are intellectuals. Many are politically committed. Most are disillusioned. Others are just plain horny. But there is one thing that we have in common: we have no sense of humor."

As the article began to circulate over the next few days, the adjectives flew. Andrea Brenneke, a third-year law student and one of many women to speak out, called the parody "a perpetuation of the forces that killed Mary Joe Frug." In an open letter, nearly every member of the Harvard Law faculty called it "contemptible and cruel." As usual, Laurence H. Tribe and Alan Dershowitz weighed in with their observations. More criticism came—to his many critics, belatedly and begrudgingly—from Dean Robert C. Clark.

Then came the apologies. The eight editors who oversaw the Revue called the takeoff "tasteless" and "offensive." This group included David Ellen, the Review's outgoing president, and Paul Clement, who will clerk one year hence for Justice Antonin Scalia at the United States Supreme Court. The two women among them filed a concurring mea culpa. Mr. Coben and Mr. Fenyo abjectly apologized as well, though they noted that none of their colleagues ever objected to what they wrote, at least until the whole school came down on them.

Mr. Coben, Mr. Fenyo and Mr. Ellen did not return a reporter's phone calls. But in the fecund tradition of Harvard analyzing Harvard, others offered ample explanations for the debacle: the moral vacuousness of legal education; the sexist zeitgeist; the fractious political climate at Harvard; jangled gender politics in the era of Clarence Thomas, William Kennedy Smith and Mike Tyson; the peculiar combination of intelligence and isolation, sophistication and uncouthness, ignorance and arrogance that characterizes a few students at a few elite law schools.

Particularly those students with clerkships in hand. Judge Douglas H. Ginsburg of the United States Court of Appeals in Washington, for whom Mr. Coben will work next year, did not return a phone call. But Mr. Fenyo's future mentor, Judge J. Clifford Wallace of the Court of Appeals in San Diego, seemed disinclined to reconsider his offer in light of the parody. "I haven't seen it," he said. "I haven't heard anything about it. I'm really not even interested in it." ❏

Mr. Coben and Mr. Fenyo have moved on to prestigious posts, at Sullivan & Cromwell and McKinsey & Co., respectively. Ms. Frug's murder remains unsolved.

ONCE AGAIN, THE 'BEAUTY CONTEST'
LAW SCHOOLS LOUDLY DISDAIN
(BUT SECRETLY SCRUTINIZE).

4/19/91

IN WHAT IS BECOMING THE U.S. NEWS & WORLD REPORT ANNUAL SURVEY of American law schools, the magazine's number crunchers grade institutions the way arithmetic teachers grade tests. The top score is 100; everything else descends from there.

On that scale, America's law school deans would give the survey, which is based on admissions and placement figures and the opinions of assorted educators, lawyers and judges, about a 5. Their assessments tend to fall into one of four camps: "flawed," "seriously flawed," "extremely flawed" and "fundamentally flawed."

A year ago, after his school was ranked a pathetic fifth in the 1990 survey, the dean of Harvard Law School, Robert Clark, went ballistic. His interview with the student newspaper sounded a bit like Ed Koch and Don Rickles playing "Password." At various times Mr. Clark described the survey as "Mickey Mouse," "just plain wacko," "highly dubious," "incomplete," "screwed up," "silly," "totally bonkers" and "crazy."

The brickbats did not stop there. In an article titled "Rankings, Ratings, Rantings, Ravings," the president of the Law School Admissions Council, Peter Winograd of the University of New Mexico, dismissed the survey as a "beauty contest."

"Just as Sports Illustrated has found a sure-fire way to sell out in the dead of winter by featuring a swimsuit on the cover, so too has U.S. News discovered its key to maximizing sales," he complained.

Then the legal education establishment—represented by the Association of American Law Schools, the American Bar Association's Section on Legal Education and Admissions to the Bar, the Law School Admissions Council and the National Association of Law Placement—joined even before the March 1990 survey came out, calling it "meaningless" and "grossly misleading."

And, in a law review-like interpretation on the matter, Richard Lempert, a law professor at the University of Michigan, concluded that the study was "fundamentally flawed." Its methodology, he said, was "akin to combining measures of the quality of apples, lamb and soda straws and using them to rate the overall quality of grocery stores," he wrote. He, at least, was honest enough to add an asterisk.

"I would, I must admit, not have attempted to document the many flaws in the U.S. News rankings had they purported to show that Michigan was No. 1 rather than No. 7," Mr. Lempert admitted. "So if the next poll lists Michigan as No. 1, forget what you read here, even though it will remain true. And there will be a next poll."

Next Monday the 1991 U.S. News poll hits the stands. In places like Ann Arbor, Mich.; Cambridge, Mass.; Evanston, Ill.; New Haven; and Palo Alto, Calif., kiosks and Kinko's will be doing a brisk business in magazines and Xeroxes. And law deans, who despite protestations and pacts cooperated with the U.S. News researchers, will be licking their chops or nursing their wounds.

"People are taking this much more seriously than ever before," said Prof. Yale Kamisar of the University of Michigan (No. 6 this time). "Last year, people were sort of laughing about it and saying 'we won't cooperate.' But all of a sudden the mood has changed. We can laugh about it all we want, but the alumni aren't laughing about it and students picking schools aren't laughing about it. So we'd better wipe the smiles off our faces."

Of course, no one admits to caring about the results. But for the record, at the top, for the second year in a row, is Yale. Thus its dean, Guido Calabresi, once more has the delicious luxury of saying he couldn't care less; last year, he called the survey "an idiot's poll." This time around, Harvard is right behind, and Mr. Clark is almost placid. "You can debate whether Harvard or Yale is first, but to have us fifth was ridiculous," he said.

Rounding out the top five are the University of Chicago, Stanford and Columbia. New York University rated seventh over all, but scored first in clinical training. Vermont Law School, an institution that has acquired in legal academia the same image of counterculturish quality that its neighbor, Ben & Jerry's, has with ice cream, leads in environmental law. One of five schools listed as "up and coming" is Cardozo Law School in New York.

Deans of schools that do not top any list, like Jesse Choper of the University of California at Berkeley or Thomas Jackson of the University of Virginia, will once more have to explain to anxious alumni why the poll's criteria seemed intended to undervalue their alma mater's strengths and exaggerate its weaknesses.

"You get letters from alumni asking 'Why have you fallen from 8th to 10th?' " said Mr. Jackson. This year, he can report to them that their beloved school has bounced back—to No. 8. He can also tell them his assessment of the entire enterprise. "It's fundamentally flawed," he said. ❑

HARVARD'S LONGTIME LAW DEAN,
WHO SAW MUCH IN A LONG AND ILLUSTRIOUS CAREER,
REVEALS LITTLE.

11/29/91

NO ONE IN AMERICA HAS KNOWN MORE LEGAL MOVERS AND SHAKERS THAN Erwin N. Griswold. As a student, professor and longtime dean at Harvard Law School, Mr. Griswold watched generations of young men (and, eventually, a few young women) evolve from hobbledehoys to honchos.

Consider, for instance, Mr. Griswold's unique perspective on the "Saturday Night Massacre" of 1973. Archibald Cox, the Watergate special prosecutor cashiered by President Richard M. Nixon, was a former student. So was Elliot L. Richardson, the Attorney General, who resigned in protest over the dismissal, and William D. Ruckelshaus, Mr. Richardson's deputy, who also quit.

Harvard ruled the elite legal community and, from the Fair Deal through the Great Society, the crusty, curmudgeonly Mr. Griswold ruled Harvard.

Mr. Griswold, now 87 years old and still practicing law, has just published his autobiography, "Ould Fields, New Corne: The Personal Memoirs of a Twentieth Century Lawyer" (West Publishing Company). One would not expect anything sidesplitting or titillating from Mr. Griswold, a stern, teetotaling type whose greatest passions are the Federal tax code, postage stamps and state boundary markers. A book dedicated to the legal profession ("With all its faults," it "stands up well against other varieties of mankind") can hardly be an indictment of it.

But while Mr. Griswold is no Geraldo Rivera, nor is he a Winston Churchill. His book, unfortunately, is heavier on childhood memories, case synopses and foreign itineraries than on anything particularly insightful about his own undeniably distinguished career.

This is not due to either inattention to details or a faulty memory. We do learn about four centuries of Griswolds. We hear about his elementary school teachers, Miss Sapp and Miss Leach. We follow him from Cleveland to Camp Pemigewassett to Oberlin and Harvard, and his cars from a Model A Ford (1930) to a second-hand Chevrolet (1934) to a Buick (1940). At last it can be told that during lunches in Hoover-era Washington he had pie for dessert—he does not specify which flavor—and that his law school roommate, later a prominent Connecticut judge, "snored vigorously and violently."

There are a few revealing anecdotes: Mr. Griswold's Marshall Plan to humanize Harvard Law School, for example, consisted of dismissing a crotchety receptionist, planting a few shrubs around Langdell Hall, starting a glee club and hanging Christmas decorations each December. Otherwise, he sheds little light on his years at Harvard's helm, a bygone time when deans could still be despots.

He does examine Harvard's belated decision to admit women, beginning in 1950, a move opposed by one professor (the model for Professor Kingsfield of the movie and television series "The Paper Chase") because he would have to change all his notes. But Mr. Griswold glosses over his own disputed role in Harvard's brush with McCarthyism, when the Lubell brothers, Jonathan and David, were kept off student organizations for refusing to testify before the Senate Internal Security Subcommittee. He offers even fewer insights about Vietnam-era Harvard or into his philosophy of legal education, except to gripe that law professors write too little and that too much of what they do write is inside baseball.

Character analysis is not Mr. Griswold's strong suit. Longtime acquaintances from Alger Hiss to J. Edgar Hoover go largely unexamined. Innumerable others are described as "able." Moreover, though both as dean and Solicitor General of the United States from 1967 to 1972 he argued dozens of cases before the United States Supreme Court, he sheds light on none of the Justices he met along the way.

William O. Douglas, John Marshall Harlan, Hugo Black, Earl Warren, William J. Brennan Jr., all are either mentioned only in passing or ignored altogether. Of Benjamin Cardozo, he says only that he was "a remarkably interesting man." As for his onetime faculty colleague, Felix Frankfurter, whose chambers were a virtual annex to the law school's alumni and placement offices during his High Court years, we are told only that he had a "somewhat mercurial disposition."

If Mr. Griswold has no more to say about Washington than Cambridge, in this instance he can at least plead ignorance. He concedes that he was "not aware of the extent to which the Vietnam involvement affected President Johnson's political situation," that he had known nothing in advance about Justice Abe Fortas's resignation from the Supreme Court and that he had been entirely taken aback by Watergate.

"Though I recognized that the higher levels of government were necessarily and appropriately 'political,' " he writes, "I assumed in my naive way that they were rational and essentially honest." ❏

Dean Griswold died in November 1994.

At Columbia Law School,
An Uncommon Ebullience and
Evangelism at the Top.

11/27/92

FOR AS LONG AS ANYONE CAN REMEMBER, COLUMBIA LAW SCHOOL HAS been regarded as a very prestigious, very dull and very unpleasant place to be. Students are happy to get in, happy to get out and say they went there, and unhappy about almost everything in between. Then the school named Lance Liebman as dean.

Mr. Liebman, 51 years old, has been at Columbia's helm for barely a year, hardly enough time to change an institution's personality. Indeed, maybe no law school can ever be fun, least of all one in New York to which people often repair only after rejections from Cambridge, New Haven or Palo Alto, sites of what are generally rated as the nation's three top schools.

But under Mr. Liebman, a weary refugee from war-torn Harvard, something unprecedented has come to Morningside Heights: joie de vivre. Surely no one—not Harlan Fiske Stone, not Charles Evans Hughes, not any of the other deans whose portraits hang grimly on the office walls—can have approached the job with as much energy and ebullience.

Mr. Liebman gossips with élan, has a goofy and infectious laugh and exhibits a sense of humor worthy of Calvin Trillin's second cousin. He drops names aplenty, but naturally and inoffensively. Law professors, judges, journalists, politicians—Mr. Liebman knows them all, either from his days in P.S. 89 in Elmhurst, Queens, or as chairman of The Yale Daily News, president of the Harvard Law Review, law clerk to Justice Byron R. White or adviser to Mayor John V. Lindsay of New York. His Rolodex must rival that of Bill Clinton—a man, remarkably enough, he has not yet met.

In contrast to his predecessor, Barbara Black, whose only visibility during her six-year tenure came when her appointment as Columbia's first female dean was announced, Mr. Liebman is suddenly ubiquitous. He evangelizes endlessly for Columbia, whether before groups of Federal judges on the shores of Lake George or over lunches with Columbia graduates at New York's 30 largest law firms, with barristers in London or with bengoshi in Tokyo.

The Liebman administration can already point to several achievements: some new and unorthodox faculty appointments; increased fund-raising among alumni; a requirement that students perform 40 hours of public-service work in their last two years and participate in an experimental program on professional responsibility. Mr. Liebman has also begun the latest and most ambitious plan to renovate the school's congenitally uncongenial building, the late architect Wallace K. Harrison's curse on generations of Columbia law students.

Many graduates consider the building so dreadful that it should be razed, and that renovations should begin at ground zero. But even with his formidable fund-raising skills, Mr. Liebman views this option as unrealistic under current economic conditions. Instead, there are plans to fix up the entrance and build a student lounge—in Mr. Liebman's words, "a place with a glass roof and a cappuccino machine."

At the same time, his goals include getting students out of the awful building more often. Even though New York is the capital of the American legal community, Mr. Liebman complained, Columbia has historically turned its back on—or its nose up at—the place. Another aim is to expand career options, so the school stops sending so many of its own to the large law firms, only to watch them leave disillusioned a few years later.

For all his efforts to seem solemn and speak like a dean—"It could hurt Columbia Law School if I said something stupid," he explained—Mr. Liebman is a naturally extroverted, exuberant sort.

Nothing pleases Mr. Liebman so much as contrasting his old institution with his new one. He brandished a copy of Robert Clark's recent letter to Harvard alumni, in which the Harvard dean described sit-ins in faculty offices, apologized for the "thoughtless and cruel" parody of a murdered law professor's work published last year by the Harvard Law Review and announced the creation of a panel intended to create a stronger sense of community at the school.

By contrast, in his letter to Columbia alumni Mr. Liebman recounted how "grand" his first year had been. Judging from it, the greatest crisis he faced came last June, when the Latin word for "dean" was misspelled on all 350 diplomas.

Mr. Liebman was passed over for the Harvard deanship in 1989. It was perhaps his first professional setback, and, as it turned out, a great professional break, for it left him available when Columbia came calling.

Some people find New York cold and brutal, but Mr. Liebman is finding it positively placid. "Only someone coming from Harvard Law School," he said, "would view New York as a haven of civility." ❑

X

PERSONALITIES

HOWARD WIEDER *(page 134)*

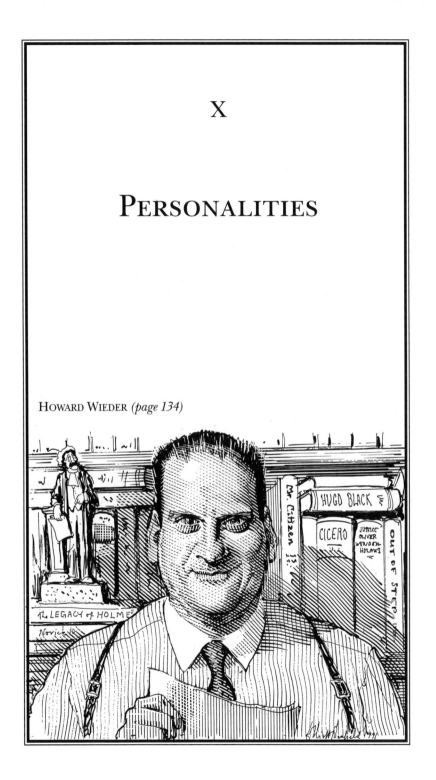

STREET-SMART DEFENDER OF REPUTED MOBSTER, 'SIMPATICO' WITH CLIENT, DISDAINS STIGMA.

4/21/89

WHEN IT COMES TO REPRESENTING NASTY PEOPLE, CRIMINAL DEFENSE lawyers have an all-purpose alibi, a Teflon-coated cure. Everyone is constitutionally entitled to a lawyer of his choice, they say; by representing the bad guys, they are actually guarding the liberties of us all.

But John Gotti's lawyer, Bruce Cutler of New York, doesn't stop there. He will tell you that Mr. Gotti, whom the authorities describe as boss of the Gambino family in organized crime, is also a fine fellow. As to his Mafia ties, he says, how can one belong to a group that does not exist?

Even lawyers who see nothing wrong with defending John Gotti wonder why Mr. Cutler so relishes the task. In the four years he has counseled Mr. Gotti, winning him two acquittals and now fighting for another, Mr. Cutler has not only represented the "Dapper Don"; at times, he has also appeared to replicate him. He has been said to look like John Gotti, laugh like John Gotti, dress like John Gotti, eat like John Gotti, strut and swagger and swear like John Gotti.

And he is proud of the resemblance. "My client is a very handsome man," said Mr. Cutler, who at 40 is eight years younger than Mr. Gotti. "If someone says I look like him I have no problem with that."

But he disputes the notion that Mr. Gotti is his role model, a distinction he reserves for his father, Abraham Lincoln, Clarence Darrow and Lou Gehrig. Their backgrounds—Mr. Gotti's spent on the mean streets of the South Bronx and Brownsville and his in middle-class Flatbush and at Hamilton College—are just too different. "I can't live John's—Mr. Gotti's—life," he said.

In one more respect he resembles "John—Mr. Gotti," to whom he usually refers simply as "my client": both, he contends, are victims of snobbery. Just as prosecutors loathe Mr. Gotti's lifestyle, they disdain Mr. Cutler as a mob lawyer, more bully than barrister. In fact, he says, he is doing nothing more than defending his client as ferociously as he can.

"Why don't they ask Arthur Liman if Michael Milken is his role model?" Mr. Cutler asked. "Did they ask Howard Weitzman if he looked at John DeLorean as a role model?"

Like most defense lawyers who inveigh regularly against government prosecutors, Mr. Cutler was once one himself, for seven years in Brooklyn. He then went to work for Barry Slotnick, who before defending Bernhard Goetz was best known for representing people like Aniello Dellacroce, then alleged chieftain of the Gambino family. It was there that Mr. Cutler was assigned to Mr. Gotti, who the authorities said was an underling in the organization.

Young lawyers hitch themselves to rising stars. Some clients turn out to be mere meteorites, others supernovas. And as Mr. Dellacroce fell to cancer and Paul Castellano to a hail of bullets, Mr. Gotti allegedly rose. He stuck with Mr. Cutler, with whom he meshed well. Or as Mr. Cutler puts it, "There was a simpatico with regard to government intrusion."

Like most top lawyers, Mr. Cutler is a man of protean personality. In court he slam-dunks indictments into garbage cans, throws around verbs like "retch" and "vomit" and epithets like "scum" and "lowlife." He knocks out informers with the brutal efficiency of Sugar Ray Robinson dispatching Gene Fullmer; his slashing cross-examinations have been dubbed "Bruceifications." But in his office, flanked by a bouquet of artificial orchids, he is soft-spoken and gentle, like a prep school wrestler at a headmaster's tea.

Mr. Cutler is not the smooth, cool consiglieri of the Robert Duvall school. He is big and beefy, at 210 pounds a third again as large as in his wrestling days at Bay Ridge's Poly Prep. He is street-smart and scrappy, the kind of carnivore who favors rib steaks over filet mignon, or Lenny Dykstra over Rickey Henderson. He speaks in raspy, breathless Brooklynese; if he uses a phrase like "raison d'être," he usually appends a "so to speak" after it. This is a style jurors like. "They believe what I'm saying," he said. "I'm not putting one over on them."

The twice-divorced, childless Mr. Cutler is married to work, which he compares to combat. But colleagues caution that while it is all right to represent an occasional mobster, or "black-collar" client, it should not become a habit. Otherwise he risks a certain stigma, known in the defense bar as the "people-will-think-I'm-a-gangster-if-I-go-to-a-lawyer-who-represents-gangsters" problem.

Mr. Cutler is unconcerned about any taint. "You can represent John Gotti and a major corporation," he said. "I've represented doctors, policemen, lawyers. If you're good enough and work hard enough, you'll have all kinds of clients."

With that he took out a True cigarette, which he bit as he lit it.

From the two packs a day he once smoked he is now down to only five cigarettes. Still he hates himself for it. "It's a weakness, and I don't like weaknesses," he said. "It's the one thing I'm most ashamed of." ❏

Prosecutors finally got John Gotti—and his lawyer. In June 1994, Judge Thomas Platt sentenced Mr. Cutler to house arrest for three months—and suspended him from practice from some Federal courts—because of comments he made to the press during Mr. Gotti's last trial, in defiance of a court-imposed gag order.

THE CONTINUING LAWYERLY, LINCOLN-LIKE LIFE OF SIMON H. RIFKIND (VOL. III).

4/20/90

FOR MANY YEARS, SIMON H. RIFKIND SPURNED ALL ENTREATIES TO TELL HIS life story, except for frequent autobiographical luncheon speeches to Paul, Weiss associates. But recently his law firm, Paul, Weiss, Rifkind, Wharton & Garrison, did the next best thing: it published the third—and for now, at least, the last—volume of "One Man's Word: Selected Works of Simon H. Rifkind."

The series, which took six years, $250,000 and cadres of lawyers, secretaries and paralegals to produce, chronicles the career of one of New York's most celebrated lawyers. Just as clamorous crowds induced an ostensibly reluctant Caesar to accept the laurel crown, it took a bit of collegial coaxing before Mr. Rifkind consented to open up his archives and remove some of the photographs from his office wall. "If my own partners considered it useful, I thought I would suppress my own humility and modesty," he said in an interview.

The local Marc Antony was Ernest Rubenstein, a Paul, Weiss partner who proposed the project in 1981 to coincide with Mr. Rifkind's 80th birthday. By Mr. Rifkind's 85th, the first two volumes of "One Man's Word" were complete. Now, as No. 90 approaches, there's Volume III. Some 2,500 copies of each have been printed, for distribution to various school libraries, friends of the firm and newly hired Paul, Weiss lawyers. (It's not officially for sale, though one of the handsome boxed sets, with Mr. Rifkind's signature embossed on each book, was recently spotted atop a table of secondhand books outside Grand Central Terminal.)

At Paul, Weiss, where Mr. Rifkind has practiced since 1950, the Roman metaphor is not inapt. "He's regarded there as a semi-divine figure, like Julius Caesar," said Adam Bellow, an editor at the Free Press (and son of Saul) who assisted in the project along with William Keens. That much is clear from the introduction, which attests to Mr. Rifkind's "unique and powerful blend of intellect, imagination, creativity, vision, energy, generosity, integrity and compassion."

The material falls into several distinct categories, including "The Man," "Judge and Arbiter," "Lawyer and Advocate" and "Public Figure." The work includes opening statements, oral arguments and summations, including one that, according to a Paul, Weiss associate who was there, left some jurors with tears in their eyes. (But Mr. Rifkind lost that case.)

With space apparently no constraint, a hagiographic profile of Mr. Rifkind in The New Yorker is reprinted in its entirety. So is Mr. Rifkind's "Money as a Device for Measuring Value," from a 1926 issue of the Columbia Law Review. So is "Industrial Recovery," a speech he gave to the ninth annual convention of the National Fertilizer Association in 1933. So, too, is an address to the Columbia Law Alumni Association that was interrupted by laughter 28 times (and laughter and applause once).

The collection also includes Mr. Rifkind's letters to newspapers, civic groups and friends, and eulogies for Arthur Szyk, Aaron Rabinowitz and Milton Steinberg. And there are some of the decisions he wrote while on the Federal District Court bench in New York in the 1940's, a post he left because, he complained in a letter to President Harry S Truman (reprinted in Volume III), the pay was too low. (Like most judges unhappy enough to quit, Mr. Rifkind was happy enough to keep the honorific; of the 50 years he's been called "Judge," only 10 were actually spent on the bench.) Reading the rulings was "a special joy," the editor states, though choosing among them was excruciating because "they are all so stunning."

In the logrolling department, there are exchanges of encomiums between William O. Douglas, Jacqueline Onassis and Judge Irving Kaufman. Thus in one speech Mr. Rifkind salutes Judge Kaufman for his "stubborn courage," "professionalism" and "flawless" performance in the Rosenberg case. In another, Judge Kaufman salutes Mr. Rifkind as "New York's premier litigator" and, somewhat redundantly, as "a decent mensch."

There are photographs of Mr. Rifkind, a painting of Mr. Rifkind, a bust of Mr. Rifkind and, for future generations, a two-record set of a Rifkind speech, in a pocket at the rear of Volume II. "I always wondered what Abraham Lincoln's voice sounded like," Mr. Rubenstein explained.

Interspersed through the materials are Mr. Rifkind's curmudgeonly assessment of the decline of the legal profession. They are captured best in a 1978 letter to Associate Justice Lewis F. Powell Jr. shortly after the United States Supreme Court had upheld lawyer advertising.

"I could not help feeling that the notion I had all these years that I was engaged in a great and noble profession was a presumption and a fantasy—that, really, I was a plumber or a butcher," he complained. "I am glad that the time I have left for the continued practice of that kind of a profession is now short."

In that, Mr. Rifkind proved more practitioner than prophet. Twelve years later, he remains hard at work—amassing, as it were, the ingredients of Volume IV. ❏

Though the 93-year-old Mr. Rifkind still comes to his office daily, he is practicing little law. According to Mr. Rubenstein, there will be no Volume IV.

Gone are the tie-dyed shirts and marijuana as a Woodstock-era guitarist covets judicial robes.

5/29/92

♪♪ *1 . . . 2 . . . 3 . . . who are we voting for?* ♪♪

For voters on either end of the demographic bell curve, the musical slogan on Barry Melton's letterhead and campaign placards does not make much sense. But for people between, say, 35 and 50, it conjures up a host of images, among them the Vietnam War, Max Yasgur's farm and songs with lyrics like "be the first one on your block to have your boy come home in a box."

Mr. Melton is a 45-year-old lawyer who is locked in a tight race for a seat on San Francisco's Municipal Court. It is his second career. From 1965 to 1970 he was lead guitarist for Country Joe and the Fish, the folk-rock group that produced what became the closest thing to the national anthem of the antiwar movement.

Sixties aficionados know the song as "The I-Feel-Like-I'm-Fixin'-to-Die Rag." But most everyone else, including anyone who attended Woodstock the music festival or Woodstock the film or owned Woodstock the record album, knows at least its opening lyrics, which are an obscene variant of a familiar high school cheer.

It was "Country Joe" McDonald, the Francis Scott Key of the Vietnam era, who dominated the movie. Mr. Melton, 22 at the time, makes only a cameo appearance, shorter than more memorable moments with the PortoSan man and various crotchety farmers of Sullivan County. Grinning mischievously, wearing shoulder-length curly hair, rose-colored glasses and a tie-dyed shirt of many colors, the would-be judge prances in front of the camera brandishing a joint.

"Mar-i-juana!!!" the band chants. Mr. Melton then places the butt in his mouth and begins strumming.

Some of the babies born at Woodstock may well be in law school now. In your neighborhood video store, "Woodstock" the movie can be found alongside "Night of the Living Dead" and "Reefer Madness" under "cult classics." And Mr. Melton, now the father of two, has shorn—or shed—his golden locks, grown a gut, traded his tie-dyes for a suit and left his crash pad for a very, very, very fine house with a very, very, very fine mortgage. True, he once extolled, used and even inhaled drugs, but no more, he maintains.

"Hey, I've got a 15-year-old," he said.

Occasionally, faint echoes of Woodstock can be heard amid the politicking. A recent Melton fund-raiser featured remnants from Jefferson Airplane, the Grateful Dead and the Steve Miller Band. But just as Mr. Melton seems anxious to soft-pedal his psychedelic past, his opponent, Judge Donna Little, appears afraid to dredge it up. In liberal San Francisco, she reasons, such charges could backfire. Indeed, just about the only thing the campaign and Woodstock have in common is mud.

At 39, Judge Little technically belongs to the Woodstock generation. But Mr. Melton theorizes—and Judge Little acknowledges—that she spent those years listening more to Herb Alpert and the Tijuana Brass than Big Brother and the Holding Company. Indeed, Judge Little, a New Jersey native and registered Republican, passed up going to Woodstock, never sat through the film, did not buy the album, has not rented the video and does not remember any lyrics to "The I-Feel-Like-I'm-Fixing-to-Die Rag" beyond "1, 2, 3."

Mr. Melton began studying the guitar at 5 on Avenue Z and Ocean Parkway in Brooklyn, where he lived next to Woody Guthrie. He moved to San Francisco in 1965, where he passed up college for Haight-Ashbury. Country Joe and the Fish eventually swam their separate ways. Mr. Melton enrolled in what he called "the Holiday Inn School of Law," cramming in correspondence courses in contracts and torts between concert gigs.

In his campaign literature he likens himself to such other legal autodidacts as Clarence Darrow, John Marshall and Abraham Lincoln. In fact, his practice is considerably more routine than that, consisting of criminal and entertainment law with a healthy helping of pro bono work.

Overall, he regards his past with a mixture of satisfaction and sheepishness, defiance and defensiveness.

"My generation has a lot to be proud of, but we did some stupid stuff," he said. "But I wasn't doing anything different than all the other 20-year-olds at Woodstock, and there were 500,000 of them. And I dare say that in that crowd there were all kinds of people who've gone on to lead adult lives: doctors and lawyers, Congressmen and Congresswomen, district attorneys and public defenders and judges." ❏

Mr. Melton lost overwhelmingly, and is now a deputy public defender in Mendocino County, Calif. He flirted with a visit to Woodstock II, but ultimately did not attend.

AN ALL-STAR NEW YORK LAWYER
DISPUTES THE IDEA THAT HE'S BECOME
A WHITE HOUSE BUMBLER.

6/11/93

EARLY IN THE AFTERNOON OF JUNE 3, AS THE CANDIDACY OF LANI GUINIER disintegrated and the search for a Supreme Court Justice intensified, Bernard Nussbaum slipped out of the White House counsel's office. He had an appointment in New York, and he was determined to keep it.

Months earlier, before names like Zoë, Kimba and Lani were to be bandied about as often as Oprah, the Federal Bar Council of New York made plans to honor Mr. Nussbaum, its past president. When the event rolled around, the 56-year-old lawyer received the usual lawyerly doodad—this time, an antique British wig box—but also something far more precious: a loving hometown respite from the finger-pointing, second-guessing and character-assassinating he was enduring in Washington.

"It was a wonderful evening," Mr. Nussbaum said in a telephone interview from the White House. "The fact that 450 members of the bar would come to say 'hello' in the midst of all these attacks was very touching. It gave me the strength to go back and face the wolves."

Changes of venue can produce startling results, but Mr. Nussbaum's move has proven to be the most dramatic since Simi Valley. In two decades at the New York firm of Wachtell, Lipton, Rosen & Katz—interrupted only by a Watergate-era stint as counsel to the House Judiciary Committee, during which he supervised a young lawyer named Hillary Rodham—he won a reputation for brilliance and savvy. He was literally a lawyers' lawyer, the man firms like Sullivan & Cromwell and Kaye, Scholer, Fierman, Hays & Handler turned to when they got in trouble.

But a short shuttle ride away in Washington, where he was supposed to supply some gray-haired wisdom to the White House kiddie corps, a different Mr. Nussbaum has emerged, at least to his mostly anonymous critics: politically naive, ham-handed, tone-deaf. It was he, they charged, who was responsible for President Clinton's trifecta of failures—his first two candidates for Attorney General, Zoë Baird and Kimba Wood, and now, Lani Guinier, the star-crossed choice to head the Justice Department's civil rights division.

As Ms. Guinier went down, only hours after the standing-room-only crowd feted Mr. Nussbaum at the Harvard Club, so did his star inside the Beltway. Time magazine called him "bumbling." "That's strike three, Bernie," declared Newsweek. Under the headline "Nussbaum Sized Up for the Blindfold," The Washington Post speculated he was already en route to the egress.

With a Justice still to be selected and myriad other emergencies to tend to, Mr. Nussbaum is giving few interviews, even to defend himself. Only with Lani Guinier, he said, had he miscalculated, by assuming that any difficulties posed by her academic writing would be outweighed by her record as a civil rights litigator.

He boasted of the appointments that worked, particularly of Attorney General Janet Reno and her top aides. He insisted that the skills he had picked up in takeover litigation—toughness, the ability to keep cool in a crisis and make quick decisions on imperfect information—mattered more than more Washington seasoning. And he laughed off the press criticism. "It's sheer nonsense," he said. "It goes with the territory."

He said he retained the confidence of the only man who mattered. "When you're down to one client—the President—the only thing that counts is your relationship with that client," he said. "If that relationship is good, then bad stories mean nothing. If that relationship is bad, then good stories don't mean anything. My relationship with the President is good.

"I see the President anytime I think it's reasonably necessary," he continued. "Unfortunately, it's been necessary too many times."

Mr. Nussbaum conceded he had not anticipated how hyperscrutinizing and jaundiced the eyes of Washington are. But for all the abuse, he said there was "no grander job for a lawyer in the United States. "This President is trying to turn this country around," he said. "To be able to help him do that is glorious."

In Mr. Nussbaum's current rarefied world, even the relaxation is memorable. During the N.C.A.A. basketball tournament, for instance, he and his family joined the Clintons and Barbra Streisand at the White House to watch the Arkansas-North Carolina game. His 83-year-old mother has also visited the White House. His wife and daughter got an inscribed photograph of themselves with Mr. Clinton, who wrote: "To Toby and Emily. Thanks for visiting me and my lawyer at the White House."

Mr. Nussbaum's days start around 7:30, when he leaves his apartment in the Watergate Complex. Seldom does he return before 10 at night. Simple pleasures, like dinners or movies, have become rare treats.

"This is an all-consuming job," he said. "Every fiber, every talent that I have is being used. And to some extent, I'm still learning." ❏

The lessons stopped abruptly. Beset by criticism for his role in the Whitewater affair, Mr. Nussbaum resigned on March 5, 1994, and returned to the more sympathetic corridors of Wachtell, Lipton.

"Now that I am back in New York, I realize that Andy Warhol was right: anyone can be famous for fifteen minutes," Mr. Nussbaum told the New York City Bar Association in November 1994. "What Warhol did not explain—but what I now know—is that fifteen minutes is plenty."

AFTER 10 YEARS, UPSTART PUBLISHER
AND HIS ICONOCLASTIC MAGAZINE
BOTH HAVE MELLOWED.

3/24/89

STATELY, PLUMP STEVEN BRILL STOOD TRIUMPHANTLY IN A CROWDED RAIN-bow Room last week. Ten years had passed since he launched his iconoclastic American Lawyer magazine. And all around, bowing and scraping before him, were emissaries from the very institutions that he has opened up, dissected and attacked.

There was a partner from Sullivan & Cromwell, a firm whose "fatal arrogance" Mr. Brill described in a recent piece. Not far away was a lawyer from Winthrop, Stimson, Putnam & Roberts, which he once depicted in precipitous decline. And over there stood a partner from Shearman & Sterling, the firm that once threatened to run Mr. Brill out of town.

Not so long ago, most of the lawyers who gathered last Thursday atop Rockefeller Center would not have returned Mr. Brill's phone calls. But a decade has passed, a time The American Lawyer describes with a Churchillian flourish as "Ten Years of Upheaval." And these same lawyers were now drinking Mr. Brill's liquor, slurping Mr. Brill's oysters and, at least metaphorically, kissing Mr. Brill's ring.

This month The American Lawyer published its gala 10th anniversary issue, five times as thick and many times as glossy as its mangy inaugural number. James B. Stewart, a charter reporter at the magazine who is now at The Wall Street Journal, recalled an era of "gray linoleum floors and battered furniture" and how Mr. Brill, "imbued with boundless enthusiasm, optimism and idealism," inspired his tattered troops.

A photograph, circa 1980, shows American Lawyer staff members in his Pound Ridge swimming pool, the same pool where the hypercompetitive Mr. Brill once bit one of his reporters, James Cramer, in a game of water polo. (The wounds have apparently healed; Mr. Cramer now writes the magazine's financial column.) Also reprinted were vintage letters from irate readers and some "AmLaw Trivia." (Question: Name the firm whose partner told one law student that wives "tend to get bored unless you move so often they constantly have a new home to redecorate." Answer: Milbank, Tweed, Hadley & McCloy.)

Most of the issue consists of long profiles of 10 who made the "upheaval" happen, including Rudolph W. Giuliani, Joseph Flom and the late Edward Bennett Williams. But none did more than Mr. Brill, now 38 years old. It was he who decided that lawyers and the law business were "too important to be boring"; who discerned, chronicled and catalyzed the revolution in large-firm legal practice, an era of ruthless competition and cost-consciousness; who pierced the firms' genteel facades, bared their finances, aired their dirty laundry and rated their work.

Mr. Brill's empire now includes legal periodicals from Washington to Texas to California. And as his magazine has grown bulkier, so has Mr. Brill himself. Physically, he has grown into the mogul he has long thought himself to be, with the throw-weight and swagger of Orson Welles's Charles Foster Kane or Robert DeNiro's Al Capone.

True, the party did not attract the cast of politicians and power brokers that attended last fall's centennial dinner for the rival New York Law Journal. But what it lacked in lawyers it made up for in alumni, who, given Mr. Brill's eye for talent and his explosive temperament, are abundant. Notably absent were Jay Kriegel, the magazine's cofounder, with whom Mr. Brill has been feuding, and Mr. Giuliani, whose face was visible only on the cover of the current issue. The story inside, laced with terms like "disingenuous," "self-promoting" and "skewed," could explain his boycott.

As the party attested, the magazine is more respected than it once was. But it is also less scrutinized, less discussed and less feared. Perhaps it was inevitable; the novelty had to wane. And, Mr. Brill concedes, the magazine has been largely purged of the anonymous quotations, "snide adjectives" and "immature 'We Gotcha' headlines" it once favored.

But while Mr. Brill's universe remains one of winners and losers, bests and worsts, ins and outs, he seems to have become kinder over the years. In many instances, his bark exceeds his bite. For at bottom, what intrigues him most is not so much character as power and money—to use his terms, "clout" and "rainmakers," "big deals" and "heavy hitters." And in those commodities, at least, the bar abounds.

For all their grumbling, lawyers who once labored in obscurity have learned to love the attention Steve Brill lavishes upon them. In the current issue, the venerable Washington firm of Arnold & Porter praised The American Lawyer, which had, it said, "pushed, prodded, challenged, and enlightened our profession." More amazing still, it paid $3,000 for the privilege. ❑

Though he remains American Lawyer's publisher and guiding light, Mr. Brill has turned his attentions to his latest—and still more significant—inspiration: Court TV.

CATAPULTED FROM OBSCURITY
BY A TEEN-AGE RAPE SUSPECT
WHOM HE ACTUALLY LIKES.

5/12/89

HOWARD J. DILLER BEGAN LEAFING THROUGH THE BLUE MESSAGE SLIPS strewn about his desk. "Here's Wanda from Channel 2," he said. "Jim Kunen from People magazine. Here's Magee Hickey from Channel 4 and Terry Landau from NBC. Tim Minton, Channel 7. Pablo Guzman, Channel 5. Michael Stone from New York magazine.

"These," he added, "are just from the last two or three days."

Lawyers, like everyone else, have their 15 minutes of fame, usually when they find a client 30 seconds into his own. In Mr. Diller's case, that client is Kevin Richardson, one of eight boys arrested in last month's rape of a young jogger in Central Park.

For Mr. Diller, this 14-year-old boy represents deliverance from 27 years of obscurity; a chance to at least approximate his lifelong ambition of becoming a radio talk show host. In a matter of a few days he was interviewed by Sam Donaldson ("delightful"), Phil Donahue ("a very dynamic, very bright guy"), Larry King ("he looks very bad") and George Will ("I get the feeling he thinks the kids really ought to be executed, without wasting any more time"). He was even interviewed by Walter Cronkite's daughter, Kathy, a thrill rivaled only by meeting Mickey Mantle recently at a Chinese restaurant.

For a frustrated newshound like Mr. Diller, who worships Edward R. Murrow far more than Edward Bennett Williams, the experience is a dream come true. It is also a homecoming of sorts for the 59-year-old New York University Law graduate, who spent his first eight years in practice in a storefront on Eighth Avenue and 127th Street in Harlem.

With all the attention, Mr. Diller has taken his fair share of heat—from friends, from fellow lawyers, from people who now recognize him on the street, from strangers by phone. "You ought to be ashamed of yourself," he was recently told at a black-tie dinner. "These people are not entitled to lawyers," a fellow elevator passenger insisted. "If you needed money so badly, you should have said so," needled a patron at the West Sider restaurant on 69th Street and Broadway, where Mr. Diller eats breakfast.

But Mr. Diller not only believes his client; he likes him. He said the teenager is "not all there," having forgotten within a few hours that he had been visited by John Cardinal O'Connor. "Kevin is a sweet boy," he said. "But he has no notion of the enormity of this case."

With its frosted-glass doors and their gold-leaf lettering, the offices at 401 Broadway, where Mr. Diller practices with his son Jonathan, are a throwback to the era of Sam Spade and Miles Archer. Mr. Diller's quarters are furnished in Naugahyde and linoleum, with a business card taped hastily to the door. The only rug in sight is the one atop his head.

He got here by way of East New York in Brooklyn, Thomas Jefferson High School and City College, a well-worn path for one of his generation. What makes him distinct are two subsequent stops: a year at what became Skadden, Arps, Slate, Meagher & Flom, now New York's largest law firm, then only an eight-man office. That was followed by five years with the Federal Bureau of Narcotics.

Seventy percent of Mr. Diller's clients are Hispanic, most of them Dominicans and Colombians. For them, as well as for the occasional police officer or corrections official, he handles criminal work: trials, parole questions, appeals. It's a living. Mr. Diller appears to have profited more from real estate—15 years ago he was prescient enough to buy a nine-room West Side apartment—than he ever did in practice.

His home is 40 blocks south and worlds away from the rape site. But shortly after Kevin was charged, one of his relatives called Mr. Diller. It seems he'd represented her years earlier in a matrimonial matter. Since then, he has seen his client five times and has met twice with his family—first in their Harlem apartment, then in his own on Central Park West. "I wanted them to feel comfortable with me in all regards," he explained. "I didn't want them to think they were welcome to pick me up but not come in."

The next day, they dropped by again. This time, they brought $500—cash—and left it with the doorman. Mr. Diller expects to devote $50,000 of his time to Kevin's defense. If he's lucky, he says, he'll eventually recoup a third of that.

Mr. Diller is no William Kunstler or C. Vernon Mason out to make some larger point about the treatment of blacks by the criminal justice system; he dismisses the charge that the system is racist as "a lot of hogwash." He is the sort who gets goose bumps watching "12 Angry Men," who thinks there are Henry Fondas in every jury room. "I believe in the system," he said. "I'm a hard-liner, and I'm appalled by what happened here. But that doesn't mean the accusations against one person are necessarily true." ❏

In January 1991, Mr. Richardson was sentenced to 5 to 10 years in prison, the maximum term for a juvenile. And in May 1994, Mr. Diller was suspended from the practice of law for six months for failing "to maintain intact" some client funds.

THE STREET-SMART LAWYER
WHO ALSO KNOWS THE WAY
AROUND THE RICH AND FAMOUS.

2/5/88

AT THE BEGINNING OF TOM WOLFE'S "THE BONFIRE OF THE VANITIES" there is the disclaimer, so beloved of lawyers, that all of the characters are imaginary. But that is only partly true. The prosecutors and policemen and defense lawyers who populate the book may technically be fictional, but they are also the people Edward Hayes has known all his life.

It is to "Counselor Eddie Hayes" that Mr. Wolfe dedicates his best-selling novel. The two met 10 years ago, when Mr. Hayes worked in the homicide bureau of the Bronx District Attorney's office. When the author began his research, Mr. Hayes was his Virgil, guiding him through the nether regions of the criminal justice system and the moth-eaten law offices of lower Broadway.

"There is no stratum of life that Eddie can't walk right into," said Mr. Wolfe. Or, as the book's dedication put it, Mr. Hayes "walked among the flames, pointing at the lurid lights."

One of the book's figures, a defense lawyer named Tom Killian, is loosely modeled after Eddie Hayes. Like Killian, Mr. Hayes is slim and dapper, favoring trench coats and double-breasted blazers. He is serious but fun-loving, hard-boiled but sentimental, the type who hides his book learning under layers of profanity, who talks tough but is moved to tears at the mere mention of his mother.

But, in a sense, there are many other Eddie Hayeses in the book, published by Farrar, Straus & Giroux. They, too, are self-made and street-smart, and speak New Yorkese. And whatever their background, theirs is the argot of the working-class Irish from the outer boroughs, whose influence still haunts the precinct houses. "Fughet aboudit!" they say. "Gedouttaheh!" "You gotta problem, pal."

"Tom has achieved literary glory by using the kind of language the nuns would have given me a good beating for when I was a kid," said Mr. Hayes, a 40-year-old native of Sunnyside, Queens.

These days, Mr. Hayes's claim to fame is more than literary. Five minutes after Andy Warhol died suddenly a year ago, his executor, Frederick W. Hughes, asked Mr. Hayes to handle the artist's estate.

The ritual after what Mr. Hayes called Mr. Warhol's "stupid and unnecessary" death was much like that in your average murder case: you eyeball things, find the documents and players, seal off the premises. Things are calmer now, but no less complicated. Mr. Hayes continues to handle other work, like the estate of the fashion designer Willi Smith, but can be found at the Warhol studio, a onetime power station on East 33rd Street. There, he runs the cottage industry of litigation that invariably emerges when the rich and famous die.

He has filed Mr. Warhol's will, begun selling off the artist's assets, set up a Warhol foundation and filed negligence charges against New York Hospital, where the artist died. Then, assisted by Paul J. Hanley Jr., a copyright expert at Richards & O'Neil who once battled bogus Louis Vuitton luggage, Mr. Hayes has gone after the bootleggers of unlicensed prints, posters, calendars, neckties, dolls, T-shirts and shopping bags bearing Warhol's depictions of Marilyn Monroe, Mao and others.

And those violations are everywhere. The other day at the studio, Brigid Berlin, star of "Bikeboy," "****/Four Stars" and other early Warhol films, was needlepointing some shoes for a friend on Interview magazine. On one shoe was Mr. Warhol's famous Campbell's Soup can, and on the other, one of his self-portraits. It was a tribute to the man she describes as her "best friend." But it was also, at least technically, an infringement of his copyright.

Anyone who follows high-profile cases expects to encounter lawyers with a certain pedigree. Not surprisingly, when word spread that Mr. Hayes was in charge of the Warhol estate several fancy law firms tried to muscle him out. They contended he was too small-time, too unfamiliar with the art world and had too unsavory a clientele.

In fact, Mr. Hayes is a graduate of Columbia Law School, a place which, like Tom Killian's Yale in the book, "is terrific for anything you wanna do, so long as it don't involve people with sneakers, guns, dope, lust, or sloth." But he learned more about trying cases by tending bar than attending class, and while others marched to Wall Street and have their names on legal briefs, he worked on the Grand Concourse and was quoted in The Daily News. He then went out on his own, spending the first two weeks of practice reading Raymond Chandler in an empty office at 225 Broadway.

Gradually, business grew. "Criminal law is the only profession in which the better you get, the worse the class of people you represent," he says. But even as he prospers, the old insecurities remain. Mr. Hayes is a man obsessed with proving he is not, as Mr. Warhol himself once put it, simply passing through his 15 minutes of fame. "I really honestly believe all that stupid stuff about America being the land of opportunity," he said. "I'm the most grateful guy in the world, but I still get up every day and think I've got to prove myself again." ❑

Mr. Hayes went on to have a well-publicized scrape with the Andy Warhol Foundation for the Visual Arts, from which he has demanded as much as $11.5 million in legal fees.

FROM A LONELY PRISON CELL, AN INMATE WINS AN IMPORTANT VICTORY FOR CIVIL LIBERTIES.

3/6/92

SOMEWHERE IN THE BOWELS OF CAMP J OF THE LOUISIANA STATE PENITENtiary at Angola, not far from where three guards kicked, punched and pummeled him nine years ago, prisoner No. 91888, Keith J. Hudson, may be savoring something few lawyers anywhere have known in recent years: he took a civil liberties case to the Supreme Court of the United States, and won.

Last week, by a vote of 7 to 2, the Justices agreed with Mr. Hudson that prison beatings can be unconstitutionally "cruel and unusual" even if they result only in split lips and bloody noses rather than concussions and broken bones. "When prison officials maliciously and sadistically use force, contemporary standards of decency always are violated," Justice Sandra Day O'Connor wrote for the High Court.

For the 32-year-old Mr. Hudson, the ruling was the culmination of nine years of legal work, in which he read precedents from the law books brought to his cell by prison messengers, and hunted and pecked his legal briefs on a portable typewriter. Mr. Hudson, serving a 20-year sentence for armed robbery, could not argue his case personally; that task was handled by Alvin Bronstein of the American Civil Liberties Union's national prison project.

Unhappy with Mr. Bronstein's refusal to handle an ancillary matter, Mr. Hudson dismissed him two weeks before oral arguments. But with the High Court's approval, Mr. Bronstein proceeded anyway. Mr. Hudson has not spoken to him for months, nor to any reporters. If he is exulting, he is exulting alone.

In a handful of homemade documents, written in a patois of street talk and legalese, Mr. Hudson offered his version of events in the early morning of Oct. 30, 1983. He was cleaning his clothes in his toilet, he wrote, when a guard named Jack McMillian, using racially abusive language, ordered him to stop flushing and to go to sleep. Convinced he was doing nothing wrong, Mr. Hudson kept doing his laundry.

Mr. McMillian promptly placed him in handcuffs and shackles and began transporting him to a more isolated cell known as the dungeon. On the way, the guard threw Mr. Hudson against a wall. "Hold him," Mr. McMillian told another guard. "Let me knock his gold teeth out." As Mr. McMillian punched Mr. Hudson in the mouth, a third guard looked on amusedly. "Don't have too much fun!" he told the other guards.

The pummeling split his lip, broke his dental plate and left him "bleeding and swelling about the face and bruised about the body," Mr. Hudson wrote in a typewritten account dotted with misspellings, typos, fractured grammar and uneven margins. He said he quickly filed a complaint seeking "fifty thousand dollors" in damages and an order to "prohibit further crulity to myself and other inmates housed at Camp J."

At a hearing in March 1987, Mr. Hudson produced and questioned two corroborating witnesses, cited his rights under the First, Eighth and Fourteenth Amendments to the Constitution, recounted the guards' racist, crude, curse-ridden comments, and told the judge that he had suffered "not only mental and physical anguish but a permanent psychological scar for life."

Convinced, the judge awarded Mr. Hudson $800 in damages. But in July 1990, a three-judge panel of the Federal Court of Appeals for the Fifth Circuit reversed the decision. The judges—Henry A. Politz, W. Eugene Davis and Rhesa H. Barksdale—concluded that the force the guards used was unreasonable, excessive, unnecessary, wanton— and constitutional. Mr. Hudson asked the Supreme Court to review the case.

In his typewritten petition, he contended that the appellate judges had misread the Constitution. "This ruling falls short, because of its negligence in also considering the 'mental injury' sustained, which is more significant than physical damage," he argued. The Court resoundingly agreed.

Although 65 percent of the prison's 5,200 inmates are illiterate, word has spread around Angola—once a plantation named after the African country—that one of its own had secured an important legal victory. Word has also quickly spread that one of the two Justices dissenting in the case was Clarence Thomas, who, like Mr. Hudson and 85 percent of Angola's residents, is black.

"This guy has forgotten his roots, or may remember them too well and, like many black professionals, is trying to distance himself from them," said Wilbert Rideau, editor of The Angolite, the prison's news magazine. "There's no sense of obligation, no sensitivity, no nothing. We might have had a better deal with David Duke on the Court."

From Mr. Hudson's cell in Camp J, there is only silence—except, perhaps, for the tapping of a typewriter. ❑

IN HONORING HIS PARENTS, THE ROSENBERGS' YOUNGER SON FINDS A MISSION FOR HIMSELF.

7/16/93

SPRINGFIELD, Mass.—WHEN HE GOES ON THE ROAD THESE DAYS, ROBERT Meeropol has two stock speeches.

The first, entitled "Crime of the Century: The Trial and Execution of Ethel and Julius Rosenberg and the End of the Cold War," is pretty much the one he has given the past 20 years, ever since disclosing that he was the younger of the two sons the Rosenbergs left behind.

But the 46-year-old Mr. Meeropol says his second spiel—"Realizing the Dream: Overcoming a Traumatic Childhood and Corporate Law"—excites him more. In it, he recounts how, after having been orphaned at 6, adrift at 33 and a frustrated lawyer at 40, he has fashioned a fitting monument to his parents—one meant to spare other children from what he had to endure.

Three years ago Mr. Meeropol—who kept the name of the couple that adopted him and his older brother, Michael, after the Rosenbergs were killed—left his Springfield law firm to create the Rosenberg Fund for Children, whose stated purpose is "to provide for the educational and emotional needs of children whose parents have been harassed, injured, lost jobs, or died in the course of their progressive activities."

By the time of the 40th anniversary of the Rosenbergs' execution in June, what was a middle-of-the-night inspiration for Mr. Meeropol had become his life's work. The fund will soon have awarded nearly $50,000 to several dozen children. They are black, white, Hispanic and American Indian children, the sons and daughters of political activists, prisoners, assassination victims, refugees and union organizers. The grants, ranging from $180 to $2,000, cover everything from school tuition to music lessons.

For instance, a $900 grant will enable two children of a black woman who lost her job with the Los Angeles Police Department after complaining of racism in the force to return to summer camp. These children, like most grant recipients, are not named.

"We don't have any poster children in this," Mr. Meeropol said. "One of the things that saved Michael and me was that the press went away."

To date Mr. Meeropol, who receives $30,000 a year for his work, has collected $185,000 from 5,300 donors for the fund's endowment. Eventually, he hopes to raise $1 million, enough to award a total of $100,000 annually to 100 children. The task could consume the rest of his life, a life that has already outlasted his mother's by 9 years and his father's by 11.

"When people come up to me and say, 'You look like your father' or 'You look like your mother'—and it's purely random; 50 percent say one and 50 percent the other—I reply: 'Yes. But older,' " he said.

In the three years it took to arrest, prosecute, convict and electrocute their parents, Robert Meeropol and his brother bounced between grandparents, friends and orphanages. They eventually landed with Abel and Anne Meeropol, a writer and teacher in Manhattan. (Abel Meeropol wrote such songs as "Strange Fruit" and "The House I Live In" from which both his adopted sons still receive royalties. Both adoptive parents are now dead.)

Throughout the 1970's Mr. Meeropol, who has a master's degree in anthropology from the University of Michigan, worked to reopen his parents' case. Then, concerned about living a life merely as someone else's son and intent on becoming the kind of father his father never had the chance to be, he enrolled in Western New England College School of Law in Springfield. He joked of specializing in "left-wing estate planning." Instead, he toiled in tax and corporate law, work that was uncongenial but useful for his current tasks.

Time passes. Michael Meeropol's two children are grown and Robert's are not far behind; come September Ethel and Julius Rosenberg will have one granddaughter at Harvard and another at Wesleyan. Judge Irving Kaufman, Roy Cohn, the Soviet Union—all are gone.

But to Robert Meeropol—whose memories of his parents, which come almost entirely from prison visits, are hazy—things like guilt and innocence no longer loom so large. "Just clearing my parents' name—while that's important to me, I don't know what that creates," he said. The fund excites him precisely because it promises to turn tragedy into something positive.

It also has given him a chance to honor his mother's admonition, contained in her last letter to her sons before her electrocution, a letter beginning, "Dearest Sweethearts, my most precious children," a letter Mr. Meeropol can quote from memory.

"She wrote, 'We were comforted in the sure knowledge that others would carry on after us,' " he said. "The Rosenberg Fund for Children is my attempt to make sure that others carry on after me." ❑

THROUGH A GLASS, FURTIVELY:
THE 'PEEPHOLE LAWYER'
TAKES ON HOLIDAY INN.

10/16/92

NORTH CHARLESTON, S.C.—E. PAUL GIBSON IS A MARITIME LAWYER, A Navy veteran with a master's degree in the law of admiralty. But nowadays the 38-year-old Mr. Gibson is as much of an authority on peepholes as on portholes.

Mr. Gibson represents 21 people who say that the rooms of the Holiday Inns they patronized in South Carolina, Tennessee and Florida were riddled with peepholes, and that voyeuristic or dishonest employees could use the peepholes to monitor their every move. Mr. Gibson's clients have taken the hotelier to court.

Legally, the cases might sound suspect, particularly because none of the plaintiffs can prove anyone saw them do anything. Instead, it is Holiday Inn that has been caught with its pants down. Earlier this year a jury awarded $10.1 million in damages to five of Mr. Gibson's clients, members of a country-rock band called Sons of the South, who discovered peepholes behind a vanity mirror in the Holiday Inn in Walterboro, S.C.

The trial judge later trimmed the award to $500,000. But the highly publicized case was to peephole litigation what the shelling of nearby Fort Sumter was to the Civil War. Now nary a day passes in which Mr. Gibson does not hear from another traveler convinced of having been spied upon in a hotel room. Mr. Gibson said thousands of rooms in hotels—Holiday Inns and others—have designs identical to the Walterboro model, in which service corridors separate two rows of guest rooms. Snoops can enter these D.M.Z.'s, drill through the Sheetrock walls, remove the silver coating on the mirrors' reverse side and play Peeping Tom.

Mr. Gibson is taking on the hotel chain with ambivalence. As a Navy brat he traveled extensively with his parents, and always, Holiday Inns were like oases. In those early Eisenhower days, when roadside standardization was still a novelty, everything about Holiday Inns— the swimming pools, the sanitized drinking glasses, the lobster dinners complete with illustrated plastic bibs, the mass-produced

Rembrandts, the paper seal around the toilet seat—smacked of cleanliness and class. "Staying in a Holiday Inn was like being in high cotton," Mr. Gibson recalled wistfully.

But since then the company has been absorbed by Bass P.L.C., a British conglomerate. And in the process, Mr. Gibson contends, hospitality gave way to hostility. Rather than apologize, they stonewalled.

"For some reason, treating people with a modicum of human decency seems to be something large corporations have forgotten," he said. "The ethic of the 1980's was, 'Get yourself a smart lawyer and I'll see you in court.' "

Heyward McDonald of Columbia, S.C., counsel for the Walterboro Holiday Inn, declined to comment.

In April 1990, when the five musicians came to Mr. Gibson and told him about the peepholes, he was initially unimpressed, even though the sheriff who had investigated their complaint found hundreds of peepholes. "I was certain that the hotel would acknowledge the problem, blame it on some rogue employee and take steps to improve things," he said. "Saying you're sorry is an incredibly powerful defense."

Instead, the hotel presented a defense with more layers than a slice of baklava. There weren't any peepholes, it argued. Or if there were, they were construction holes. Or if they were peepholes, they were too small to see through. Or if you could see through them, no one ever did. Or if someone did look through them, we didn't know about it. Or what they saw hadn't hurt anybody.

At the trial, the jury learned of similar complaints at Holiday Inns throughout he country; that an inspector had regularly cited the Walterboro franchise for de-silvered mirrors but had never ventured into the service corridor because she was afraid of spiders, and that piles of cigarette butts could be found beneath some holes. "There must have been something real interesting going on in that room," Mr. Gibson surmised.

But the most important exhibits were a videotape taken through a typical peephole, in which a woman was clearly visible, and a scale model of a typical vanity, complete with peepholes, through which the jurors could look at one another during their deliberations.

In some ways, Mr. Gibson confessed, handling these cases is warping his Weltanschauung. No longer can he stay comfortably in Holiday Inns, and wherever he does wind up for the night he thoroughly looks the place over beforehand.

He also says he is getting rather tired of peepholes. "I'd be happy to pass the title of 'peephole lawyer' to someone else," he said.

But Mr. Gibson promised to persist. "The day Holiday Inn announces they have a problem and are taking steps to stop it, that's the last they'll hear of Paul Gibson," he declared. "But until that day, as long as they deny everything and call decent people liars, I will continue to dog them." ❑

Twenty-five additional lawsuits, against Days Inn and Motel 6 as well as Holiday Inn, came into Mr. Gibson's office. Those, and all the others, were eventually settled for between $15,000 to $20,000 apiece. Holiday Inn ultimately admitted to the problem, and directed its managers to inspect their premises for peepholes.

As he nears 90, Witkin (and 'Witkin')
remains a lighthouse
to California's lawyers.

11/19/93

BERKELEY, CALIF.—BERNARD E. WITKIN, THE MAN WHO KNOWS MORE about California law than anyone alive, was speaking about all the "adulation sessions" being held for him these days. "They're becoming more frequent as people take a more realistic view of my limited life expectancy," he said. At a love-in given by the Alameda County Bar Association, the 89-year-old Mr. Witkin confronted his own mortality.

"I told them, 'The race is nearly over, and it's time for me to turn over my task to others,' and there was a deadly silence," he recalled. " 'I have decided to retire'—I paused in order to let the silence grow more deadly—'in the year 2001.' "

It was a typical moment for Mr. Witkin, who is nearly as well known in California legal circles for his wit as for his writings. Though Mr. Witkin cut more law school classes than he attended, though he never really represented any clients or argued a case or played professor or sat behind a bench, his books on California law have been cited more often in the state's courts than Mr. Blackstone's ever were in England's—by some estimates, more than 100,000 times. When California's lawyers do research, they usually begin with him; some say it is malpractice not to.

Sixty-five years ago, Mr. Witkin ran off a mimeographed two-volume summary of California law, based on the bar review course he was teaching, and sold it for $15. He has been revising ever since, and in the process his treatise has ballooned into 32 volumes totaling 33,000 pages. Collectively, the books are known simply as "Witkin," and they sit in thousands of law libraries from Yreka to Chula Vista.

Roger Traynor, Matthew Tobriner, Raymond Sullivan, Stanley Mosk, Otto Kaus and other luminaries of the California judiciary—Mr. Witkin has read virtually their every word, along with those of hundreds of lesser judicial lights. Then, working in his home here overlooking San Francisco Bay, he has sat down at his Royal typewriter, distilled each opinion to its essence, placed it in the firmament of state law and related it to what was already there. "The law is a seamless web, and Witkin is the only spider who knows all the threads," an admirer once wrote.

Mr. Witkin's desire to lay out the law, accessibly but intelligently, grew from his frustration with what he considered the intellectual gamesmanship of his own legal education at the University of California at Berkeley. Though he sees some movement toward practicality, he thinks that elite law schools remain temples of obfuscation, and the cushy lives of their professors, he believes, explain why there are no others like Mr. Witkin in California and few, if any, anywhere else. "The best minds capable of doing this prefer the happier life of a law school professor, which is relaxed and philosophical and enjoyable," he said. "This thing takes discipline. I've worked incessantly."

Just as he has believed that legal academia prepares students poorly for practice, he believes practice prepares lawyers poorly for judging. As a result, he helped create and finance a foundation on judicial education. For new judges, reading Mr. Witkin's manual on appellate court opinions has been as much an initiation rite as ordering robes.

A native of Holyoke, Mass., who came to California at the age of 5, Mr. Witkin said he was never tempted to practice law. "I could have learned that racket, but it would have been narrow and unrewarding, and I would have tired of it very quickly," he said. Instead, he built a bar review course, then became the State Supreme Court's reporter of decisions, all the while working on his summaries. In 1949, he began devoting himself to them full time.

Tens of thousands of opinions later, he said he still considers legal opinions "more interesting than any fiction other than 'The Lord of the Rings.' " Though his long inventory of infirmities—"If I'd known I was going to live so long, I'd have taken better care of myself"—includes fading eyesight, he said he ranks court decisions above even Roller Derby and "Star Trek: The Next Generation" on his list of must-sees.

The Royal remains at the ready, but Mr. Witkin uses it less frequently now. After many anxious years, he finally thinks he has instructed the 13 lawyers and staff members who make up the "Witkin Department" at Bancroft-Whitney Law Publishers in San Francisco to carry on the work he once did by himself. Besides teaching he is bequeathing.

The more the law was complicated by judges and legislators, the wealthier Mr. Witkin became—former Chief Justice Rose Bird, one of the few California jurists he has criticized, once called him "a legend with profit in his own time"—and his books have made him millions of dollars, several of which he and his wife have already given away.

Twenty years ago the state judges association issued a medal naming Mr. Witkin "Guru to the California Judiciary" ("They didn't know how to spell 'maven,' " he theorized). But recently the praise has grown even more gushing.

Last month alone, Representative Robert T. Matsui saluted Mr. Witkin in Congress, and the California Legislature pronounced him "one of the world's unique and irreplaceable treasures." The keynote speaker at a toast in Sacramento boasted of the time he'd been called "a walking Witkin." (That called to mind the lawyer's wife who once complained of being a "Witkin Widow.") The State Bar of California created a "Witkin Award," forged a medal with his likeness and named him its first recipient.

"I only wish I had a nickel for every time the phrase 'go check Witkin' has been uttered in this state!" Ronald Reagan wrote him.

Mr. Witkin greeted these and all the other hosannas with what he calls "ostentatious modesty." Of the medal, for instance, he said he'd never seen a likeness of himself he did not like. "I don't go out of my way to deprecate compliments," he said.

Indeed, he suggested that his life's work could be reduced to two index entries: "LAW, see Witkin"; and "WITKIN, see Law." ❑

XI

NOOKS
AND
CRANNIES

THE TANTALIZING BOGGS CASE: ONE BALLPLAYER, TWO WOMEN AND THREE NATIONAL PASTIMES.

3/3/89

BASEBALL, SEX AND LITIGATION. THEY ARE THREE OF AMERICA'S NATIONAL pastimes, and they are all on the docket of a Southern California lawyer names James McGee.

Mr. McGee represents Margo Adams, the onetime lover and traveling companion of Wade Boggs, who has filed suit against the Boston Red Sox's celebrated third baseman in the wake of their breakup. As such, Mr. McGee is the architect of perhaps the country's best-known pending court case.

For Mr. McGee, a serious, intense man of 37 years, the hoopla of the Boggs case is far removed from the usual torpor of corporate litigation. And things heated up still further recently, when Penthouse magazine printed Ms. Adams's steamy memoirs.

For Ms. Adams, a 34-year-old onetime mortgage broker, the article, entitled "Designated Swinger," was both lucrative and cathartic, casting Mr. Boggs as the most villainous ballplayer since Shoeless Joe Jackson. But for Mr. McGee, it marked only the latest in a series of strikes against his client.

Already the courts have hacked away at what was once a $12 million case. Mr. McGee fears that kiss-and-tell memoirs may not play well to jurors in Orange County, where the airport is named for John Wayne. Nor should things improve when, as Penthouse says, "Margo Adams bares all" in next month's issue.

Mr. Boggs's lawyer, Jennifer King of Tustin, Calif., calls the suit "extortion" and says it should never have been brought. "Anybody can sue anybody for anything, but it's something lawyers shouldn't get away with," said Ms. King, who calls herself a "bimbo buster." "Mr. McGee's too smart to believe there's a legitimate cause of action here."

But Mr. McGee, who grew up in Montclair, N.J., sees nothing frivolous in the case. Besides, he must know that whatever its outcome, the sins and silliness of clients rarely rub off on their lawyers. Where sex meets law, any publicity is good publicity.

Indeed, in recent months he has been besieged by calls from the jilted lovers of philandering sportsmen, who play hockey, football and basketball as well as baseball.

Mr. McGee calls the Boggs matter "a standard, albeit not garden variety, oral contract case." But to collect the $500,000 to which he says his client is entitled, for lost income and services, he must spot in California case law what Ted Williams managed to find whenever he singled through Lou Boudreau's Cleveland Indians infield: an exceedingly small hole.

Under the Lee Marvin "palimony" decision, there can be no cash awards for lost sexual services. Nor can there be compensation for the value of emotional sustenance as long as the couple cohabitates. That explains why Mr. McGee's court papers seem prudish, if not bowdlerized. Nowhere do words like "paramour" or "mistress" appear. Instead, he terms the tie a "business relationship," with Ms. Adams playing chauffeur, financial adviser, travel agent, autograph broker, clothier, valet, seamstress, washerwoman—everything, in short, but lover.

All these duties paled next to what is, in Mr. McGee's case, perhaps her most important task: to placate the army of leprechauns, demons and dybbuks that apparently guide Mr. Boggs. If anything, his ranking for superstitiousness is even higher than for career batting, where he currently places fifth on the all-time list. In 64 road trips over four seasons, Mr. McGee contends, Ms. Adams made sure Mr. Boggs got certain lucky hotel rooms with certain lucky layouts, placed herself in certain lucky seats, drove him to the ballpark along certain lucky routes, wore certain lucky clothes of certain lucky colors, and made sure he ate only certain lucky foods, especially chicken.

Simply keeping track of all these things was serious business. "It's one thing to order a pizza for someone, and another to order dinner for Wade Boggs," Mr. McGee asserted. And it worked: when she was with Mr. Boggs, he batted .341, as opposed to the anemic .221 he hit when accompanied by his wife.

Mr. McGee explored the subject further in Mr. Boggs's deposition. (In his 14-hour deposition, Mr. Boggs's legendary concentration was displayed: he looked at Ms. Adams only once.) While Penthouse's questions for Ms. Adams sounded like "The Newlywed Game"— "What was your first date like?" "How was your sex life?"—Mr. McGee's poultry probe seemed better suited to an interrogation of Frank Purdue.

Were there, as Mr. Boggs had once stated, "hits in chicken?" How did chicken help his hitting? Did Ms. Adams cook it for him on the road? How did she prepare it? Mr. Boggs, author of a recipe book called "Fowl Tips," explained that lemon chicken, chicken cacciatore or barbequed chicken worked best, but that other birds were turkeys.

"I think I had duck one time," he explained. "I went 0 for 4." ❑

That December, Judge James Gray of Orange County Superior Court dismissed Ms. Adams's case and placed a gag order on both players. Ms. Adams reportedly married the Penthouse photographer; Mr. Boggs moved from Fenway Park to Yankee Stadium, but still eats chicken and bats .300.

THE BAR CHIEF CONFRONTS HIS
BELIEF IN FREE SPEECH WHEN HIS
DAUGHTER EXPRESSES HERSELF, OPENLY.

9/6/91

BY AND LARGE, PRESIDENTS OF THE AMERICAN BAR ASSOCIATION LEAD good, staid lives. They travel first class, hobnob with politicians and dignitaries, speechify on safe subjects. But Talbot (Sandy) D'Alemberte, a partner in the Miami firm of Steel, Hector & Davis, has been president of the bar group barely a month and has already faced his first flap, one he could never have anticipated in his nearly lifelong quest for the post.

It came this week, when the October issue of Playboy hit the newsstands. In it there is a photograph of his daughter, 21-year-old Gabrielle. She is featured in an article on "The Girls of the Big Ten," and she is almost entirely unclad.

Both the A.B.A. and Hugh Hefner's Playboy empire are based in Chicago. And both entities are all for the First Amendment. Beyond that, though, they are an incongruous match. A few years ago the two organizations briefly shared office space but the bar group quickly skedaddled—at least partly because traditionalists and feminists within it were uncomfortable working in a building with a bunny on it.

But with the publication of this month's Playboy, the two are joined anew. Ms. D'Alemberte can be seen on page 143, bare-breasted, dressed in unzipped denim cutoffs and standing in what appears to be the backyard of an Iowa farmhouse. In her hand is a blue-jean jacket, with the words "Kiss Me" stitched on. "Gabrielle D'Alemberte came to the U of Iowa from Miami—and has yet to slow down," the caption states. "A former member of the Pompom Squad and a Gamma Phi Beta sorority sister, she has auditioned for 'Santa Barbara' and would love to be a Laker Girl."

The appearance of the bar president's daughter in such surroundings has caused its fair share of snickering and Schadenfreude both inside and outside the A.B.A. This is particularly so given some of the stances the 58-year-old Mr. D'Alemberte has taken—positions considerably easier to espouse when one's own daughter is not involved.

He has always championed women's rights, particularly within the legal profession and court system. While dean of Florida State University Law School, he helped initiate and finance the first statewide survey of sexism within the state's courts. The Playboy philosophy, he said, is "quite contradictory" to what he stands for himself. He has also served on the A.B.A.'s commission on women in the profession. Moreover, he has fought for press freedoms on behalf of clients like The Miami Herald, The Palm Beach Post and Post-Newsweek Corporation.

That he seems certain to ride out the hubbub is a sign of how much the once-stuffy bar group has changed. So, for that matter, was its unanimous selection of Mr. D'Alemberte, a steady backer of federally financed legal services for the poor, increased counsel for death row inmates and other civil libertarian issues.

And if the brouhaha is ephemeral, it will also reflect the directness with which he has faced and defused an embarrassing situation. Rather than issue press releases or surround himself with spin doctors, Mr. D'Alemberte has spoken of the episode freely, confronting simultaneously his love for his daughter, their own pained relationship, his unhappiness with her decision and his concern for her well-being.

"This is a choice she made, and it would not have been my choice," said Mr. D'Alemberte, who said he had still not looked at the magazine. "I'd rather see her emphasizing her talents than relying on her good looks. But most of us who've been parents have been through some heartache and most of us who've been young have made mistakes ourselves."

Ms. D'Alemberte says she never told Playboy officials who her father was and considered using a fake name to protect him. In a telephone interview between calls from "A Current Affair" and "The Maury Povich Show," she said she was "more or less exhilarated" by the experience. "My father's not happy, but on the other hand he realizes that I'm 21 years old and very capable of making judgments for myself," she said.

In some ways, she conceded, she is not like her father; she is a registered Republican and does not consider herself a feminist. But like him, she said, she is headstrong and wants eventually to be a lawyer. Nothing, she said, should preclude a woman who likes wearing makeup and short skirts and otherwise flaunting her femininity from becoming a respected and respectable member of the bar.

The whole episode, in fact, has given Jeff Cohen, Playboy's managing photo editor, some food for thought. "Maybe it's time to do a 'Women of the Bar,' " he said. "Hmm. I like that." ❏

HOW THREE MISSING ZEROS BROUGHT
RED FACES AND COST MILLIONS OF DOLLARS.

10/4/91

THE CABLE READ: PARDON. IMPOSSIBLE TO BE SENT TO SIBERIA.

In one of his famous "Believe It or Not" columns, Robert Ripley wrote about that cable, and how a man's life had been spared when some Czarist apparatchik mistakenly placed the period after the first word of it instead of after the second.

The occasionally errant typography emerging from New York's corporate law firms rarely has such life-and-death consequences. But the omission of three figures from a routine mortgage agreement five years ago, a mistake overlooked by numerous supposedly crackerjack lawyers at several New York law firms, has generated a spate of litigation, hundreds of thousands of dollars in legal fees, millions of dollars in damages and an untold fortune in embarrassment.

What Erle Stanley Gardner might have called "The Case of the Terrible Typo" began in the early 1980's, when both the Prudential Insurance Company and the General Electric Capital Corporation lent money to United States Lines. A fleet of ships was the collateral, with Prudential holding first dibs in the event of foreclosure and General Electric Capital entitled to whatever was left.

When the deal was restructured in early 1986, United States Lines still owed Prudential $92,885,000. But when a secretary at Haight, Gardner, Poor & Stevens in New York, which officially represented G.E.C.C. but by agreement of the parties was to draft the revised mortgage, typed up the document she forgot three crucial things: a zero, a zero and a zero. As she recorded the deal, Prudential's interest was only worth $92,885.

Even though it was ultimately repeated on almost 100 different documents, neither the Haight lawyers nor Prudential's in-house counsel spotted the mistake. Nor did the insurance company's outside counsel, at Dewey, Ballantine, Bushby, Palmer & Wood. Nor did the lawyers for United States Lines, from Gilmartin, Poster & Shafto. James R. Gillen, Prudential's general counsel, called the oversight "astonishing."

In November 1986, United States Lines went bankrupt. But while its problems were thereby temporarily placed on hold, Prudential's had just begun. First the shipping company argued that under the clear terms of the mortgage, Prudential's interest in its ships was a matter of thousands, not millions of dollars. It was a powerful claim, particularly because under a quirk in the bankruptcy law, whatever United States Lines actually knew about the parties' intent was irrelevant.

Nowhere in the voluminous court records is it disclosed who discovered the missing zeros. But rather than put its entire entitlement at risk, Prudential gave United States Lines $11.4 million of the $65.4 million it raised from the sale of the ships to drop the claim.

Then in March 1988, G.E.C.C., too, tried cashing in on the mistake. In what Manhattan Lawyer magazine called "the kind of claim that only a lawyer could love," General Electric Capital insisted that Prudential should get the smaller amount, thereby leaving G.E.C.C. tens of millions of dollars it wouldn't have otherwise gotten.

The lawyer for General Electric Capital, Nathan Bayer of Freehill, Hogan & Mahar, made the argument, but only after assuring Federal District Judge Richard Owen he could still "look himself in the mirror" after doing so. Prudential eventually prevailed in two Federal courts, but not before it had forked over hefty fees to another set of lawyers, at Weil, Gotshal & Manges.

What with the payment to United States Lines, its own legal fees and the costs of holding on to and maintaining ships it would otherwise have sold, Prudential reckoned that the typo had cost it at least $31 million. In September 1989, the insurance company, represented by Howrey & Simon of Washington, sued Haight, Gardner; Dewey, Ballantine; and Gilmartin, Poster for malpractice. All three, of course, had thereupon to hire counsel of their own: Parker, Chapin, Flattau & Kimpl (for Dewey, Ballantine); Gair, Gair & Conason (for Haight, Gardner), and Bower & Gardner (for Gilmartin, Poster).

A State Supreme Court Justice dismissed Prudential's claim against Gilmartin, Poster, a decision the company is appealing to New York's highest court. Meantime, Haight, Gardner and Dewey, Ballantine have quietly bought peace from Prudential. As is usually the case when lawyers make mistakes, the settlement is shrouded in secrecy.

"I'd really like to talk you out of doing an article about this," said Dewey, Ballantine's managing partner, L. Robert Fullem, who described the episode as "really unnewsworthy," saying it was "just a plain typographical error that we've resolved."

William J. Honan 3d, a member of Haight, Gardner's management committee, was marginally forthcoming, declaring that whatever his firm shelled out was "well, well within" the firm's malpractice insurance coverage. He also disclosed that the firm knew the name of the erring secretary. He described her as contrite. He also said her current whereabouts were unknown. ❏

IN 'REGARDING HENRY,' ART IMITATED LIFE. OR SO SAY A COUPLE WHO HAVE LIVED THE LIFE.

2/18/94

IF THERE WERE AN ACADEMY AWARD FOR LAWYER MOVIES, THE 1991 FILM "Regarding Henry," starring Harrison Ford, would garner few votes. But its premise, at least, was provocative. It is that an exceedingly obnoxious and dishonest lawyer can suddenly become a nice guy—that he can stop philandering, swaggering, suppressing evidence, abusing his secretary and neglecting his family—but only after his brains have been blown out by a robber.

The unconvincing nature of the transformation was only one of the film's many problems. But to at least one viewer, Joan Cox of Evansville, Ind., the story was all too painfully plausible. In fact, she had lived through it twice: first when her own husband, a lawyer, suffered brain damage in a traffic accident, and then when she turned their experience into a 325-page manuscript.

"It was devastating to sit there and watch this thing," she said, recalling the night she and her husband played "Regarding Henry" on their videocassette recorder. "At first I thought all the similarities were just a coincidence. But pretty soon I was pacing around and saying, 'There's that scene!' And my husband was saying, 'There's another scene!' We turned it off and looked at each other and thought, 'This is just unreal.' "

So last fall, long after it had been deservedly relegated to the back shelves of Blockbuster Video, "Regarding Henry" began a run in Federal District Court in New York. Mrs. Cox and her husband, John, had sued the film's screenwriter, Jeffrey Abrams, along with its producers, Mike Nichols and Scott Rudin, and Paramount Pictures on grounds of copyright infringement, misappropriation and assorted other infractions.

In their suit, the plaintiffs list 112 ways in which the stories of the fictional Henry Turner and the real-life John Cox coincide. Many concern the nature of the injury and the symptoms afterward—drooling out of the left side of their mouths, dragging their left legs, failing to recognize their wives or remembering what was where in their old closets, acting oddly enough that people who had once held them in awe now dismissed them as "retards."

Each man's law firm is depicted as similarly treacherous, demoting him to a smaller office, denying him access to his old files. Professional colleagues, too, are similar: in the words of the complaint, "unscrupulous, want to win at all costs and avaricious." And each man undergoes the same involuntary metamorphosis. "Unlikable pretrauma and becomes very likable by end," says No. 45 on the Coxes' list of similarities.

The Coxes face a problem: they cannot explain how the manuscript found its way into the hands of Mr. Abrams, the film's screenwriter. But Carl Person of New York, who is representing the couple, says copyright law holds that if the similarities between two products are striking, then access to the original can be inferred. "If you don't think these similarities are 'striking,' " he said, "then I don't know what 'striking' means."

Fifteen years ago, Mr. Cox, then 36, was flying high. A handsome and charismatic man, he had put together a successful law practice, had served in the Indiana Legislature and, a few years earlier, had been named corporation counsel of Evansville. As a result of all that, he was a fixture on local television. And all the success, his wife says, went to his head. "My husband was an arrogant ass," she recalled. "He was kind of on an ego trip."

But things changed on July 2, 1979, when a car hit his motorcycle, throwing him 28 feet. For a month he was unconscious. When he came to, he was paralyzed and could not speak. It took him nearly two years, filled with various therapies and constant ministration by his wife, to get him back to his law office. Now he has a practice of his own, negotiating his way around by walker and wheelchair. "A movie ought to be made about your life," Mrs. Cox says she once told her husband.

And so one was. Or so she claims.

For solace and catharsis, Mrs. Cox had recorded her thoughts during her husband's rehabilitation. "I was writing a page a night," she said, "while taking care of four kids, helping start his law practice and stirring the chicken noodle soup with my left foot." After three years, she sent off to various publishers a manuscript that she called "Breaking the Tape." All rejected it.

In 1989, she says, she tried again, sending the manuscript this time to Daphne Merkin, then an associate publisher at Harcourt Brace Jovanovich. This time it took 15 months for the rejection to arrive. Ms. Merkin, the Coxes' suit says, "had frequent contact with movie producers seeking properties upon which to base a movie or screenplay." During those 15 months, the Coxes surmise, the book found its way to

Mr. Abrams, and a real-life lawyer redeemed by brain damage became the basis for a fictional one.

Ms. Merkin says she does not even remember "Breaking the Tape," and laughs off the suggestion that she forwarded it to friends in Hollywood. "If I had the access to these movie producers that this woman delusionally imagines," she said, "my whole life would be different."

None of the defendants would comment on the case. But their lawyer, Les Fagen of Paul, Weiss, Rifkind, Wharton & Garrison in New York, called the suit "meritless" and said he would soon ask the court to dismiss it. "Nobody connected with this motion picture ever heard of the Coxes before this lawsuit was brought," he said. ❑

HE IS A VIRTUOSO ON THE
COURTROOM KEYS, BUT HE MAY BE
PLAYING AN ENDANGERED INSTRUMENT.

12/11/92

THERE ARE NOT MANY MEMORABLE MOMENTS IN HIS 25 YEARS IN THE MANhattan Surrogate's Court that Nathaniel Weiss has failed to record. Whether art experts were testifying in the Estate of Mark Rothko, or Al Pacino was testifying in the Estate of Lee Strasberg or 15 workers were disrupting the proceedings in the Estate of J. Seward Johnson, Mr. Weiss, his fingers dancing over the keyboard of his trusty stenograph, got it down.

Last May, however, something occurred that even Mr. Weiss missed documenting. In a cost-cutting measure, Matthew Crosson, chief administrator of New York's courts, replaced Mr. Weiss and 36 other court reporters in the state's Surrogate's Courts with tape recorders.

Mr. Crosson, it is true, merely transferred Mr. Weiss and his colleagues to other local courts. But they face a far more implacable foe in New York's Comptroller, Edward V. Regan, who last month labeled stenographic reporting "an anachronism" and called for jettisoning it.

Court reporters, their views seconded by many judges and lawyers, argue that electronic recording is unreliable, cumbersome and more costly. They note, too, that most of them, Mr. Weiss included, now use computers to transcribe their notes. But for court reporters seeking to defend their craft and preserve their jobs, Mr. Weiss himself is perhaps the best exhibit of all. For half a century, through a combination of erudition, wisdom, curiosity, conscientiousness and an insatiable love of words, he has given judges, lawyers and litigants what is by common consensus a most consistent and reliable recapitulation of reality.

Mr. Weiss is one of those increasingly rare reporters who need not spell out "Brobdingnagian" or "epimenorrhea" or "in pari passu" phonetically until he can look them up in a dictionary. Better than just about anyone, he manages the increasingly difficult task of capturing and clarifying what decreasingly articulate lawyers and witnesses seem to say.

He is a nimble practitioner of linguistic triage, choosing what matters most when lawyers, judges and witnesses speak at once. He can understand mumbles, the jargons of various professions, the thickest Ukrainian accent. He knows whether laughter or tears or screams or italics belong in the record or whether they intrude on it. But his greatest attribute is his inconspicuousness.

By personality and temperament, Mr. Weiss's peers are no more given to hyperbole than he is. But to William Cohen, a 45-year veteran of the trade who works in Federal District Court in Manhattan, Mr. Weiss is "the finest court reporter in the English-speaking world." Befuddled periodically by some lawyerly malapropism or neologism or unintelligible burble, Mr. Cohen, like many others, invariably asks Mr. Weiss for help.

Perhaps because they rarely get the respect they deserve, court reporters stick together. They have their own clubs, their own publications, their own rituals and role models. Sometimes they are quite literally family; the profession is filled with siblings, husbands and wives, fathers and sons. Mr. Cohen's twin brother, Arnold, is also a renowned reporter; Mr. Weiss's son, Robert, works in Family Court.

In 1939, when the elder Mr. Weiss was still in Brooklyn College and the country did not quite realize it was out of the Depression, he saw shorthand as a route to a steady job. Three times, in 1958, 1959 and 1960, Mr. Weiss won the speed contest given by the National Shorthand Reporters Association. Twice he matched the mark for accuracy set in 1926 by one Martin Dupraw, who still transcribes part time in Westchester County. After turning it down for years, in 1986 Mr. Weiss accepted the New York State Court Reporters Association's Louis Goldstein Memorial Award honoring contributions to court reporting.

His landmark 1963 guide to medical terminology, for instance, teaches reporters how, by understanding prefixes, suffixes and roots, they can differentiate between a colotomy, a colostomy and a colectomy and handle an occasional jejunojejunostomy as well. His 1971 study of punctuation contains individual chapters on paragraphing, colons, semicolons, question marks and quotation marks, plus two chapters on different sorts of dashes and five chapters on commas.

The bar is a status-conscious breed, and throughout his career, Mr. Weiss has been largely overlooked—or, on occasion, barked at—by people who, for all their skills at bombast and legerdemain, may be nowhere near his intellectual equal. In no way has that, nor his profession's recent trials, diminished his enthusiasm.

"Anatole France said that 'children are the unrecognized geniuses of the world,' and reporters are the unrecognized human computers of the court system," Mr. Weiss said. ❏

After some political maneuvering, the court reporters seem poised to return to their jobs, but Mr. Weiss will not be among them. He is due to retire in March 1995, after 52 years of conscientiousness.

FOR A FALTERING PIONEER IN JURY SELECTION, THE SMITH CASE PROVIDES NEW INSPIRATION.

11/22/91

IT IS BITTERSWEET INDEED TO RECEIVE A LIFETIME ACHIEVEMENT AWARD AT the age of 40.

This month, Cathy Bennett put aside her tasks in West Palm Beach, where she is helping William Kennedy Smith select the six people who will decide his fate. She went to New Orleans, where the National Association of Criminal Defense Lawyers honored her for her contributions to the evolving art of picking juries.

There was a certain urgency to the ceremony. Five and a half years ago, Cat Bennett learned she had breast cancer. The disease has since metastasized to her lymph nodes, her bones, her stomach, her intestines, her skin. In late October, only a few days before the luncheon and the beginning of jury selection in the Smith case, a doctor warned that unless she resumed her chemotherapy, she could die within a month.

But Ms. Bennett quickly concluded that living mattered less to her than living with herself, and to her, that meant serving her client. She checked herself out of the Houston hospital and went to Florida, where she sits daily alongside Mr. Smith, helping frame questions that his lawyer, Roy Black of Miami, is posing to the citizens of Palm Beach County.

By now, what might have been Ms. Bennett's last month has passed—time in which Ms. Bennett meditated, ingested 150 different kinds of herbs and took Japanese mushroom extract intravenously rather than have herself bombarded with radiation.

Those who know and love her are shocked by how pale and tired this once-vital woman now looks, and some who do not share her enthusiasm for the defendant might question whether the tawdry confrontation between Mr. Smith and his accuser provides a fitting swan song for a woman who has toiled on so many important civil rights cases. But Ms. Bennett maintains that working for Mr. Smith has given her renewed strength. She believes in his innocence, she says, and she is fond of him as well.

It was Morris Dees, the famed civil rights lawyer and longtime friend of the Kennedy family, who suggested that the defense team hire her. And it was Mr. Dees who presented Ms. Bennett with her award. He was given the job not just because he had worked with her more often than almost anyone, in various death penalty and racial discrimination cases, but because organizers of the event thought he could say the words without breaking down.

They were wrong. Mr. Dees, veteran of a thousand hostile court-rooms, faltered as he introduced her. "Come on up here, sugar," he finally said to her. "I can't do this by myself." Once she took her place, he told the group: "If Rosa Parks was the mother of the civil rights movement, Cat Bennett is the mother of modern criminal law practice in America. She has taught lawyers to be feeling, loving human beings, and that comes across to the jury."

Since beginning her work in 1974, equipped with little more than a couple of psychology degrees and an uncanny intuition about people, Ms. Bennett has helped pick scores of juries, for clients ranging from Indians at Wounded Knee to John Z. DeLorean to members of the Hell's Angels and the Irish Republican Army. Last year, she helped Mr. Dees win a $12.5 million verdict for an Ethiopian student who had been beaten by skinheads in Oregon. Jury experts like Ms. Bennett are generally luxuries that only well-heeled defendants can afford, though in the Oregon case, as in many others, Ms. Bennett worked for free.

In articles and speeches and seminars, Cat Bennett's message has been both disarmingly simple and surprisingly elusive. Picking a jury is the most crucial phase in many criminal cases. It is the time not only to learn the views of prospective jurors, but for a defense lawyer to start making his own case, to start defusing the prosecution's, to create ties to jurors.

Too often, Ms. Bennett maintains, trial lawyers are too busy putting on an act, too busy exuding omniscience and arrogance, either to listen or to learn. Thus, the jurors they select are not as sympathetic as they might be. They see through all the phoniness.

But just as jurors resent a con job, they respect what is real. She tells lawyers to ask open-ended questions, the kind through which jury candidates can disclose something about themselves. She also instructs them to be "open, sincere, vulnerable, receptive" with those they interview.

Whether Ms. Bennett's work will help Mr. Smith will not be clear until the jury returns its verdict. But there is no doubt that the case has helped her.

"This whole experience has been better for her than chemo," said her husband, Robert Hirschhorn, a lawyer who assists his wife. "Where there was cancer, there's now this love and dedication. There's no room for the cancer to grow." ❏

In December 1991, Willie Smith was acquitted. Six months later, Ms. Bennett died. Her friends at the National Association of Criminal Defense Lawyers have created both a Cathy Bennett scholarship (at its teaching arm, the National Criminal Defense College) and a law school moot court competition in her memory. One of Ms. Bennett's disciples, Jo-Ellan Dimitrius, brought new visibility to the trade: she helped O. J. Simpson's lawyers pick a jury.

In tribute to a dedicated scholar and ambassador of New York's highest court.

11/15/91

WALTER MORDAUNT NEVER SAT ON THE NEW YORK COURT OF APPEALS, OR argued before it or parsed its decisions for a law school class. But no one ever cared for it more, or studied it more lovingly, or knew so well its every alcove or imparted his erudition about it so enthusiastically. When he died last week, at the age of 72, New York's highest court lost one of its most authentic scholars as well as its most effective ambassador.

Benjamin N. Cardozo, who served as Chief Judge of the Court of Appeals from 1926 to 1932, when he was named to the United States Supreme Court, once defined the mission of New York's highest court to be "translating into law the social and economic forces that throb and clamor for expression." Too often, however, the expressions emanating from it or any other court are unintelligible to the naked eye, and the process by which they are reached incomprehensible. Sometimes, it seems, lawyers and judges prefer it that way.

It was to combat that tendency that, in 1973, Charles D. Breitel, one of Cordozo's most distinguished successors, overcame his instinctive aversion to hype and, for the first time, hired a spokesman for the court: Mr. Mordaunt, who had been a reporter for The Albany Times-Union and served as deputy press secretary to Gov. Averell Harriman. From that moment on, Mr. Mordaunt proved that to demystify need not mean to degrade or debunk.

From 7:30 or so five mornings a week for the next 17 years, until his retirement in September 1990, Mr. Mordaunt toiled away in his small office in the court's southwest corner. He took phone calls from anxious reporters, explaining a convoluted court system like New York's, in which an appeals court is supreme and a Supreme Court is inferior.

It was Mr. Mordaunt who parceled out the court's decisions, placing them on Greyhound buses for some downstate newspapers. He kept reporters apprised of the court's caseload, a task that required him to comprehend the legalese of lawyers from Tonawanda to Montauk, as well as the judges' own often impenetrable prose. Mr. Mordaunt never got a law degree—World War II precluded that—but his grasp of legal issues would have shamed many who had.

A tall and elegant man with a mellifluousness inherited from his thespian parents, he went about his work with modesty and gentlemanliness, no mean feat in the cloistered, egocentric world of the judiciary. Some spokesmen for important courts take on the coloration of the institutions they serve—the higher and more prestigious the tribunal, the more begrudgingly these people help, the more self-importantly they say no.

Mr. Mordaunt took it upon himself to explain the court's past as well as its present. A history buff who spent his spare time touring Civil War battlefields, he schooled himself in the court's law and lore, then imparted what he learned about it to thousands of schoolchildren and ordinary citizens who took his court tours.

He could tell you how the portrait of John Jay, New York's first Chief Judge, hung directly behind the seat reserved for his most recent successor, and how, from that position, Jay stares in perpetuity at Robert Livingston, New York's first chancellor, whose statue stands on the other side of the room. He would explain how the hand-carved courtroom had been designed by Henry Hobson Richardson, and been moved over piece by piece from the old state Capitol in 1916, and would point out the seven brass spittoons that still sit under the bench.

Shortly before he retired he gave one last tour to a peculiarly attentive audience: the seven judges themselves, none of whom knew nearly as much about the place as he. It was, said one of the judges, Joseph W. Bellacosa, "a showstopping finale."

So great was Mr. Mordaunt's love for the institution that even the milestones of others working there gave him personal pleasure. Sept. 12, for instance, marked the date that Judith S. Kaye, the court's first woman, had been named to the bench. Mr. Mordaunt observed the anniversary each year by bringing Judge Kaye a sprig from a florabunda rosebush in his front yard, containing the appropriate number of blossoms. Sure enough, when Judge Kaye arrived in her chambers shortly before 7 A.M. last Sept. 12, she discovered that Walter Mordaunt had preceded her. "Now, Judge!" the accompanying note scolded her, "I hope you did not think I'd forget."

All seven members of the court attended a memorial service for Mr. Mordaunt on Wednesday night in East Greenbush, across the river from Albany. "He could deal with governors or schoolchildren and show them the same concern and grace and dignity," said Chief Judge Sol Wachtler, who spoke at the service. "He opened up the court, and our process lost a lot of its mysteries. He showed them that this was not simply a sterile courthouse, but a part of history." ❑

Lawyer, hereinafter
"Broken Heart,"
sues to mend it.

9/11/92

CHICAGO—IN A YEAR WHEN LAWYERS ARE FODDER FOR JUST ABOUT EVERY-
one else, Maria Dillon has another beef with the profession. Because
her former fiancé is so much the lawyer, she contends, her broken
courtship has ended up in court.

Last month, precisely a year after the couple had met, nine months
after her fiancé had placed a 1.06 carat diamond ring on her finger,
and only two days before they were to have wed, Frank D. Zaffere 3d, a
corporate lawyer here, sued Ms. Dillon for breaking off their engagement weeks earlier.

Hell hath no fury, it seems, like a lawyer scorned—particularly a
lawyer familiar with chapter 40, sections 1801-1810 of the Illinois Revised Statues of 1991, which covers breach of promise to marry. In a
document loaded with heretos and wherefores and in reliance upons,
Mr. Zaffere demanded that Ms. Dillon, a 21-year-old hostess at an Italian restaurant, repay the $40,310.48 he spent wooing her.

That would cover the costs of the fur coat, the car, the typewriter,
the engagement ring and, he said, even the champagne with which he
toasted his bride-to-be in Chicago's Pump Room. That figure could
grow even higher. In his complaint, filed in Cook County Circuit
Court, Mr. Zaffere is also seeking interest, fees and court costs. And,
he said, the latest statements from Visa and MasterCard had not arrived.

But he has hope. Mr. Zaffere, a 44-year-old Georgetown Law
School graduate with a daughter nearly Ms. Dillon's age, declared in
the court papers he prepared himself that he remains willing to marry
Ms. Dillon, subject to a few provisos.

Or, as he wrote to Ms. Dillon three days before filing suit, "I am
still willing to marry you on the conditions hereinbelow set forth."
Those conditions include faithfulness, truthfulness and a commitment to marry him within 45 days of receiving the letter—that is,
next Thursday.

"Please feel free to call me if you have any questions or would like
to discuss any of the matters addressed herein," the letter concluded.
It was signed, "Sincerely, Frank."

The suit has forced Ms. Dillon to consult two lawyers, the first of whom suggested she marry Mr. Zaffere, then procure a generous divorce down the road. She rejected the advice.

"I've wasted a year's worth of tuition in two months," said Ms. Dillon, who is saving to attend law school, referring to her lawyers' bills. It has also given her sleepless nights, prompted her to think of leaving Chicago and driven her back to cigarettes, she said. And, she adds, she has also stopped dating. "Somebody really major has to walk into my life for me even to go out for a cocktail."

Contacted this week at his law office, Mr. Zaffere was reluctant to discuss his lawsuit. "I'm in an awkward position," he said. "I'm the plaintiff and I'm also an attorney, and I've got severe ethical constraints on what I can say. I'm not permitted to say anything that could reflect positively or negatively on my opponent's character or reputation."

He did acknowledge, however, that he loved his opponent very much, and that he still wanted to marry her. But on the list of enticements, a breach of promise suit apparently ranks far below bouquets, nosegays, candies and Valentines for Ms. Dillon. "I think he's trying to use this as a way to make me say 'O.K., O.K., Frank, I'll marry you. I'll marry you,' " she said. "But there's nothing romantic about it. I can't imagine telling my children as a bedtime story that mommy and daddy got married because of a lawsuit."

Indeed, as Mr. Zaffere's deadline approaches, the case has destroyed whatever small chance remained of reconciliation. "It makes me want to swim across Lake Michigan to the other side to get as far away as possible from him," she said.

Such cases are extremely rare, particularly since the Illinois State Legislature limited them 45 years ago. The restrictions seem to have discouraged most jilted would-be spouses from filing suit. Ms. Dillon's current lawyer, Ronald S. Fishman of Chicago, asserted that Mr. Zaffere is representing himself because few lawyers would take on such a case.

Ms. Dillon said the suit reflected several truisms about lawyers: their arrogance, their tendency to see everything through a legal prism and thus seek legal solutions, and their ability to exploit a system that only they know and are licensed to operate.

"I think he has his own personal problems and is taking them out where he knows he can," she said. "He thinks he can stomp on me as much as he wants because he's a lawyer."

Ms. Dillon also offered a more benign interpretation: court papers are just about the only way he has of keeping in touch with her, albeit through such intermediaries as filing clerks, law secretaries, lawyers and reporters. "It's working," she said. "I'm thinking about him all the time."

As for the formality of his pleadings she said that even when their love was young, Mr. Zaffere had a disconcerting tendency to lapse into legalese. "I constantly told him to talk like a person, that I wasn't familiar with all these lawyer terms," she recalled as she puffed on a Salem Light. "It was difficult for him to just have a conversation. It was always as if we were in his office and I were one of his clients."

But Mr. Zaffere denied that he was exploiting his position as a lawyer. "I really don't understand why I should be precluded from availing myself of a statute that's been on the books since 1947 any more than any other citizen of the state," he said. As for addressing his former fiancée so formally, he said he was simply following the procedure laid out by the law.

Mr. Zaffere and Ms. Dillon, who met in August 1991, got off to an auspicious start. Their courtship included her first trip to New York City, featuring tickets to "Phantom of the Opera" and dinner at the Rainbow Room.

"I've dated doctors and lawyers before who were jerks," she said. "He was just a good guy to me." By November, a month short of her 21st birthday, they were engaged.

But the next seven months proved stormy, and in June Ms. Dillon told him she wanted out. On Aug. 3, Mr. Zaffere sued Ms. Dillon in the Municipal Department of the Cook County Circuit Court, demanding the return of several items, including a red pullover he valued at $22, a $7.99 Patsy Cline cassette and a Notre Dame umbrella listed at $23.95. The same day, as specified under Illinois law, he sent his letter to Ms. Dillon.

Three days later, Ms. Dillon received a summons at the Como Inn, the grotto-like Italian restaurant where she works. It listed Mr. Zaffere's various courtship-related expenses. That included $5,200 for the engagement ring, which, at her lawyer's suggestion, she plans to keep for the time being. "I don't even care for the damn thing," she said. "As far as I'm concerned, you can toss that in Lake Michigan, too, but I'm listening to my lawyer."

Ms. Dillon said she had no appetite for the coming court case, in part because she had more important things to do—like going back to school and getting a law degree for herself. "I think lawyers are great," she said. "I just think this is one lawyer who makes other lawyers look bad." ❑

At the urging of Mr. Fishman, Mr. Zaffere dropped the lawsuit, and it turned out to be his wisest course: the couple soon reconciled and, in May 1993, mar-

ried. *"I'm taking 5 percent credit for this,"* Mr. Fishman boasted. *"By convincing all sides that litigation is the wrong way to solve just about any problem in life, the hostility ended."* Mr. and Mrs. Zaffere are now the proud parents of a baby boy. Soon he may hear that bedtime story about how Mommy and Daddy married.

Owning History: Does Film of
Kennedy Assassination
Belong to All or to One?

11/25/88

ABRAHAM ZAPRUDER, THE DALLAS DRESSMAKER AND COINCIDENTAL FILM chronicler of the assassination of President Kennedy, died in 1970. His 486 famous frames of Kodachrome now sit in the United States Archives, alongside Eva Braun's home movies. But the question of who should own the Zapruder film, like the matter of just what it reveals about the killing, is still hotly debated.

Two days after the shooting, Time Inc. bought the film from Mr. Zapruder for $150,000, then gave it back to his survivors in 1975. Ever since, whenever the film appears, whether in a book, magazine, newspaper or television show, the Zapruders are entitled to a fee. And in the silver anniversary of the shooting, these are banner days. In the last few months news organizations have paid them tens of thousands of dollars to use it.

But should the law allow people to copyright so crucial a piece of Americana? What constitutes "fair use" for which compensation need not be paid? Are some photographs so much a part of history that the First Amendment protects the right to use them? Does a policy of sales only to the highest bidder, which some say is the case with the Zapruder film, skew scholarship toward mainstream views? All these issues were raised in a case filed against the Zapruders last month in Washington.

Abraham Zapruder did not set out for Dealey Plaza on Nov. 22, 1963, with money on his mind. He had left his Bell & Howell camera at home and had fetched it only when his secretary urged him to record the President's visit. Mr. Zapruder later told Richard Stolley of Time that the night of the killing he dreamed of hearing a Times Square huckster hawking his film. It was his way of saying he wanted his accidental artifact handled with care, Mr. Stolley recently recalled.

There were other considerations. Fearful that news of a Jewish man's profiting from the assassination could set off a wave of anti-Semitism in Dallas, Mr. Zapruder's lawyer, Sam Passman, suggested his client donate the first $25,000 payment to Mrs. J. D. Tippet, widow of the policeman killed by Lee Harvey Oswald. Mr. Zapruder readily agreed.

Individual frames of the film—but never the infamous number 313, which shows a bullet shattering Kennedy's head—appeared in

Life magazine. But only in 1975, when a bootleg version was broadcast, did the American people see the shocking film in full. The sight reignited debate over the killing, and demand for the film intensified.

Reluctant to police its use, Time sold it back to the Zapruders for a dollar. Henceforth, Henry Zapruder, Abraham's son, who is a tax lawyer with Morgan, Lewis & Bockius in Washington, would decide who could use the film and how much they should pay. Bootleg copies abound, but Mr. Zapruder could sue anyone using one for copyright infringement.

In April 1985, Gerard Selby Jr., a University of Maryland graduate student, sought Mr. Zapruder's permission to use the film in a documentary on the Kennedy killing. He says his letters and phone calls were repeatedly ignored. Eventually, Mr. Zapruder's assistant quoted a price: $30,000. It was twice what Mr. Selby's film had cost to make and was apparently non-negotiable. Last month, Mr. Selby took Mr. Zapruder to court. Joining him was Harold Weisberg, who asserted that Mr. Zapruder had reneged on promises to let him see the previously uninspected portion of the film along the sprocket holes.

They noted how, in 1968, a Federal judge ruled that the public's extraordinary interest in the Kennedy killing mandated that "fair use" of the Zapruder film be broadly construed. They also cited Melville Nimmer, the copyright scholar, who once wrote that some photographs are so newsworthy that they should not be copyrightable. He gave two examples: pictures of the My Lai massacre and Abraham Zapruder's home movie. Finally, they argued that by failing to curb unauthorized uses of the film, the Zapruders had in effect abandoned their copyright.

The tension between free speech and copyright has arisen before, most recently in cases over The Nation magazine's publication of former President Gerald R. Ford's memoirs and a biographer's use of J. D. Salinger's letters. It was not resolved then, nor would it be now; Mr. Selby wanted his show to air before Nov. 22. The case was settled: Mr. Selby's documentary, with the Zapruder film, aired last week. Mr. Weisberg will soon see the sprocket areas, and Mr. Zapruder kept his copyright.

Mr. Zapruder said he charged only commercial interests, not scholars, for the use of the film. Mr. Selby and Mr. Weisberg, he said in an interview, just fell between the cracks. Neither he nor his mother, Lillian, will say how much their family has made from the film, except to insist it could have been far more. "I think we've been pretty good about it," Mrs. Zapruder said. "We could have made copies and peddled it on street corners. Someone else would have made millions on it." ❑

CLASSIC CARDOZO RULING IN
A NEGLIGENCE CASE OF THE 20'S
IS STILL REVERBERATING IN AN 80'S APPEAL.

6/16/89

IN HIS APHORISTIC, INVOLUTED OPINIONS, JUDGE BENJAMIN N. CARDOZO depicted the same bygone New York, of trolleys and els, "Broad-way" and Coney Island, that John Sloan captured on canvas and Rodgers & Hart set to song.

But the world Cardozo drew as Chief Judge of the New York Court of Appeals is also timeless. In his vignettes of long-forgotten people are the universal themes of the law and life. One such issue is the nature of negligence. Who must bear the cost of carelessness? How remote and unpredictable must an injury be for the law to overlook it?

Cardozo's successors on the bench still struggle with these issues, as a recent case involving a banking executive named Grace Marenghi attests. That story harks back to a character from Cardozo's era, as familiar to every American lawyer as it is unknown to everyone else. Her name was Helen Palsgraf.

Mrs. Palsgraf earned the limited immortality of the lawbooks simply by standing in the wrong place on a Long Island Rail Road platform in August 1924, when she was taking her daughters from East New York to Rockaway Beach in Brooklyn on a hot summer Sunday. As two trainmen helped a passenger board the Jamaica express, they dislodged a small package of fireworks he was carrying. It fell to the rails and exploded.

Twenty-five feet away, a penny weighing machine jarred by the blast fell on top of Mrs. Palsgraf. She went into shock, was hospitalized and never really recovered. Until her death in 1943, she was plagued by stuttering, dizziness, headaches—and indignation. Reversing a Brooklyn jury, the New York Court of Appeals held that she was not entitled to damages from the railroad.

The reason, Cardozo wrote in his landmark 1928 decision, was that her injury was simply too remote and unforeseeable. "Nothing in the situation gave notice that the falling package had in it the potency of peril to persons thus removed," he observed. "Life will have to be made over, and human nature transformed, before prevision so extravagant can be accepted as a norm of conduct."

Elsewhere in the ruling, he put it more bluntly: "The risk reasonably to be perceived defines the duty to be obeyed." It may have seemed heartless, but Cardozo felt he had no choice. For as he wrote, "The judge is not the knight-errant, roaming at will in pursuit of his own ideal of beauty or of goodness."

In his equally famous dissent, Judge William Andrews conceded that a causal chain has to stop somewhere: "A murder at Sarajevo may be the necessary antecedent to an assassination in London 20 years hence," he wrote. "An overturned lantern may burn all Chicago." But the trainmen's negligence was close enough in time and space, he wrote, to be considered the "proximate cause" of Mrs. Palsgraf's injury.

It might all appear nitpicky, like so much of the law. But not to Ms. Marenghi, after she boarded a Manhattan-bound A train in October 1981.

What followed was what she calls "a typical New York horror story, something to feed tourists from the Midwest." Just as she stepped off the train onto the platform on the Chambers Street station in Manhattan, the 40-year-old woman saw a man with an attaché case hurtling down the stairs. "Open the doors!" he yelled. The conductor did, long enough for the man to flatten Ms. Marenghi, shatter her knee, hop over her and onto the departing train.

For four months she could not walk. She still cannot run, cannot ride a bicycle and has trouble with stairs. Her knee can detect meteorological changes better than Willard Scott.

Ms. Marenghi, who is an assistant vice president at Dean Witter Reynolds Inc., sued the New York Transit Authority, and last year a Manhattan jury awarded her $174,976.85. The authority appealed, thereby confronting another appellate court with issues of predictability, superseding negligence, chains of events. Once more, it split. Once more, it reversed.

Even if the conductor had been negligent, the conduct of the man "was an unforeseeable, superseding act," stated the opinion, issued last week by Justices David Ross, John Carro and Bentley Kassal of the Appellate Division of State Supreme Court in Manhattan. As authority in exonerating the city, they cited Cardozo in Palsgraf.

And in dissent, Justices Sidney Asch and Israel Rubin echoed Judge Andrews. By reopening the doors, they wrote, the conductor effectively, predictably invited the man to bolt for the train. That is the argument Ms. Marenghi's lawyers, Sol Zepnick and Norman Frowley, will make anew when they bring the case before the State Court of Appeals.

But when her case reaches Albany, Grace Marenghi will have yet another painful encounter to worry about, and not with some anonymous hit-and-run businessman. This one is with the ghost of Helen Palsgraf. ❏

Ms. Palsgraf's ghost proved formidable, indeed: the Court of Appeals ruled unanimously against Ms. Marenghi.

A BIG HOUSTON FIRM FACES A
MALPRACTICE CHARGE BECAUSE
A LEGAL BRIEF WASN'T BRIEF ENOUGH.

5/24/91

OF ALL THE OXYMORA IN THE ENGLISH LANGUAGE, NONE MAY BE AS EGREGIOUS as "legal brief."

Lawyers seems constitutionally incapable of writing brief briefs. Lest they omit any potential winners, they lard their documents with all manner of arguments. No citation is too obscure to invoke in the service of ersatz erudition. Moreover, there are no Maxwell Perkinses editing legal briefs. Most are written not just with stultifying solemnity but remarkable repetitiousness.

Not surprisingly, courts faced with a steady diet of such paper polenta have imposed strict space limitations. Even in Texas, a place famed for its expansiveness, the state Supreme Court is cracking down. So it is that one of Houston's mightiest law firms, Vinson & Elkins, could face legal malpractice charges for its loquacious handling of an architectural malpractice case.

Earlier this year, in appealing a $550,000 judgment against a Texas architectural firm, Vinson & Elkins asked the state Supreme Court for permission to file a 103-page brief—that is, 53 pages longer than the limit the court adopted in 1987. That motion was rejected, whereupon the firm tried to file a streamlined 52-pager. When that, too, failed to pass muster, Vinson & Elkins trimmed its submission to 45½ pages.

Unfortunately, it did so at least in part by cutting the size of the print rather than the amount. The opposing counsel, Jon Burmeister of Beaumont, charged that had Vinson & Elkins not resorted to typographical tricks, the brief would have been 75 pages. The court, clearly in a no-nonsense mood, concurred. The brief was not just hard to read, it ruled, but violated the spirit and maybe the letter of the rule. It threw out the appeal.

Guy Lipe, the Vinson & Elkins partner on the case, moved for a rehearing. So, too, did John Holloway, a Houston sole practitioner whose case had been dismissed on similar grounds. As a result, a court more accustomed to handling writs and motions had to consider typefaces, pica counts and density of typographical characters.

Vinson & Elkins took a polite, contrite approach, insisting it had neither meant to pull a fast one nor show the court any disrespect.

The turn of events, it argued, reflected only "a misunderstanding over type size and margins"—neither of which are specified in the rule—and "an unknown quirk" in its word processor, one that squished the letters tighter than usual.

Mr. Holloway was considerably more caustic. If marginalia like margins could be scrutinized, he asked, where would the court stop? Can a brief be struck because it is printed on insufficiently "heavy" paper? How many indentations should be made before each paragraph? How many staples should be used and where? Should the typeface be Courier or Prestige, Orator or Gothic, and should it be set at 10 or 12 pitches an inch?

Four other lawyers—including a former Texas Supreme Court Justice, James P. Wallace of San Antonio, and W. James Kronzer, an appellate specialist from Houston—weighed in, too. They noted that through word processing wizardry, "hyperfootnoting" and other stratagems, resourceful lawyers everywhere had tried to squeeze 75 pounds of manure into 50-pound bags. Some judges, notably Frank Easterbook of the United States Court of Appeals for the Seventh Circuit in Chicago, seem obsessed with the problem. So is the United States Supreme Court, whose rules are so elaborate, they note, it takes a table to explain them.

But given the limited potential for abuse, the four lawyers say, courts should not get too exercised about the problem. "The threat posed by an occasional 70-page brief in a 50-page package is probably not sufficient to warrant creation of a Pica Patrol," they wrote. The Texas court was not convinced. Last month, it denied the rehearing motions.

Mr. Holloway said he may just take his case to the United States Supreme Court, but he doubts it will agree to hear it. Annoying, vexatious, petty, hyperlegalistic—all these things the Texas Supreme Court's policy may be, but it is probably not unconstitutional. Mr. Lipe said Vinson & Elkins has not decided whether to join Mr. Holloway's appeal, though the decision may have been made for him. Unbeknownst to Mr. Lipe, another partner in the firm recently asked a state court to dismiss charges against another client on the ground the 50-page printed brief filed by the other side was too long.

"It's rather strange to me that having been screwed up by the court, they're willing to drop the thing on someone else," Mr. Holloway grumbled. "You don't take a position that something is unfair, unequal, unreasonable and all those jolly good words and then turn around and stuff someone else with it a month later." ❑

When Sudden Baldness Is Bad
for Business, a Lawyer Decides
to Beard the Rumors.

5/27/94

UNTIL ABOUT A YEAR AGO JEREMIAH GUTMAN, A MAN WITH A MANE OF flowing, slightly unruly white hair, bushy eyebrows and moustache, was periodically mistaken for a famous physicist. Standing at a bus stop in Los Angeles once, Mr. Gutman, a fixture in Manhattan's civil liberties bar for 40 years, was even asked for his autograph. "The guy gave me whatever he was carrying and I signed 'Albert Einstein,' " he recalled.

Almost overnight, however, Mr. Gutman, who is 70, has come to look more like Telly Savalas or Yul Brynner. Disease has clear-cut his distinguished head and, for a time, threatened to decimate his law practice as well. Therein lie several lessons for lawyers about the fragility of small law practices, the fickleness of some clients, the squeamishness of colleagues and the ravages of rumors.

Mr. Gutman once wore a beard that made him look like a beat poet; now he has not had to shave for months. His hair was once luxuriant; now all that is left is the single strand growing on his nose. He trims it periodically, but there is little else either north or south.

Late last year, Mr. Gutman learned that he had alopecia generalis, an illness whose only physical effect is that it claims all of one's hair. Within a few months the man who once represented such hirsute sorts as Abbie Hoffman and Jerry Rubin has come to resemble another, balder client of his in the 1969-70 trial of the Chicago Seven: David Dellinger.

Most of the world, and the bar, however, know nothing about alopecia (pronounced ala-PEA-sha). They assumed that Mr. Gutman's hair was a casualty of chemotherapy; that he had cancer; that he was dying. And both the world and the bar began acting accordingly.

Some old allies, like Henry Schwartzchild and Ira Glasser of the American Civil Liberties Union, did not mince words. "What's the matter with you?" they asked. When he told them, they commiserated with him.

Many others in his concentric circles—groups like the National Coalition Against Censorship, the American-Israeli Civil Liberties Coalition and others with the words "civil" or "liberties" usually in their names—blanched but didn't want to ask. Others, fearful of any-thing smelling of death or dying, didn't want to know. Still others, like Norman Siegel, head of the New York Civil Liberties Union in New York City, were so steeped in the constitutional right to privacy that they didn't think they should pry.

Mr. Gutman—who used the locker he was given as editor of the New York University Law Review in 1948 to store the guns he had hus-sled up for Israel—initially agreed. He figured that hair loss, like hem-orrhoids, were not anybody else's business. But he underestimated how much some people cared.

"People were very concerned," said Lesly Lempert of Ithaca, presi-dent of the New York State Civil Liberties Union. "No one could pos-sibly imagine the N.Y.C.L.U. without Mr. Gutman's presence."

Had it remained strictly a matter of appearances, Mr. Gutman might have remained silent. But business began dropping off nearly as quickly as his hair, down 70 percent in the last half of 1993.

Part of the loss, he knew, was attributable to the recession. The small businesses that make up half his clientele—the rest are public-interest matters he handles for nothing—had economic troubles of their own, and stopped paying their legal bills.

"When half your business is not for money and half of the other half stops paying, you're in trouble," Mr. Gutman said recently in the cluttered offices of Levy, Gutman, Goldberg & Kaplan, in Suite 1776 of 275 Seventh Avenue, in the heart of the garment district. On his wall is perhaps the world's largest collection of "No Smoking" signs—in 40 different languages, stolen, er, borrowed from Italian trains, Athenian buses and the like—plus an assortment of paintings, mostly poor man's Rothkos.

There was evidence, however, that public perceptions of Mr. Gut-man's health were partly to blame for his financial perils, that old clients were taking their business elsewhere. The Levy in Levy, Gut-man, Goldberg & Kaplan has been dead since 1929; the Gutman, Mr. Gutman's father, died in 1948; and Mr. Goldberg has been dead since 1982.

Indeed, there are more lawyers in the firm's name than there are in the firm, which now comprises Mr. Gutman, Philip Kaplan and a junior associate. When one of the three gets sick, or when the world thinks that he is sick, the place founders.

Mr. Gutman pondered his options. He thought of placing a notice in The New York Law Journal, or at the bottom of the front page of The New York Times, or sending out one of those printed cardboard announcements of the sort that are thrown out thousands of times in hundreds of law offices every morning: "Levy, Gutman, Goldberg & Kaplan is proud to announced that Jeremiah Gutman is not suffering from cancer, is in good health and is looking for business," it would have said.

Instead, he decided to come clean, then rely on word of mouth. To friend and foe and client alike, he started volunteering the obvious and then providing the explanation.

It now seems that gossip runs both ways. Business has bounced back, and so has the mood of his once fearful colleagues. But the hair hasn't been so resilient. Mr. Gutman and his friends are still getting used to it.

"His new look is sort of a Wall Street corporate type," Mrs. Lempert said. "I think that's as troubling to him as anything." ❑

BEYOND CONFRONTATIONAL LAW:
THE FEEL-GOOD APPROACH,
AS PRACTICED FROM THE HEART.

4/10/92

NOT LONG AGO, THE BAR OF MIDDLEBURY, VT., WATCHED WITH BEMUSE-ment as Bill van Zyverden hung his shingle, or more accurately, his awning, over his new law office, in what was formerly the menswear department of Abram's department store. "Holistic Justice Center," it states.

"What are you practicing, wimpy law?" a local lawyer sneered, un-doubtedly anticipating the reaction of most conventional practitioners.

In typically non-confrontational fashion, Mr. van Zyverden said no, that he was merely "practicing law from my heart."

"I wasn't implying that other lawyers don't do that," he said in an in-terview. "I was just implying that the traditional practice of law seems to have no emotional empathy."

The 36-year-old Mr. van Zyverden is trying to change all this, not only in Vermont but throughout the world. He is founder, president and one-tenth of the membership of the International Alliance of Holistic Lawyers—international because one member lives in Rotterdam.

What is a holistic lawyer? It is, said Mr. van Zyverden, someone ded-icated to the use of arbitration and mediation rather than rancorous, bloodletting litigation. And, through intense questioning of his client, the holistic lawyer seeks to identify the roots of a conflict, to foster a client's self-awareness and feelings of responsibility for a prob-lem and empathy for his opponent rather than to cater to the desire for revenge.

Perhaps the prototypical holistic lawyer was Gandhi. "I realized that the true function of a lawyer was to unite parties riven asunder," Gandhi wrote in his autobiography. "The lesson was so indelibly burnt into me that a large part of my time during the 20 years of my practice was occupied in bringing about private compromises of hun-dreds of cases. I lost nothing thereby—not even money, certainly not my soul."

Indeed, if lawyers cease to see themselves as mouthpieces, hired guns and alter egos, Mr. van Zyverden says, they can free themselves from the torments of the adversary system, including stress, alco-holism, drug abuse and suicides.

Mr. van Zyverden's docket is varied, as expected in a small-town practice. But whatever the matter, he hews to certain principles.

The first has to do with the importance of fostering introspection among clients—that is, to help a person to determine why they need a lawyer. Like those newfangled laundromats where one can watch videos, get a tan or sip cappuccino, Mr. van Zyverden acts as lawyer as well as amateur psychologist, all for the bargain price (at least when compared to more conventional lawyers or therapists) of about $80 an hour.

It is no coincidence that the rendering of Justice in the Holistic Center logo has removed her blindfold. "I don't think Justice should be blind," he said. "People get into predicaments for different reasons. You can't judge a person on what they did, but who they are and why they did it."

A second precept is acceptance of responsibility. Take the case of a client charged with drunken driving who had, in fact, been drinking. "There may have been loopholes we could have used, or we could have had evidence of the test suppressed," Mr. van Zyverden said. "But it would not have been justice." Instead, the client pleaded guilty, and is now receiving counseling.

Another is civility to adversaries, even if they are loathsome. "I can be passionate about my client's case, but I will not carry their anger," he said.

Nor will he carry their water. Mr. van Zyverden insists that his clients conduct their own investigations, take their own pictures, interview potential witnesses, assemble documents—everything except research the law. "It helps them heal their own inner conflict," he said. "To go back and work things through sometimes defuses a lot of the anger."

To emphasize the notion of partnership, Mr. van Zyverden asks that he be called "Bill." His office is a friendly shade of blue, and is without those shelves of intimidating tomes that lawyers love more than they use. He wears jeans and never sits behind a desk when speaking with clients.

Among the other lawyers on Mr. van Zyverden's wavelength are Keith Rodli, a trial lawyer from River Falls, Wis., who said he had become "increasingly bothered by what I see the adversary system doing to people" after 18 years of continuous courtroom wars. Another is Randy Krause, a public defender in Concord, Calif., who in his spare time runs Holistic Justice Advocates.

Mr. Krause does not fear being called a wimp—"I'm sure Gandhi got called that many times"—but confesses that "holistic" may be a problem. In recent advertisements, he has substituted "integrative." Mr. Rodli, too, said he would never put "holistic" on his shingle. "I think the word would throw people," he said. "They'd wonder if I was going to adjust their back while they were here." ❑

Thanks to reports in Yoga Journal, New Age Journal and Good Morning, America, among other places, word about the International Alliance of Holistic Lawyers has spread, and membership now numbers 450, in 44 states and five countries. Mr. van Zyverden reports that his holistic law business has also grown, and that it's been a long time since any local lawyer called him a wimp.

New Television Stars
in the O. J. Simpson case galaxy:
The lawyer-commentators.

11/4/94

LOS ANGELES—One day not long ago, a local lawyer, Jay Jaffe, approached Roger Cossack, another member of the bar, in Nate and Al's, the venerable Beverly Hills delicatessen and agora. "Rog, my ratings are higher than yours," Mr. Jaffe declared.

"Nationally, but not internationally," Mr. Cossack replied.

The ratings the two men were talking about were not from Martindale-Hubbell but Nielsen. Both are among the spate of lawyer-celebrities spawned by the O. J. Simpson case, catering to the news media's insatiable appetite for yet more legal commentary on the most commented-upon case in history.

Like Mr. Cossack, the Simpson maven in residence for CNN, most of these lawyers practiced in untelevised obscurity until June 12. Now, they are accosted at airports and asked for autographs. Since starring on Larry King Live, Crossfire and Good Morning, America, Blair Bernholz of Los Angeles says she has even fielded calls from the William Morris Agency about doing television work full time. (She says she prefers to practice criminal law.)

If Walter Mitty has become Walter Cronkite, the transition has not always been smooth; few lawyers meet the blow-dried standards of television news personalities, let alone the glitz quotient of Los Angeles. Like the most overworked Legal Aid lawyers, dumped into cases on a moment's notice, the new commentators have had to get up to speed—and fast.

For reporters in search of Simpson commentary, there is a full menu of experts, pontificators and second-guessers. Most can be reached in their offices, though some have beepers or cellular phones. Others, like Stanley Goldman of Loyola Law School in Los Angeles, make house calls to the press center above Judge Lance A. Ito's courtroom.

A few commentators, like Ira Reiner, the former District Attorney of Los Angeles, and Leslie Abramson, of Menendez fame, were household names even when Mr. Simpson was still a pitchman and Bundy, Rockingham and Kato were not. Some, like the twin oracles of legal academia, Peter Arenella of the University of California at Los Angeles Law School and Laurie Levenson of Loyola, cut their telegenic teeth on the Rodney G. King case, though they are now more in demand, by newspapers as well as television stations, than ever.

Indeed, people deprived this year of watching Frank Thomas and Ken Griffey Jr. vie for the home run crown can consult their newspapers to see Mr. Arenella and Ms. Levenson vie with Harland Braun, a Los Angeles lawyer, for quotemeister-of-the-year honors in the print media.

By contrast, Mr. Cossack and Donald Wager were plucked from obscurity, to which they will only reluctantly return.

Mr. Wager is, by all accounts, a very good lawyer. But he is also pushing 60 and balding, and his personal trainer seems to have gone into retirement. When he first hit the airwaves for ESPN, he seemed stiff and ill at ease.

Since then an acting coach has taught him the peculiar pirouette of talking heads: for the first quarter of an interview, look at the interviewer; for the next half, look to the camera, and for the remainder, it's back to the interviewer again. Familiarity has also bred contentment: Now he spends less time worrying about how he looks and more time basking in his fame.

"People stop me on the street," Mr. Wager said recently. "I was going up an escalator in a Las Vegas hotel and two guys on the down escalator shouted, 'Hey, it's the ESPN guy!' I was coming out of barber shop in Santa Monica and a guy riding by on his bike said, 'I like your work.' A lawyer wanted my autograph for his father, who's a sports freak. A very attractive young married woman stopped me and says, 'I like what you do.' "

Better, still, the work entails no financial sacrifice. "I make substantial money doing this," Mr. Wager said, without offering specifics. "And because I can maintain my practice by scrambling, it's extra income."

Until Mr. Simpson's fate is determined, Mr. Cossack has put much of his law practice on the shelf. His on-air confidence soaring, he no longer lowers his voice to sound authoritative, as he did at the start. He's also put in contact lenses and taken off 14 pounds. "I wanted to lose weight, but could not quite find the motivation," he said. "But when I saw myself on television, I thought, 'Gee, who is that gray-haired, heavy guy?' "

For years Mr. Cossack, who has heard from Cossacks everywhere in search of long-lost relatives since his first television appearance, was the one spotting celebrities amid the Mercedes and Porsches in the hip Beverly Glen shopping center; now, people are spotting him. The experience, one might say, has been ego enhancing.

"He's cocky to begin with, but you should see him walking in now, with all that stupid makeup, singing 'Hurray for Hollywood,' " said his receptionist, Judy Shumsky. "I have to slap him. He can barely fit through the door."

Mr. Braun refuses to do any television, and even the entreaties of Ted Koppel and Larry King have not changed his mind. "It makes you look either like an umemployed lawyer or a lousy newscaster," he said. "You're forced to fill up dead time, and what you end up doing is babbling. And when you don't know the answer to a question, you can't say, 'I don't know the answer,' because you look like an idiot." ❏

XII

DOING GOD'S WORK

THOMAS B. STODDARD *(page 322)*

COLLEAGUES BID FAREWELL TO
A NAZI-HUNTER, HIS QUEST ENDED
BY MODERN MURDERERS.

12/30/88

WASHINGTON—A WEEK AFTER HE WENT DOWN WITH PAN AMERICAN FLIGHT 103, Michael Bernstein, or what they could collect of him, was still in Lockerbie, Scotland. His family had hoped to have his remains back in time for the funeral here this morning, but the bureaucratic maze was too formidable.

Temple Sinai was filled with his grieving colleagues, family and friends. Together, they heard Psalm 121 and the kaddish, the Jewish prayer for the dead. There was a tribute by Eli Rosenbaum of the Justice Department's Office of Special Investigation, where Mr. Bernstein, a 36-year-old father of two, had worked since 1985. There were the bittersweet words of A. E. Housman's "To an Athlete Dying Young".

Mr. Bernstein might have been a bit embarrassed by the praise. His colleagues at O.S.I., the office created to denaturalize and deport Nazi war criminals, describe him as modest. They talk of such a gentle man dying so violently, of how one who ferreted out murderers from one era would fall to those of another.

But if the circumstances seemed paradoxical, they were also fitting. Mr. Bernstein died at a moment of triumph. He was returning from Vienna, where he had persuaded the reluctant Austrians to take back some native sons they would rather forget, beginning with an Auschwitz SS guard, Josef Eckert. Mr. Bernstein could have come home earlier, but he stayed for the formal signing to make sure there were no hitches.

Twenty-four former Nazis have been deported from the United States in O.S.I.'s 10 years. Mr. Bernstein was responsible for seven.

Mr. Bernstein came to the office by way of history and private law practice, with the Washington firm of Covington & Burling. There, he spent much of his time on public-interest work, largely prison reform. But no matter how much pro bono work he did, he felt himself a hired gun, doing advocacy for advocacy's sake.

He was the kind of man who needed a cause, and in his Nazi-hunting work, as in his love of the Michigan Wolverines and Jimi Hendrix, that was what he found. He was Jewish, but his cause was not a sectarian vendetta. It was an expression of his faith in the law as a tool for what Mr. Rosenbaum called "tikkun olam"—Hebrew for "the repair of the world." Among Mr. Bernstein's more moving experiences was walking the "death steps" of the rock quarry at Mauthausen, the Austrian camp from which many of his cases came.

"It's almost as if he thought of it as his own piece of the world, one he could consecrate by dedicating his work to the memory of those who died there," said a colleague, Aron Goldberg. The work required him to be a psychotherapist, detective, diplomat and historian as well as a prosecutor.

To build the case against Mr. Eckert, for example, Mr. Bernstein had to grasp the intricacies of Auschwitz, a megalopolis of murder. Through witnesses, experts and documents, he essentially reconstructed the Polish subcamp of Gleiwitz, where Mr. Eckert was a guard. In his knack for spotting and extracting the guts of a case, he was perhaps more surgeon than lawyer. "Everyone else was working with scalpels," said Bruce Einhorn, another O.S.I. lawyer. "Mike worked with lasers."

In two other cases, Mr. Bernstein became the first prosecutor in the office to get confessions from two former guards, one of whom admitted under the weight of evidence amassed by Mr. Bernstein to shooting an unarmed prisoner in the back.

Mr. Bernstein never touted his success. He loathed pretense and pomposity among lawyers. Among the books he enjoyed most, and he was a voracious reader, was "The Bonfire of the Vanities." If anything, his success frustrated him. Because the opposition invariably capitulated, his cases never went to trial. He would then repair to the record room, restlessly fingering documents, searching for his next case.

Other Office of Strategic Investigation lawyers would stop by to talk law, strategy, ideas. Few matters got far before someone would ask, "Have you bounced it off Bernstein?"

The men Mr. Bernstein helped remove from America—Stefan Leili, Josef Wieland, Johann Leprich, Martin Bartesch, Chester Wojciechowski, Stefan Reger and Juris Kauls—were the foot soldiers of the Holocaust. All were guards, at Maidanek and Auschwitz as well as Mauthausen. All had entered the United States illegally.

And all learned the truth of the fortune cookie adage, now accompanied by a death notice, that Mr. Bernstein taped on his office door. It is a message that affords some small solace as the investigation into Flight 103 continues:

"The law sometimes sleeps, but it never dies." ❑

A VETERAN OF MANY BATTLES
AGAINST LAW ENFORCEMENT
GONE AMOK IS NO LONGER LONELY.

3/29/91

YEARS AGO, SHORTLY AFTER HE HAD BEGUN THE LONELY AND UNREMUNERA-
tive task of representing victims of police brutality, a Los Angeles
lawyer named Hugh Manes approached a personal injury practitioner. How much in damages, he asked, was a broken nose generally
worth? Five thousand dollars, he was told.

But what if, Mr. Manes continued, that nose were shattered, vi-
ciously and unnecessarily, by a policeman wielding a club? Three to
four thousand dollars, the other lawyer responded, explaining that juries would not believe that officers behaved that way, let alone lied
about it afterward.

Much to the relief of police officials, Mr. Manes is not representing
Rodney G. King, whose pummeling at the hands of the Los Angeles
police this month has since been seen by millions on what has become America's best-known home video. But had Mr. Manes the time
or the ego, he might view the King case as vindication of a kind.

In 37 years of law practice Mr. Manes (pronounced MAY-ness) first
created and embodied, then cultivated and led what is probably the
most extraordinary network of police misconduct lawyers anywhere.
By teaching and by example, he has trained dozens of younger
lawyers in California to do what, in a far more hostile age, he did
alone: combating law enforcement gone amok.

"He was taking on police brutality cases when nobody even believed there was such a thing," one colleague, George V. Denny 3d of
Pasadena, recalled in an interview. "It was hard to convince jurors
that police would even lie, let alone beat up and kill people."

Suddenly, thanks to the King videotape, the cause to which Mr.
Manes had dedicated much of his life is now on the national agenda.
He is hearing from reporters who have long ignored him. The Police
Misconduct Lawyers Referral Service, which he helped set up in Los
Angeles 10 years ago, is suddenly flooded with telephone calls. The
monthly workshops he leads, which usually attract 10 to 15 lawyers,
are now packed.

Sure, he said, he would have liked to have landed the King case.
But what mattered far more to him was whether the episode would reduce public tolerance for police abuses. On that, he is only guardedly

optimistic. Convincing jurors is not necessarily the problem, since claims and collections against police departments have risen astronomically in recent years. Other forces—racism, violence and a lingering belief that those in blue can do no wrong—have proved even more powerful than the iron hand of the marketplace, he observed.

"We figured that when we started hitting up cities for large judgments, they'd make some changes," he said. "It hasn't happened that way."

The 66-year-old Mr. Manes, an Edward Asner look-alike who favors open collars and clashing colors, still speaks with a hint of his native Chicago. He also speaks quietly, without the glib certitude and shrill self-righteousness so often found among true believers. Still, a Los Angeles judge once remarked that Mr. Manes had "the greatest reservoir of outrage at injustice" he had ever seen.

Mr. Manes passed up a more conventional career to work with Abraham Lincoln Wirin, chief counsel for the American Civil Liberties Union in Southern California. His activities there, along with civil rights and antiwar work, were faithfully followed by the F.B.I., he was to learn later. As with many Americans of his ilk and age, J. Edgar Hoover was his biographer.

Mr. Manes took on his first brutality cases early, and gradually began devoting himself almost exclusively to them. Though the climate has never been favorable, two factors have markedly improved it, he said. One was the civil rights movement, which empowered those communities most victimized by police misconduct. The other was the Watergate scandal and the Nixon years.

"We were able to persuade people that if the President could be shown to be a liar, then surely it was not too surprising that police could fall into that same category," he said.

Mr. Manes began training others, and now finds himself in a Wilshire Boulevard office with four other police brutality specialists— two of whom work almost exclusively for people bitten by police dogs.

The police don't like Mr. Manes much, but they pay him homage. When the son of the police chief of Alhambra was beaten up by officers from another department, it was Mr. Manes he hired. Moreover, for the last five or six years, he has been invited to speak to Americans for Effective Law Enforcement, a police group. They listen to him politely if not exactly rapturously.

He begins all such presentations the same way. "I always start by saying, 'My name is Hugh Manes, I sue cops for a living, and I want to tell you some ways you can put me out of business,'" he said. As of now, business is brisker than ever. ❏

THE SHORT LIFE AND LONG LEGACY
OF AN UNSUNG, UNDERPAID DEFENDER
OF NEW YORK'S HAVE-NOTS.

8/11/90

TO SOME, THE MEASURE OF A MAN'S LIFE IS THE LENGTH OF HIS OBITUARY. By that standard, Jack Lipson's legacy, like his life, was short. When he died of a heart attack last November at 45 years old, he rated only a few column inches of print.

But there are other measures. One is the durability and depth of the impression one leaves. Another is the residue of gratitude. Walk around the Legal Aid Society or the United States Court House at Foley Square in Manhattan and talk to those who knew him, and you learn that by those standards, Jack Lipson's legacy is long indeed.

One scholarship fund has already been set up in his memory by his fellow Federal public defenders throughout the country. Now the New York criminal defense bar and his friends from Columbia Law School's class of 1967 are establishing another. It will go annually to help pay off the loans of a student committed to defending indigent people in New York.

Maybe he or she will become another Jack Lipson, though that seems unlikely. For Mr. Lipson was one of those unsung and undercompensated heroes of the profession who not only keep the system from choking but also give it dignity. As the longtime head of the Legal Aid Society's Federal public defenders service unit, which represents the poor in the Federal courts of Manhattan and Brooklyn, he earned a reputation for modesty, integrity, good humor, conscientiousness and collegiality.

At a memorial service this year, Judge Pierre N. Leval of the Federal District Court in Manhattan paid Mr. Lipson the ultimate compliment. He compared him to three revered judges: Learned Hand, Henry Friendly and Edward Weinfeld. Like them, he said, Mr. Lipson elevated the process simply by his presence.

When Mr. Lipson got out of law school, he could have had any job he wanted. So he joined the Legal Aid Society. Unlike the vast majority of the tiny minority of law school graduates going into legal aid work, he never got ground down.

At Foley Square, United States attorneys and young assistant prosecutors came and went. Mr. Lipson, all 5 feet 5 of him, periodically strayed but ultimately stayed. He was lonely without other Legal Aid lawyers around. "He was the Phantom of the Courthouse," recalled a former colleague, Tom Concannon. "He could teach you how to save a quarter-step down a corridor, which toilets flushed better, which water fountains worked."

Eventually, he rose to the top post in the public defender's office, administering a staff of 28 other lawyers. But he did not become a bureaucrat. He always carried a full caseload and, by all accounts, represented the lowliest defendant as if he were Leopold and Loeb combined.

"I wasn't just one of a zillion clients that he had to deal with," a former client wrote. "He took time when I know he really didn't have the time. He helped me in ways that he never had to. He was my friend."

Jack Lipson was not Mother Teresa. Sometimes, the clientele and the system got to him. That was when, during recesses, he might debate with Judge Kevin T. Duffy the circle of Dante's Inferno on which a certain case belonged. And though he constantly rubbed up against the rawest edge of humanity, he remained a big kid, with toys on his office shelves and, on his wall, a framed picture of Jackie Robinson sliding into second.

Clients were not the only ones to benefit from his counsel. Colleagues, prosecutors, defense lawyers, law students, law professors: all called him regularly. Court reporters, clerks, officers and marshals gathered around him in court, just as they filled Riverside Memorial Chapel and spilled over onto Amsterdam Avenue for his funeral.

" 'Adversaries' somehow seems the wrong word when it comes to Jack," Federal District Judge Michael B. Mukasey, a former prosecutor, wrote Mr. Lipson's widow, Robin Charlow of Port Washington, L.I. "Not that he wasn't a vigorous advocate for his clients; he always was. And not that the result he wanted generally wasn't different from the result I wanted; generally it was. But things simply never got that adverse.

"I never spoke to him about a case and felt the same way about it afterward. I never heard him raise his voice in anger; and I never saw him do anything that was even close to the ethical line. If that seems an unremarkable list, I must tell you there is no other lawyer now living about whom I can say all three of these things."

For all those who miss Mr. Lipson, there are many others who may not even recognize their loss, as a New York lawyer, Julius Wasserstein, pointed out to Ms. Charlow. "Hundreds, if not thousands, of future indigent defendants," he predicted, "will find themselves in the hands of a less caring, less competent advocate." ❑

FOR A CRUSADER WHOSE TIME
OF GLORY HAS COME, EVEN AIDS
FAILS TO DAMPEN THE SPIRIT.

2/5/93

THE DICKENSIAN LINE ABOUT "THE BEST OF TIMES AND THE WORST OF times" has become the tiredest of clichés. But when it comes to capturing the state of Thomas B. Stoddard, there is simply no better description. His is a tale of two psyches.

These days, Mr. Stoddard is feeling the kind of exhilaration that Frederick Douglass must have felt in the 1860's or Martin Luther King Jr. felt a century later: the high of someone whose time has come. With the debate now raging over homosexuals in the military, Mr. Stoddard has seen his life's work move from a neglected backwater to the center of American consciousness.

Furthermore, having shed his administrative duties last year at the Lambda Legal Defense and Education Fund, the gay and lesbian rights group he led since 1986, he is free to concentrate on what matters most to him: championing the lot of homosexuals, particularly those with AIDS, by legislating, litigating, organizing, writing, reaching and preaching.

To each of these endeavors this lifelong crusader is bringing new urgency, clarity and empathy, and herein lies the key to Mr. Stoddard's glorious and perilous existence. Three years ago he learned he had AIDS. He is nursing the same wounds, taking the same medications, feeling the same fears, undergoing the same rituals as those he represents. "I became the client as well as the lawyer," he said in an interview. "The 'they' became 'we.' "

It has not been easy for Mr. Stoddard, who is 44, and not just because, as a modest man and an instinctive advocate, he is more comfortable pleading cases other than his own. Once more, he had to approach his conservative Republican parents. This time it was with news of a dire illness rather than a way of life; by this time his father had cancer, and his brother also had AIDS.

Then, like so many of his clients, Mr. Stoddard has had to meet the demands of his own illness. He must fight off the symptoms: the fatigue and the nausea, the pneumonia and the lesions of Kaposi's sarcoma, a cancer common among many AIDS patients. During a recent radio interview, he had to break for an injection, one of the battery of shots that for a time made it painful even to be hugged.

But Mr. Stoddard says that instead of dragging him down, his illness has "crystallized and purified" his endeavors. And these deeds, he said, have in turn been more therapeutic than any medication. "My most effective antiviral drug is political commitment, because it gets me so worked up," he said. "That's what I have that most people in my circumstances don't have the luxury to develop: a clear sense of mission and commitment."

"I wouldn't wish this experience on anyone, but I find it absolutely fascinating," he said. "It's rich, it's complex, it's filled with paradoxes. I'm very glad to be living this."

Mr. Stoddard said he was kinder these days to himself and to those around him. He sleeps more, starts his days later and exercises more regularly than before. He has less tolerance for wasted time, idle chatter, bickering. He says he has become a much better, more incisive lawyer because he is less lawyer-like.

In the last few months he has unsuccessfully petitioned the United States Supreme Court to protect the health benefits of people who have the AIDS virus and other catastrophic illnesses. He has also worked on a new Federal Lesbian and Gay Civil Rights Bill and continues to teach a class on gay rights at New York University Law School, the first such course at a major American law school.

He expects to play a major role in the effort to secure a Presidential order allowing homosexuals to serve in the military, and a minor role in "Philadelphia," the forthcoming film by Jonathan Demme about a lawyer who has AIDS. Working in his West Side apartment, he answers up to 50 telephone calls a day from lawyers and clients, friends and reporters. ("If you care to leave a message, please be complete, concise and, of course, amusing," his answering machine advises.)

Long before he arrived at Lambda, which he transformed from a 6-person, $300,000-a-year operation to a 22-person, $2.2 million one, Mr. Stoddard was a mentor, fixture and father figure to a generation of gay and lesbian lawyers. It was he who, by his very example, persuaded them to come out, attend law school, join the cause. For many of them, it is impossible to contemplate life without him.

At a party last fall, shortly after he had made his illness known, Mr. Stoddard offered his Lambda and civil liberties colleagues an emotional thank-you for their love and support. The very presence there of his ailing father seemed to capture the spirit of reconciliation and healing optimism that night, one that moves him still. He has precedents to set before he sleeps, and he is convinced that he can.

"I feel as though I'm on a precipice," he said. "I worry that I might fall, but my perspective is now broader and deeper. I see an all-encompassing vista, one that connects the past to the future, one that ties me to all other people who have suffered." ❏

A LONE PRACTITIONER IN THE
TRADITION OF LAWYER AS COUNSELOR,
CONFIDANT AND FRIEND.

1/25/91

A SPECTER IS HAUNTING AN EASTERN EUROPEAN COMMUNITY—THAT IS, THE community of scholars, artists and intellectuals who came to the United States from Poland after two world wars. One day, Ludwik Seidenman is going to retire, and they will have to find another lawyer.

Mercifully, it will not happen right away. Mr. Seidenman, who turned 84 years old last month, still comes to his office on Madison Avenue five or six days a week, and though his lease is up April 30, he fully intends to renew. Some things have changed: his wife, who typed his letters in English, Polish, German and maybe even Russian for 30 years, died three years ago, and he is taking on no new clients. But he keeps plenty busy tending to old ones.

Some are institutions, like the Polish Institute of Arts and Sciences of America and the Committee for the Blind of Poland. Most, though, are people. At one time, he helped many gain at least some meager recompense from the two tyrannies that laid waste their lives: the one that murdered their families or the one that "liberated" them, only to seize their property. Now, for the most part, he tends to their wills and, increasingly, their estates.

"I told him he does not dare die before I," said a client and close friend, Halina Rodzinski of Manhattan, whose husband once conducted the New York Philharmonic. "If he dies I am lost."

In an era of giant firms, it is easy to forget that sole practitioners like Mr. Seidenman still exist. Or that in an era of specialization, there are still generalists. Or that in an era of egomaniacs, some lawyers remain self-effacing to a fault and do their good deeds inconspicuously, in the way Maimonides envisioned. Or that in an era of rampant lawyer-bashing, some lawyers are still revered by those they represent.

By all accounts, Mr. Seidenman is such a man. He perpetuates the tradition of the land from which he and his clients came—the tradition of lawyer as counselor, confidant and friend. "He is a good lawyer, undoubtedly, but he is also one of the noblest men I've met in my life," said Rabbi Isaac Lewin of New York, whose scholarly work on Polish Jewry has been published partly with Mr. Seidenman's legal assistance.

Why, at his age, does Mr. Seidenman persist, long after he needs to? Perhaps he does not want to relinquish a profession he has twice trained for. Perhaps he enjoys his clients, who have ranged from Aleksandr Kerensky, the Russian prime minister whose government was overthrown in the Bolshevik Revolution, to the wife of the pianist Arthur Rubinstein, Nella, to Svetlana Stalin, whose father imprisoned Mr. Seidenman during World War II. Mostly, though, it is a matter of responsibility, the special responsibility felt by one who, like so many of his friends, could just as easily have ended up as ashes in Treblinka or beneath the trees of Katyn.

"I never viewed my profession solely as a source of income," he said in his accented but impeccable English. "Basically, I'm trying to be useful. I'm fully aware of the exceptional circumstances that made my apparent success in life possible, and I can't help thinking of all those who were equally capable but perished."

Mr. Seidenman grew up in Warsaw, where his father was a lawyer, a Zionist leader and, later, a member of the Polish Parliament. He earned his law degree from Warsaw University in 1928 and practiced civil law until the Germans marched in.

Mr. Seidenman fled eastward, eventually to the Soviet Union, where he ultimately landed in Stalin's jail on a trumped-up espionage charge. Freed in 1941, he joined the Polish Embassy in Moscow. Later, he was named counsel in New York for the Polish government in exile.

When the Communists took over in Poland, Mr. Seidenman went into the export business. But he found it boring and began studying law again, this time at New York Law School, this time at night, this time in a foreign tongue. He graduated cum laude in 1957 and opened a practice at the age of 51.

Fluent in Russian, he counseled Kerensky on several matters—for instance, whether or not it was safe to describe Lenin as syphilitic in an article he was writing on his onetime rival (Kerensky ignored his advice and printed it). He also worked for various Polish organizations, always pro bono publico, always functioning with equal ease in both the Polish and Polish-Jewish communities.

Mr. Seidenman has never looked for adulation and is a bit startled by reports that it exists. "I'm amazed at how little you have to do to earn people's gratitude," he said. "I don't know of any real sacrifices on my part." He pooh-poohs all this talk of indispensability. "There are no irreplaceable people," he said. "Nature has horror of a vacuum."

Nonetheless, when his clients greet him, they do not simply say hello. Invariably they add, "I'm glad to see you're in such good shape." ❑

A Brooklyn-Born Lawyer Finds
Himself at the Center of a
Civil Rights Case in Israel.

1/15/93

Jerusalem—Joshua Schoffman tried but failed to block the deportation of 415 Palestinians to southern Lebanon last month, and he incurred the wrath of Israel's Prime Minister for his efforts. But the experience accelerated his quest to import to his embattled adopted home the kinds of civil liberties he learned to appreciate in his native land.

On Dec. 17, as 22 busloads of handcuffed and blindfolded Palestinians, mostly members of the Islamic fundamentalist group Hamas, headed north from the Negev to the Lebanese border, Mr. Schoffman—Orthodox Jew, committed Zionist and legal director of the Association for Civil Rights in Israel—took on the Israeli Government and many of his fellow Israelis.

In the wee hours of the morning, as word of the deportations began to emerge, he wrote a four-page petition challenging their legality, then drove through a downpour to the home of Justice Aharon Barak of the Israeli Supreme Court. Later in the day, while fielding reporters' calls, battling censors and sleeplessness and sifting through rumors, he argued twice before the tribunal, with Israel's Attorney General, Yosef Harish, and Army Chief of Staff, Ehud Barak, arrayed against him.

Concerns for security won out, as they often do here, and the buses crossed the border. But Yitzhak Rabin, the Israeli Prime Minister, was not about to let Mr. Schoffman or his association off easily. (Mr. Rabin described the group in news accounts as "the so-called Association for Civil Rights" and "the Association for the Rights of the Hamas.") As Mr. Schoffman left court, there were shouts that he, too, should have been deported—back to the United States. There were also catcalls telephoned to his home, from which he was spared only when the Sabbath came and, as he does each week, he stopped answering.

The Brooklyn-born Mr. Schoffman, who is 39, said he had never felt such rancor, even when he successfully challenged the Israeli policy of demolishing the homes of suspected terrorists while refusing to respect their right to appeal before the demolitions.

But a strange thing happened after Mr. Rabin's remarks. Though polls showed that 9 in 10 Israelis supported the expulsions, lawyers, public-interest groups and members of the Israeli parliament, the Knesset, leaped to Mr. Schoffman's defense. When the dust settled, the association had won new visibility and respect—enough, perhaps, to help wean it off American dollars a bit and bring more Israeli shekels.

A civil-libertarian consciousness has taken root in Israel only slowly, and understandably so. This is a country with no written constitution, a country built on a collectivist rather than an individualistic foundation. It is also a young country; when the United States was Israel's age, Andrew Jackson was President. Most importantly, it is a country at war, a situation in which civil liberties can also be considered civil luxuries.

Mr. Schoffman moved here in 1975 after graduating from Brandeis University. After law school at the Hebrew University and a three-and-a-half-year hitch in the Israeli army, he went to Washington to study civil liberties law at American University. In 1985 he became the first full-time legal director of the 20-year-old association, whose $350,000 annual budget comes primarily from the Ford Foundation and the New Israel Fund, a New York-based charity dedicated to strengthening Israeli democracy. The father of two, Mr. Schoffman makes less than most legal secretaries in New York.

In a country in which personal politics can often be surmised from the size and style of a yarmulke, Mr. Schoffman cuts an anomalous figure. His is of the knit variety, the one favored by members of the Jewish fundamentalist group Gush Emunim, those messianic proponents of West Bank settlements with whom he has occasionally tangled in court.

But the association's docket is resolutely pluralistic. Taking on Israel's Orthodox rabbinate, the association's lawyers have fought for the rights of Reform and Conservative Jews and converts, challenging Sabbath closing laws, for instance, or securing the option of secular burials and Latin lettering on gravestones. The rights of women, prisoners, political candidates, protesters, the disabled and Bedouins have all been enhanced by association lawyers.

A modest, soft-spoken sort, Mr. Schoffman said that his recent prominence is something he would gladly have forgone. "I'd prefer it if the intifada-related problems went away and our docket looked more like the A.C.L.U.'s," he said. "There'd be more than enough work to do." ❑

NEW YORK'S OUTSTANDING YOUNG LAWYER HAS BEEN YOUNG AND OUTSTANDING FOR A LONG TIME.

1/31/92

THIS WEEK, WHEN THE NEW YORK STATE BAR ASSOCIATION ANNOUNCED ITS outstanding young lawyer for 1992, one might have thought some typographical gremlin was at work. The winner is 63 years old.

The proofreader was not asleep. Under the association's rules, lawyers are deemed "young" if they are either under the age of 37 or have practiced for fewer than 10 years. In this sense Ree Adler, a legal aid lawyer in Buffalo who began her legal career in 1983, won with two years to spare.

Legal aid lawyers tend to be the chronologically young—people who retain the idealism and independence necessary for such difficult and unremunerative work. But with her youthful energy and enthusiasm and her sense of commitment and humor, Mrs. Adler, a $1-per-annum lawyer at Neighborhood Legal Services in Buffalo, is very much at home.

For the $8 she has earned, payable each Dec. 31 in one-dollar increments, she has helped to establish a center providing schooling and child care for 60 teenage mothers; created procedural protections for water users facing service cutoffs; helped assemble a group of lawyers to aid the poor in receiving Medicaid benefits; and set up a coalition of doctors and lawyers to discuss health care issues.

She has helped immigrants and the handicapped to negotiate their way around the welfare system's intricate regulatory maze. She has coaxed large corporations into providing drugs to the poor at no cost. By her example, her colleagues say, she is a constant reminder that good lawyering is not just rattling sabers but getting real results for real people—through persuasion, pressure and ingenuity as well as through lawsuits.

Around her office, she has played law librarian, psychiatrist, legal scholar and one-woman continuing legal education service. She is a steady source of wisdom, experience, perspective, good humor and—notwithstanding her five grown children, four children-in-law and two grandchildren—youthfulness. When Ronald Reagan once visited Buffalo, Mrs. Adler's husband, Richard, a well-known thoracic surgeon, was asked to stand by in the event the President became ill. In the meantime Mrs. Adler was in the streets, protesting efforts by the Reagan Administration to gut the Legal Services Corporation, a Federally financed agency that serves the poor.

"Ree is not here because she works for free," said the director of the legal aid office, Jim Morrissey, who added that Mrs. Adler could earn $37,000 a year there if she wanted to. "We have plenty of 40-year-old codgers here. And then we have this 60-year-old ray of sunshine."

Mrs. Adler said her reaction to winning the young lawyer award was: "I know I'm young. I just can't believe I'm a lawyer." It was the response of someone who had struggled to realize her own potential and, having done so, was seeking with special fervor to bring that opportunity to others. "Like many, many women my age I'll never know what I could have been or could have done," she said. "I feel lucky I got some of it."

Born and reared in Paterson, N.J., she came of age, as she puts it, "at the wrong time to be the kind of person I wanted to be." Abandoning her dream of entering medicine, she married young and had three children. She divorced, married Dr. Adler and moved to Buffalo, where she enlisted in innumerable causes. But only with a law degree, she realized, could she be fully effective. "When you make a phone call as a lawyer, someone listens," she said. "You're the same person you were the day before, but the title means something."

She initially balked at attending law school, fearing that its rigors could harm her marriage. When she took the plunge, at age 52, it was with several promises, to her husband and herself: she would leave an hour and a half each evening to dine with him; she would never study beyond 10:30 at night; and, once she graduated, she would do legal services work, full time and free of charge.

When she first appeared at Neighborhood Legal Services, suspicions ran high that she was just another limousine liberal, a philanthropic bird of passage who would soon fly off to something easier. To allay such skepticism, she never missed work, even in the midst of Buffalo's fabled winters. And if the work did not come to her, she devised her own projects.

"When she gets her teeth into something, she's absolutely relentless," said Olney Clowe, her first supervisor. "She is so skilled in communicating with people—in shaming them, basically, into doing what they should do. She just will not let up."

Actually, she has let up a bit, working four days a week now instead of five. "When I was little, my parents called me a pest, and that's a wonderful trait for a lawyer," she said. "I never give up on anything unless I absolutely have to." ❑

BRINGING TEARS TO THE EYES
OF LAWYERS AND COMFORT TO
THE LIVES OF ALIENS.

8/16/91

WHEN MANLIN MAUREEN CHEE WAS GROWING UP IN SINGAPORE, SHE HEARD much from her parents about the Confucian hierarchy of occupations. At the top, Confucius placed the educated class, who, because of their schooling, he said, bore a special obligation to serve others. After that came farmers and laborers. Both last and least were businessmen, whom the Chinese philosopher considered exploiters of other people.

Confucius created no separate category for lawyers, though in our era of lawyers-as-businessmen, their niche is arguably clear. But by her good deeds Ms. Chee has exemplified the Confucian ideal. The 39-year-old lawyer, who lives in Greensboro, N.C., is one of five winners of this year's American Bar Association's "pro bono publico" award. But she was the only one among them who moved many of her listeners, including Justice Sandra Day O'Connor, to tears as she accepted her award.

Ms. Chee told of the assignment her father had given her on the way to the airport in 1969, when she was leaving Singapore for what she called "the American education of John F. Kennedy and Pearl S. Buck." America, her father said, was a great nation, not because it had helped liberate their country from the Japanese or had just put a man on the moon, but because it took care of its weakest citizens. "I want you to go over there and find out how they do it," he told her.

A few years later, Ms. Chee graduated from Guilford College in Greensboro. The recent Watergate scandal notwithstanding, she saw the law as an avenue to public service, which was a tradition among her ancestors, a frequent practice of her physician father and a topic of dinnertime conversation among her family. She entered Wake Forest Law School.

After graduation, she took a job with the Greensboro human relations agency and, in 1980, moved to the local office of the Legal Services Corporation, the Federally financed agency providing lawyers for the poor. Her work brought her into contact with the large population of aliens in the area: Mexican migrant workers, Asian spouses of G.I.'s at local Army bases, Vietnamese, Cubans, Haitians. They are, she concluded, "the most oppressed of our indigent population," facing problems with language, the bureaucracy and the police.

In 1983, the Reagan Administration decreed that legal services lawyers could no longer represent most aliens. So, a country that pays homage to the wretched refuse of one era on the base of the Statue of Liberty would let the detritus of another molder unrepresented in shanties, camps and detention centers. It was then that Ms. Chee decided to quit her job and open an office of her own. The office quickly became known as the place to which her former colleagues sent people they were too busy or were not allowed to handle.

Her life has its disadvantages. She works long hours, juggles three daughters when her husband, Juan Forgay, a flight attendant with US-Air, is not around, drives a beat-up Toyota, shops at yard sales. But there are compensations.

Like job security. Throughout the country, in firms large and small, lawyers are receiving pink slips. The New York City Bar Association recently issued guidelines to help firms ax lawyers more humanely; "MAKE THE RIGHT MOVES NOW IF YOU'RE LOSING YOUR JOB," the cover story of the group's Barrister magazine advises. That's one problem Ms. Chee will never have.

Moreover, a recent study by the North Carolina Bar disclosed that 22 percent of the state's lawyers have stress-related diseases; 23 percent say they would not become lawyers again; 24 percent are depressed. Ms. Chee, who was not among those surveyed, suffers from none of these symptoms.

Characteristically, when Ms. Chee accepted her award on Monday, it was not of herself that she spoke. Instead, she talked about her father, and about other lawyers—the lawyers she has seen working for the homeless, the hungry, the mentally ill and the alien.

"My father died last year," she said. "But I was able to tell him, 'Dad, you sent me across to the United States for an American education. I'm sorry I did not come back. But Dad, I found out how America does it. It is the American lawyer. I am so proud to be an American lawyer.'"

Justice O'Connor dabbed her eyes, then rose to speak—about pro bono work. Anyone looking to avoid controversy, as Justices on the stump are forever trying to do, can hardly find a safer topic, particularly when, as in the case of Justice O'Connor, they tell their lawyer listeners they must please try to do more—voluntarily, of course.

Afterward, Ms. Chee told a reporter: "Everybody believes in what Jesus said about helping the poor, but whether you get into the trenches is a different question. My Dad didn't tell me to do it. My Dad did it." ❑

A PROBATE LAWYER TURNS
IMPRESARIO, REVIVING MUSIC SO
SWEET TO HIS CLIENT'S EARS.

2/19/93

ASK JULIUS BURGER TO DESCRIBE WHAT HIS LAWYER DID FOR HIM, AND HE
responds as best a 95-year-old man, the victim of two strokes, can. His
eyes water, and as he reaches for an elusive encomium he pounds his
cane on the floor in frustration. Finally, the mot juste wends its way
through the damaged neurological maze.

"Everything!" he exclaims. "Everything!"

Through tax tips and testamentary tricks, probate lawyers spend
their days helping people die in peace. But Ronald Pohl, a probate
lawyer at Rothfeld & Pohl in Manhattan, did more for Mr. Burger
than tidy up his estate. He gave him new life by giving him back his
music.

When the two first met in April 1990, Mr. Burger, once an assistant
conductor of the Metropolitan Opera, was a new widower, grieving
and depressed. He was planning for his own death and told Mr. Pohl
his posthumous wishes: to turn what he had managed to save—earn-
ings from his days as a conductor in Europe and America along with
German war reparations—into scholarships for young Israeli musicians whose careers, he hoped, would never know a Holocaust. Mr.
Burger, a Jew, had been an assistant conductor at the Berlin Staat-
soper before World War II when he was stripped of his job by the
Nazis and forced to flee.

As Mr. Burger shared his memories, he also disclosed a dream.
Tucked away in the closets and desk drawers of his apartment in
Elmhurst, Queens, he told Mr. Pohl, were sheafs of his own, almost
entirely unperformed musical compositions: sonatas, symphonic frag-
ments and songs, most of them also refugees from his incinerated Europe. Among them was a cello concerto; after the war he had
dedicated its second movement to his mother, whom the Germans
shot on her way to Auschwitz. How nice it would be, he said, to hear it
performed before he died.

Exit Mr. Pohl, lawyer; enter Mr. Pohl, impresario. Persuading musicians to perform something new, he quickly learned, was an arduous
task, far more complicated than devising trusts or writing codicils but
ever so much more rewarding.

Mr. Pohl's first task was to determine whether Mr. Burger's music
was any good. He turned to Maya Beiser, an Israeli cellist, who went to

Mr. Burger's home and, with Mr. Burger accompanying her on the piano, performed the piece. Suddenly, music that had been imprisoned on paper for decades filled the room. Mr. Burger wept. Mr. Pohl resolved to have the concerto performed by a full orchestra, and quickly, because in 1990 Mr. Burger had suffered two nearly fatal strokes.

Words, names, arias—Mr. Burger remembers them all, but he can no longer summon them on demand. Nowadays the German of his youth is more accessible than his English. Only when he has a musical score before him can he communicate as he once did; on Monday it was with a Mozart sonata, K. 533, which he performed on his upright Steinway.

In March 1991, Mr. Pohl persuaded the Orchestra of St. Luke's to perform the cello concerto, along with four other compositions, at a concert to be held that June. Mr. Pohl booked Alice Tully Hall at Lincoln Center, found a conductor, prepared the programs, had the music copied, hired a publicist and arranged for a digital recording.

The concert got rave reviews, and it was repeated in Israel and New York. Tomorrow night the New York Virtuoso Singers will play his "Miserere," a composition for chorus and organ, at St. Peter's Church on Lexington Avenue at 54th Street in Manhattan.

"My goal has been to have Julius hear all of his music before he dies, and by enough people so that it could last on its own merits," Mr. Pohl said. "We're close to accomplishing that."

Besides being lawyer and impresario, Mr. Pohl has played grandson, too. He and his wife, Diane, have invited Mr. Burger to a family seder as well as to outings at the New York Botanical Garden. When Mr. Burger dined with his niece at the Palm Court, Mr. Pohl secretly arranged to have a violinist serenade them with a Burger arrangement of a Dvořák melody. Mr. Pohl secured a new housekeeper and physical therapist for Mr. Burger, and helped him buy new glasses, new dentures, a new hearing aid and a new suit. He has done much of the work free because, like most of those who spend any time with Mr. Burger, he has come to love him.

With Mr. Pohl's help, Mr. Burger also bought a new stereo. Now he can play recordings of his music, including his cello concerto. As the mournful, Hebraic sounds of its second movement filled his apartment recently, Mr. Burger listened silently, rocking, and then began crying anew. For all his infirmities, he still managed to make clear just what the tears were for: the vanished world of his youth and family.

"It disappeared," he said. "All of a sudden, nothing." And then he moved his hand clockwise, as if turning on a faucet. "The gas—" ❑